RETHINKING COMMUNITY RESILIENCE

Rethinking Community Resilience

The Politics of Disaster Recovery in New Orleans

Min Hee Go

NEW YORK UNIVERSITY PRESS

New York

NEW YORK UNIVERSITY PRESS
New York
www.nyupress.org

References to internet websites (URLs) were accurate at the time of writing. Neither the author nor New York University Press is responsible for URLs that may have expired or changed since the manuscript was prepared.

Library of Congress Cataloging-in-Publication Data
Names: Go, Min Hee, author.
Title: Rethinking community resilience : the politics of disaster recovery in New Orleans / Min Hee Go.
Description: New York : NYU Press, 2021. | Includes bibliographical references and index.
Identifiers: LCCN 2020050163 | ISBN 9781479804894 (hardback) |
ISBN 9781479804900 (paperback) | ISBN 9781479804917 (ebook) |
ISBN 9781479804955 (ebook)
Subjects: LCSH: Hurricane Katrina, 2005—Economic aspects. | Hurricane Katrina, 2005—Social aspects. | Disaster relief—Louisiana—New Orleans. | Disaster victims—Services for—Louisiana—New Orleans.
Classification: LCC HV636 2005.N4 G6 2021 | DDC 976.3/35064—dc23
LC record available at https://lccn.loc.gov/2020050163

Chapter 2 was previously published as a book chapter in *Disasters, Hazards and Law* titled "The Federal Disaster: The Failed Logic of Disaster Prevention in New Orleans." 17: 155–174.

Chapter 3 was previously published as an article in *Journal of Urban Affairs* titled "The Tale of a Two-Tiered City: Community Civic Structure and Spatial Inequality in post-Katrina New Orleans." 40 (8): 1093–1114. Used with permission.

Chapter 4 was previously published as an article in *Urban Affairs Review* titled "The Power of Participation: Explaining the Building Permits Explosion in post-Katrina New Orleans." 50 (1): 34–62. Used with permission.

New York University Press books are printed on acid-free paper, and their binding materials are chosen for strength and durability. We strive to use environmentally responsible suppliers and materials to the greatest extent possible in publishing our books.

Manufactured in the United States of America

10 9 8 7 6 5 4 3 2 1

Also available as an ebook

CONTENTS

List of Abbreviations   vii

Introduction: Do Resilient Communities Make
a Resilient City?   1

1. Resilient Communities in a Vulnerable City   27

2. Federalism and the Construction of Protection from
   Betsy to Katrina   47

3. Rebuilding the City: Reconstruction and the Paradox
   of Participation   83

4. Returning to the City: Community Civic Structure
   and Spatial Inequality   112

5. The Making of Resilient Communities   143

Conclusion: Rethinking Civic Capacity and
Urban Resilience   181

Acknowledgments   199

Methodological Appendix   201

Notes   207

Bibliography   225

Index   253

About the Author   265

LIST OF ABBREVIATIONS

ABFE Advisory Base Flood Elevations

ACORN Association of Community Organizations for Reform Now

APA American Planning Association

BDC Broadmoor Development Corporation

BFE Base Flood Elevation

BIA Broadmoor Improvement Association

BNOBC Bring New Orleans Back Commission

BP British Petroleum

CBD Central Business District

CDA Housing and Community Development Act of 1974

CDBG Community Development Block Grant

CDC Community Development Corporation

CLURO Comprehensive Land-Use Regulation Ordinance

DDD Downtown Development District

EIS Environmental Impact Statement

FDPA Flood Disaster Protection Act

FEMA Federal Emergency Management Agency

FIRM Flood Insurance Rate Map

FNC Freret Neighborhood Center

GMP Growth Management Program

GOHSEP Governor's Office of Homeland Security and Emergency Preparedness

HFIAA Homeowner Flood Insurance Affordability Act of 2014

HMGP Hazard Mitigation Grant Program

HOME Home Ownership Made Easy

HUD United States Department of Housing and Urban Development

LPVHPP Lake Pontchartrain and Vicinity Hurricane Protection Project

MIR Make It Right Foundation

MRGO Mississippi River–Gulf Outlet

NENA Lower Ninth Ward Neighborhood Empowerment Network Association

NEPA National Environment Policy Act

NFIP National Flood Insurance Program

NHS Neighborhood Housing Services

NORA New Orleans Redevelopment Authority

NSP Neighborhood Stabilization Program

NU Neighbors United

OECD Organisation for Economic Co-operation and Development

SPH Standard Project Hurricane

THE RESTORE ACT Resources and Ecosystems Sustainability, Tourist Opportunities, and Revived Economies of the Gulf Coast States Act

USGS United States Geological Survey

Introduction

Do Resilient Communities Make a Resilient City?

The greatest social capital in Broadmoor is us. Because we
live here, and I don't want to lose my house. I don't want to
lose my neighborhood, so I have more incentive than literally any human being on the planet to make this work.
—Hal Roark, executive director of the Broadmoor Development Corporation

Hal Roark was sanguine about the prospects for his neighborhood and
greater New Orleans when I interviewed him in February 2010, about
five years after Hurricane Katrina. As executive director of the Broadmoor Community Development Corporation, Roark firmly believed
that the residents' collective desire to save their neighborhood was the
most critical resource available for repairing the immediate damages
from Katrina and restoring Broadmoor to the viable community it had
once been. In fact, his belief was not just wishful thinking. Broadmoor,
a predominantly Black community with an average household income
below the city-wide average, has since been recognized nationally as
a successful model of post-Katrina recovery and community development. With the help of prestigious organizations, including the Clinton
Foundation and Harvard University, Broadmoor regained nearly 80 percent of its pre-Katrina population within three years of the hurricane.[1]

One salient fact less known about this extraordinary success story,
however, is that Broadmoor is the lowest lying of the seventy-three
neighborhoods in the city.[2] Located at the "bottom of the bowl," Broadmoor collects all the floodwater that flows into the city and passes it into
the Mississippi River. Since the late nineteenth century, the drainage systems have been built to go around neighborhood boundaries to facilitate
this water flow and protect the area's population. The most recent was

a large-scale project constructed immediately before Katrina inundated the neighborhood. As part of the Southeast Louisiana Urban Flood Control Project, the Army Corps of Engineers and Orleans Parish built a pump station expansion and box culvert in 2004 to transport rainfall-induced floodwaters away from the area.[3] This drainage work, also called the Napoleon Canals Project, was part of a larger public works project that included an $18 million expansion of a pumping station as well as a $21 million construction of a canal beneath South Claiborne Avenue, a main thoroughfare that runs just south of the neighborhood.

Yet these technological solutions would only go so far. Despite the century-long effort to improve drainage problems, these facilities often failed to mitigate the heavy rainfall and flooding because Broadmoor, after all, is so low and flat. In fact, hurricanes were not the only reason for the neighborhood's chronic flooding. Even half an inch of rainfall would cause a problem by exceeding the local drainage capacity. Many houses suffered repetitive flood losses pre-Katrina, and the owners of these properties filed multiple claims each time their houses were submerged. Since 1978, the homeowners of these "repetitive-loss properties" have received approximately $5.8 million in total flood claims paid—about $160,000 per property—all before Hurricane Katrina swept through the neighborhood.[4]

Given the accumulating cost of rebuilding, not everyone was so hopeful about the resident-oriented recovery. A senior fellow at the Urban Land Institute stated that "the confidence [of Broadmoor's recovery] is misplaced," warning against an incomplete and sparse repopulation. Although he acknowledged that the financial and emotional investment was beneficial for the homeowners, he showed skepticism toward the rise of neighborhood movements for repopulation. "Rather than pull together to say how do we design a city that we can all live in that's better and safer for everyone, they're simply saying, 'I want my neighborhood back, the hell with you, I want my neighborhood back.' And they're pulling against a concerted, cooperative citywide effort, and it is possible that their efforts will cause the concerted citywide efforts to fail, and that each of these little neighborhoods will Balkanize the city, and they'll win, and be left with a city that can't support them."[5]

Given Broadmoor's permanent geographic predisposition to hazards, the neighborhood's revival presents a dilemma—rather than a pure victory—for the city. Famously sitting close to sea level and surrounded by or adjacent to major bodies of water—the Mississippi River, Lake Pontchartrain and the Gulf of Mexico—New Orleans is susceptible to flooding from normal weather events. It has also been hit by a hurricane at least once every fifty years, and the cost of hurricane recovery is nothing but escalating. The Great Storm of 1915 damaged 25,000 structures and took 275 lives in Louisiana. Thirty-two years later, the 1947 Fort Lauderdale Hurricane inundated the city once again, causing fifty-one deaths and $100 million in damage. The next devastating hurricane arrived in 1965, when Hurricane Betsy killed eighty-one people and incurred $372 million in damage. Then came Hurricane Katrina, in 2005, which caused 1,800 deaths and $81 billion in property damage and remains one of the nation's deadliest disasters.[6]

Given the frequency and escalating costs of disasters, it is hardly surprising that some proactive policies have been proposed to prevent a similar, or even greater, degree of loss. The rationale was based on the city's unavoidable reality: as a coastal city, New Orleans has been, and will be, exposed to hurricanes and flooding, and climate change will only accelerate the frequency and magnitude of these large-scale events. And, as it happens, one in ten cities in America is shrinking in population size, New Orleans among them. Considering the city's changing climate and declining economy, experts saw post-Katrina recovery as an opportunity to promote a more compact design and thus to "rightsize" the city—by clustering the population in a smaller area and deferring development in less populated, high-risk areas.[7] Through careful design and planning, they believed that rightsizing could rehabilitate the city's social and economic vitality by reconstructing neighborhoods in a selective manner.

Shrinking the city size was an unconventional, if not irrational, idea. Residents, including those in Broadmoor, did not share enthusiasm for this idealistic plan and fervently resisted it. In public meetings and hearings, people vehemently opposed shrinking the city's footprint. What they preferred was not to retreat or relocate for safety, but to stay and focus on redeveloping their original neighborhoods. With the post-Katrina repopulation process seen by many residents as part of a neoliberal attempt to gentrify and dislocate the poor, they actively claimed that they had a right to rebuild their neighborhoods. Consolidating the city size was equally unpalatable to many who lived on higher ground, who did not want to invite newcomers into their neighborhoods and make their communities densely populated.[8] Facing a popular backlash, the city government eventually abandoned the idea and allowed all residents to come back and rebuild their homes.

Broadmoor stands in the middle of this shrinking-city debate as a glaring example of a grassroots victory against the attempt by government to make a smaller city. This success story, however, is seldom discussed in relation to how vulnerable the city of New Orleans was well before Katrina, and how much repeated development would cost the city in the event of another hurricane. This dilemma of how to foster civic resilience in a vulnerable city requires us to address a set of questions: In the face of the undeniable sinking of the city proper and amid a shrinking population, what makes citizens reluctant to leave their neighborhoods, even when the risks of staying there are high? What are the consequences of such resistance? In other words, what are the consequences of letting people return to any location of their choosing? More generally, to what extent is civic capacity, defined broadly as the collective resources of community members to achieve a common goal, good for the sustainable and managed development of cities?

These questions point to the central inquiry of this book: Do resilient communities make for a resilient city? To most people, the answer may seem straightforward. In an era when cities are exposed to the dangers of natural hazards more than ever before,[9] empowering local communities sounds like a natural solution for building resilience, which is usually defined as the capacity to recover from hardship. This is a well-known narrative. Here, civic capacity, understood as the collective social resources of community members, often plays a crucial role in achieving difficult goals, such as saving lives, providing food and shelter, and helping people return to their homes after a disaster. Therefore, the argument goes, nurturing the social and civic strength of communities can make the city livable again by filling the void created by inefficient government and alleviating many of the negative effects from external shocks such as hurricanes and earthquakes.

What is missing in this line of thought, however, is whether and how these community-based civic resources accrue to reduce the vulnerability of a *whole city*. While many studies highlight the astounding resilience of individual neighborhoods, they often do so without considering the larger economic and political consequences of promoting civically oriented rebuilding efforts. In this sense, the conventional wisdom on the importance of community spirit in times of crisis, based on the short-term experiences of select communities, leaves us with a limited view of the larger picture.

The Argument of the Book

In this book, I argue that successful community-based civic activities after a catastrophic event may generate *vulnerable resilience*, a state in which active neighborhood recovery efforts escalate the larger city's susceptibility to future risks. I contend that while local communities can exert a considerable influence on post-disaster recovery efforts, they do so in a more complicated way than what previous research has hitherto suggested. Instead of casting uniformly positive effects, I argue, civic capacity presents both opportunities and challenges with regard to overcoming crises and building resilience in a city. On the one hand, the civic capacity of communities can help people concentrate resources on restoring damage and facilitating reconstruction immediately after disaster. By rebuilding a ruined community with their own hands, residents gain a sense of greater belonging and empowerment over the fate of their neighborhood and the city. In this sense, strong civic capacity is closely associated with community resilience. On the other hand, the same capacity and sense of belonging and empowerment may also reinforce challenges that can ultimately undermine the city's overall resilience. While the civic capacity of communities may facilitate revitalization at the smaller spatial scale of distinct neighborhoods, a collective pursuit of recovery and rebuilding by affected residents tends to generate conflicts at the city level. As civic actors continue to request protection and pursue development in a city's unsafe areas, as was the case in New Orleans, they may generate greater vulnerabilities for certain sections of the city than existed before, with the result that they distance themselves from the communities that have advocated for sustainable, resilient redevelopment during the same period. This haphazard approach to spatial recovery compromises the city's ability to mitigate future disasters and reduce urban inequality.[10]

While this book is a cautionary tale about the power of civic activism, *Rethinking Community Resilience* is by no means a critique of those who strove to return to their vulnerable neighborhoods. Rather, it adds weight to the argument against narrowly conceptualizing civic capacity as something that is invariably positive and desirable.[11] Furthermore, I take into account the fact that civic capacity does not solely lead to resistant actions but also creates a proactive force that can determine the course of urban policymaking and practice. In post-Katrina New Orleans, residents were not only resistant to the government's proposals— they also organized to define their own goals, strategies, and plans for rebuilding, which were in large part incorporated into the city's comprehensive vision for the future. These communities did not always work in harmony; they sometimes clashed and had to compete with other neighborhoods. Civil society, in this sense, is not a single, uniform entity but an organism of multiple, spatially demarcated neighborhood units whose capacity and success may vary. This book pays attention to this dynamic of conflict and contention within the city and its unintended consequences. Assessing the negative consequences of civic capacity, however, does not and should not mean desensitizing race and class issues. Instead, this book highlights the proximate and often paradoxical relationship between neighborhood-based civic engagement and the city's persistent social inequalities, and shows how civic engagement can be intertwined with the uneven patterns of post-disaster recovery. This is why New Orleans in particular has shown signs of resilience yet still remains vulnerable to future disasters in the long run.

To better understand the contemporary response to Katrina, I offer a historical narrative about how civic actors have interacted with various levels of government to grapple with the aftermath of disasters. Throughout the twentieth century, citizens mustered their civic strength to demand government protection for private property, and as a result, national disaster policies have been designed in such a way so as to compensate property loss *after* a disaster rather than mitigate hazards before they occur. Most citizens believe that natural disaster response should be the primary responsibility of the federal government—despite that it has little say in regulating local land-use issues, building codes, and zoning, all of which have the potential to prevent hazardous development in the first place. Nevertheless, in response to these demands, the federal government offered New Orleans structural protection by constructing floodwalls, levees, canals, and drainage systems, all of which proved to be insufficient for mitigating natural disasters. With federal funds earmarked for these public works projects, citizens developed a perhaps false sense of security and resilience out of proportion with the safety that the physical structures designed for storm protection could actually provide.[12]

Historically grounded analysis helps us understand why citizens organized around rebuilding, rather than retreating from, their vulnerable homes and communities. In a disaster-prone city like New Orleans, post-disaster civic organizing is derivative of a continued fight against natural constraints. As the city prospered by expanding its territory into wetlands and low-lying grounds, residents developed a strong attachment to their land, properties, and community. When natural disasters disrupted this urban identity, citizens negotiated with the federal, state, and local governments to increase spending on protecting and compensating for the unexpected loss of their homes. New Orleans occupies a unique place in this process, as two major events in the region—Hurricane Betsy and Hurricane Katrina—marked important junctures for creating and implementing federal disaster programs, especially in terms of defining the role of the federal government as one that protects private properties and communities located in flood-prone areas.

Against the historical backdrop, this book provides a set of analyses that connect the short- and long-term patterns of recovery after Katrina. Some might claim that post-disaster recovery and resilience building are essentially separate processes, as the former involves speedy reconstruction and recuperation from loss and trauma, while the latter emphasizes deliberation and comprehensive discussion of the city's future.[13] While this view highlights the difference between immediate response (such as evacuation and emergency operations) and multistage planning (such as land-use regulations and comprehensive zoning), the two processes are neither entirely isolated nor clearly separable from each other.[14] The early momentum for civic-oriented recovery had a lasting consequence by shaping and spreading the belief that nurturing social relations among people is critical to forming an urban space that is resilient against natural disasters. For example, many of the civic organizations that introduced first responders to New Orleans were not disaster-focused organizations, like the Red Cross, but everyday establishments, such as churches and neighborhood associations. After Katrina, a Catholic church in a devastated neighborhood called Village de l'Est quickly turned into a place where disaster victims—mostly Vietnamese immigrants—shared information for rebuilding and collectively protested the city government's plan to build a landfill in the area where their homes were. Again, while these everyday organizations have traditionally had little to do with disaster mitigation in ordinary times, they served broader purposes in the post-Katrina disaster period as recovery organizations. In turn, the city government responded to these civic organizations. Taking heed to the impacts of local communities, the city government established the Mayor's Neighborhood Engagement Office in 2011. The office launched the Neighborhood Participation Plan, and its introductory document proclaims that "there is wisdom in government and wisdom in neighborhoods," giving weight to neighborhoods as important voices for governance and decision-making.[15] The short-term recovery efforts by local organizations, therefore, were realized not only by physically rebuilding broken homes but also by influencing long-term governmental priorities.

Juxtaposing the short- and long-term temporal horizons yields two seemingly contradictory, yet reconcilable, propositions. For short-term recovery, strong civic capacity facilitates repopulation and reconstruction in a democratic and expeditious manner. This fits the traditional argument in disaster recovery that social capital facilitates immediate recovery after a disaster.[16] I further argue, however, that these positive immediate effects may have detrimental long-term consequences. First, when focusing on immediate reconstruction rather than adaptation, civic actors continue to request physical protection against rising water, even when such structural measures have failed to anticipate the actual conditions present during massive disasters. Second, people's collective capacity affected an uneven distribution of government services and facilitated repetitive development in hazardous areas. Tracking where reconstruction and repopulation occurred in the early period of post-Katrina recovery, I find that civic-oriented, unplanned rebuilding reproduces, or magnifies, pre-Katrina vulnerabilities. Third, inequality in communities' civic resources led to a two-tiered recovery pattern across the city, whereby safe communities could further reduce vulnerabilities while low-lying communities accumulated them. The adverse effects of spatial inequality are disproportionately felt by the city's most disadvantaged population—the poor people of color, who are once again placed in a socially and geographically perilous situation. Finally, community resilience materializes in the form of privatized governance, in which neighborhoods pursue their own strategies for survival rather than make concerted efforts for progress. Civic claims were made and policies implemented based on spatial boundaries and reinforced as a de facto unit of post-Katrina governance and recovery.

Acknowledging these long-term consequences of civic capacity, *Rethinking Community Resilience* contributes to shifting our discourse from encouraging civic involvement anywhere and anytime to weighing both the possibilities and limitations of civic participation in the context of urban resilience.

Charting a New Territory: Bringing Nature Back In

Compared to the many studies that approach Katrina and other disasters as human-made catastrophes, this book highlights New Orleans's natural history, particularly the city's constant struggle with water, as both its biggest asset and constraint. I define Katrina as a natural disaster not to underestimate its social, political, or economic consequences; rather, I emphasize Katrina as a natural phenomenon to highlight the ways resilience can and should take into account ecology, and recalibrate the boundaries of useful civic engagement therein. When disasters are understood as solely socially constructed events, recovery entails restoring and revitalizing distraught individuals and destroyed places at all costs. Defining Hurricane Katrina strictly as a human-made disaster, therefore, justifies the claim that all civic actions must be benevolent in both their intentions and consequences. In sociology and political science research, then, the central premise—that community civic capacity is a positive good—holds firm.[17] And yet, by focusing lopsidedly on the positive aspects of civic participation, we may lose sight of the fundamental dilemma of resilience building—a trade-off between revitalizing local communities on the one hand, and deferring redevelopment in certain communities on the other. This trade-off is inevitable given New Orleans's vulnerable natural environment, where half of the city lies below sea level and remains exposed to coastal and riverine threats. The normative value of civic participation notwithstanding, this dilemma compels us to think critically about the meaning, scope, and effect of community-based civic actions within such a geographically constrained situation.

Bringing this natural dimension to the fore, I revisit the existing parameters of standard recovery plans—such as rebuilding, repopulation, and community development—and discuss them in the context of the city's ecological conditions, including land subsidence, sea-level rise, and climate change. As explained in the following, the topography of New Orleans is susceptible to various water-related hazards such as flash floods, hurricanes, and tropical storms. As such, the city's history of urbanization has been inseparable from the process of overcoming the challenges of those natural hazards while expanding the city's physical dimensions. During this process of territorial expansion, the high-risk neighborhoods have traditionally been occupied by the city's most vulnerable populations, and part of the "human-made" aspect of disaster points to the failure of the wet infrastructure—such as levees, floodgates, and water-storage facilities—that was designed to shield those communities from being inundated. However, despite these engineering efforts, Hurricane Katrina demonstrated that armoring the shoreline may not be the ultimate solution to mitigating the ecological and topographical vulnerabilities of coastal cities. By factoring in natural constraints, we may gain a better sense of the potential consequences of individual or collective civic actions without overstating their long-term impact on the city's sustainable future.

In conceptualizing Katrina as a natural disaster, it further helps to situate it along the "transitory-perpetual" spectrum and compare it to other disasters. Transitory disasters are those "limited to smaller geographic scales, with fewer jurisdictional spillover effects."[18] According to this definition, the 1906 San Francisco Earthquake and 1871 Great Chicago Fire, although similarly detrimental natural disasters in urban settings, fit squarely within the category of a transitory disaster, having a great impact yet limited durability in temporal scope. Although these large-scale events did cause massive damage within their respective urban settings, their impacts and subsequent responses relied less on the geographic conditions of either city than in the New Orleans case. Seismic threat is not particularly confined to the city of San Francisco, but rather spread widely along the coastal region of California.[19] Moreover, being a transitory disaster, the geographic location was not a significant causal factor in the occurrence of the Great Chicago Fire. Thus, development in these cities was less constrained by the exposure to natural hazards than what New Orleans has endured.

In contrast, perpetual disasters like Katrina have a gradual-yet-continual impact, and in this sense, recurring hurricanes that strike New Orleans and the Gulf Coast are closer to the definition of perpetual disasters. Although there have been temporal breaks in frequency, hurricanes have continually affected intergovernmental relations, urban development, and the patterns of human habitation in the Gulf Coast region. Furthermore, not only do these disasters occur as a result of transient meteorological factors; these water-related events are also based on the city's geographic location in the Delta, where the threat of water-related catastrophes is a permanent condition and serves as a critical determinant for the city's socioeconomic outcomes. New Orleans's racial and economic topography is interwoven with the distribution of environmental hazards in the region, so that African Americans (and later Vietnamese immigrants) and those who are economically disadvantaged have historically inhabited the most perilous parts of the city and disproportionately fallen victim to hurricanes. In this regard, restoring pre-Katrina conditions would satiate the feelings of loss and depravation but would not address the city's fundamental injustices and inefficiencies, reproducing the risks that the city's most underprivileged populations have consistently suffered. In this book, I seek to explain how civic responses are associated with this reproduction of risks.

Why New Orleans? A Vulnerable City

Despite its significance, the memory of Katrina was almost perversely forgotten far too soon after the event itself, written off as a rare meteorological disaster that happened to strike a region of the United States almost uniquely ill equipped to handle it.[20] Despite the wealth of studies on either side documenting the city's epic failures or successes thereafter, the most profound conclusions about New Orleans's post-Katrina recovery have yet to be explored. In this book, I shed new light on the city's economic geography as a crucial example of a sinking and shrinking city—a city that lies in the crosshairs of two great crises: climate change and economic decline.

The Sinking City

In the Organisation for Economic Co-operation and Development (OECD) report on *Cities and Climate Change* (2014), New Orleans is listed as one of the world's top ten cities for highest projected losses due to floods by 2050. Comparing coastal cities in both developing and developed countries, the report paints a grim picture for New Orleans's geographic sustainability. Overall, New Orleans scored the second highest in projected losses, estimated to lose about 1.5 percent of its urban GDP each year from socioeconomic changes as well as from land subsidence induced by climate change. Losses from land subsidence are projected to be the most severe in New Orleans, followed by only Abidjan in Côte d'Ivoire. The US Geological Survey's (USGS) subsidence survey also reports that New Orleans is sinking at a faster rate than the sea level is rising, and that the subsidence is partly caused by the efforts to keep the metropolitan area dry.[21] According to the survey, the average subsidence rate for New Orleans is about 5 millimeters per year or higher, while mean sea-level rise is measured at 4.8 millimeters per year.[22] This brings us to the conclusion that in the next one hundred years, the New Orleans area will have an elevation more than one meter below the current mean sea level. If a hurricane were to hit the city under such circumstances, the storm surge would be four to five meters above the city's present elevation. The cumulative effects of land subsidence, sea-level rise, and storm surge, therefore, dramatically increase the chance of loss of life and property due to flooding. Considering that the projected loss is calculated relative to the city's GDP, the absolute amount of loss is greater in New Orleans than in any of its counterparts in developing countries.

Located in the Mississippi Delta, New Orleans has depended heavily on the ability to drain the water out of the city to sustain itself. Throughout the twentieth century, New Orleans's low-lying areas continued to develop in step with the city's drainage system improvements. In the 1920s and 1930s, residences and recreational facilities were built on the lakefront, as the scenic view attracted affluent residents to Lake

Pontchartrain. The Lower Ninth Ward also became urbanized during the 1950s, following an installation of drainage systems designed to store sudden and excessive rainfall. In the 1960s, middle-class African Americans found their homes in New Orleans East, a low-lying expanse of land east of the Industrial Canal. The region had remained mostly rural until World War II, but developers began to build residential and commercial buildings once Interstate 10 connected Eastern New Orleans with the city core and thus improved accessibility and mobility. These areas—Lakeview, the Lower Ninth Ward, and New Orleans East—had only been built thanks to the reassurances provided by the city's supposedly improved drainage system and yet suffered greatly from massive flooding and wind damage during Katrina's landfall in 2005. By continuing to redevelop and reinvent what will always be flood-prone communities and by focusing on constructing levees rather than restricting development in hazardous areas, these communities will surely be exposed again to ever-greater risks from natural hazards.[23]

Resilience in the face of vulnerability was not a characteristic unique to the Broadmoor neighborhood, as other parts of New Orleans that were heavily flooded have also showed remarkably expedient recovery. Village de l'Est, in Eastern New Orleans, is another good example of how community spirit can transcend economic and social hardships. Over 90 percent of its Vietnamese residents returned, whereas only half of their African American cohabitants came back after the disaster.[24] Scholars attributed this difference to a high level of cohesiveness among the Vietnamese community, arguing that their tight social network enabled the entire community to recover faster than socioeconomic conditions would have predicted. Vietnamese Americans of New Orleans shared a collective memory of refugee resettlement in a remote suburb of a Southern city and had accumulated strong ties with Catholic community leaders, who served to activate their tight bonds at every step of the post-disaster response. Despite a paucity of linguistic, economic, and political resources, Vietnamese Americans weathered the disaster thanks to their social resources.[25]

The civic victory had a weak geological foundation, however, as their neighborhood had been built upon sinking ground. Although social scientists touted the unexpected rebound of this resource-deprived Vietnamese immigrant community, the recovery raised equally important concerns about their future safety. Geographers, urban planners, and architects have long warned against the gradual sinking of Eastern New Orleans, and Village de l'Est is part of this at-risk area. Stretched far away from the city core, New Orleans East sits below sea level and has gradually subsided since the beginning of its development as a residential area. A dissertation that surveyed homeowners in East New Orleans in the 1970s presciently warned that land subsidence was a major and ongoing problem, and that homeowners may have to bear the hidden costs of subsidence, such as damaged pavements, water, and sewerage systems, and high utility rates.[26] The continued development of East New Orleans, the study concluded, would eventually impair homeowners:

> Present land reclamation practices do not provide stable trouble-free residential land and result in long-term costs to consumers. The present practice of shallow drainage and immediate development is serving only to reduce developer costs by passing long-term subsidence costs on to the homeowners. Village de l'Est is a good example. Its thick organic soils are now being dewatered and oxidized and the residents whose homes are built on the land will be paying a premium for many years to come. . . . Governmental planning and housing agencies have an obligation to direct growth away from wetland zones and to inform the consumer about potential problem conditions.[27]

As this study predicted thirty years ago, residents in Village de l'Est and Eastern New Orleans did have to bear a high cost when Katrina hit in 2005. More than 50 percent of residential properties in Eastern New Orleans were substantially damaged;[28] the Six Flags theme park, once a popular attraction in New Orleans East, was afflicted so severely by wind and water that the site remained abandoned and rotten ten years later, with naked metal structures, graffiti, and debris left all over the place. Any potential resurrection of the amusement park, now surrounded by overgrown marshes and with little sign of human habitation, seems unlikely in the foreseeable future. As of March 2014, only two proposals had been submitted; they suggested rejuvenating the abandoned site into "Jazzland," a theme park with a New Orleans feel.[29] Like the Broadmoor case, the rebuilding of Village de l'Est represents a mixed blessing: while it is encouraging that people with limited resources make use of their strong civic capacity to reclaim their properties and community, the reconstruction of this sinking wetland is also aggravating the problems of land subsidence, housing deterioration, and ultimately, vulnerability to future disasters.

Submergence and recovery from a vulnerable terrain, therefore, have been part of the city's lived experiences. In this context, the unprecedented magnitude of damage and misery inflicted by Katrina should not be understood as a unique, singular event; rather, the nation's most devastating disaster is on the continuum of disasters that have wrought havoc since the birth of the city. Hurricanes Betsy, Camille, Georges, and Ivan have all swept through the Big Easy in the twentieth century alone. Thus, the greater New Orleans area has had to confront a cycle of destruction and address its effects with continual reconstruction. In 1965 Hurricane Betsy, for example, caused material and human damages of $372 million and claimed eighty-one lives across Southeast Louisiana. In 1969 Hurricane Camille, a Category 5 storm, proved to be one of the most formidable hurricanes of the twentieth century, causing $350 million worth of damage and 335 deaths in Louisiana.[30] The increasing cost of hurricane damage culminated in Katrina's wake. Among all affected regions, the magnitude of damage was by far the greatest in Louisiana, where the number of deaths reached 1,577 and far surpassed fatalities in neighboring states, such as the 238 deaths in Mississippi and 14 in Florida. In Louisiana, Orleans Parish sustained the most significant devastation. Katrina flooded about 80 percent of the city, and the depth of flooding varied from one foot to more than ten feet of water. The hurricane also facilitated the population decline of the city, which lost about half of its population—more specifically, the number of residents in the city plummeted from 484,674 in 2000 to 254,502 in 2006. About 70 percent of the occupied housing units in 2005, totaling almost 134,000, were damaged by the hurricane.[31]

As the most catastrophic natural disaster in American history, Hurricane Katrina resulted in substantial financial losses in both public and private sectors, amounting to an estimated cost of $200 billion.[32] The bulk of recovery funding came from the federal government. US Congress appropriated more than $100 billion over eight years to facilitate immediate relief as well as long-term recovery.[33] Insurance companies received more than 1.7 million Katrina-related claims and spent

$41.1 billion in payments, accounting for more than twice the insurance payments from the federal National Flood Insurance Program (NFIP). In fact, the size of insurance payments from natural disasters has increased dramatically over the years, as most of the largest disasters in the United States have happened in recent decades. Among the ten most expensive hurricanes in American history, seven occurred in the fourteen months between 2004 and 2005,[34] and the cost of these disasters amounted to $88.6 billion in total.[35] The continued presence of geographic vulnerabilities, coupled with the rising cost of flood protection, makes it more important than ever to resolve the dilemma of resilient communities in a particularly vulnerable city such as New Orleans.

The Shrinking City

Just as encounters with hurricanes have made the city chronically susceptible to natural hazards, the macroeconomic downturn has also constrained the city's capacity to mitigate natural hazards. Adapting to climate risk is expensive, and financial capacity is one of the most formidable barriers to adaptation.[36] In this sense, New Orleans has been constrained by depopulation and economic decline. Before Katrina, the population of New Orleans had already dwindled by about 30 percent—from about 627,525 in 1960 to approximately 452,170 in 2005[37]—and this trend was accentuated by the arrival of the storm, when the count hit the nadir with slightly more than 250,000 in 2006. While the city gradually recovered some of its population to reach 343,829 in 2010, the downward pattern continues to compromise the city's ability to adjust to the accelerating challenges of climate change.[38]

To put this in a comparative context, data show that the trajectory of New Orleans parallels that of many post–World War II Rust Belt cities that have suffered from consistent decline since the 1960s. Figure I.1 plots population changes during the twentieth century in several cities across the United States.[39] Overall, population changes in these cities commonly show an inverse U-shaped pattern, with a sharp increase during the early period of the twentieth century, plateauing somewhat in the 1930s and 1940s, and then decreasing at various paces after the 1960s. In terms of population size, these cities were among the twenty largest urban places in the 1900 Census. However, by 2000, only two

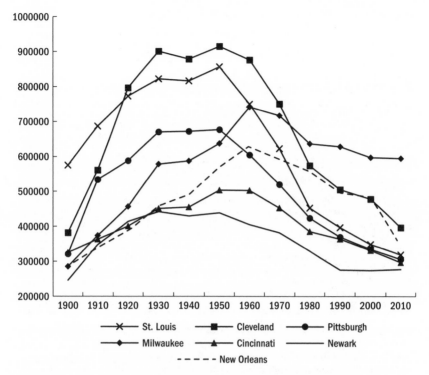

Figure I.1. Population change in Rust Belt cities, 1900–2010. Source: Historical Census Data. Compiled by author.

cities—Detroit (tenth) and Milwaukee (nineteenth)—made the top twenty. The biggest drop occurred in Saint Louis, which had the fourth-largest population in 1900 (575,238) but dropped to forty-ninth place by 2000, with 348,189 people living within city limits. New Orleans also sustained significant population loss over the century, and by 2000, the size of the city had reduced to what it was in 1940. Like many cities in the industrial Northeast, the number of post-Katrina inhabitants has diminished further, to almost approximately the population of the early twentieth century.

While the city lost much of its population, its southern competitors caught up. In 1900 New Orleans was the twelfth-largest city in America, with a total population of about 290,000. The second-largest city in the South at the time, Louisville, Kentucky, was far behind New Orleans,

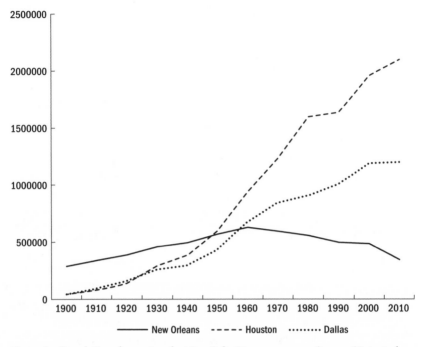

Figure I.2. Population change in select Sun Belt cities, 1900–2010. Source: Historical Census Data. Compiled by author.

with a population of 200,000. The decline presents a sharp contrast with the rise of "Sun Belt" cities in the South (Figure I.2). Despite continued growth until the 1960s, the relative rank of New Orleans has been dropping as a result of the rapid expansion of other cities in the South and Southwest. In 2000 New Orleans fell to thirty-first place, whereas other cities, such as Houston, Phoenix, and Dallas, were among the top ten most populous cities. Houston, for example, was the fourth-largest metropolis in 2010 with a total population of 2.1 million, and Dallas was the ninth-largest city with 1.2 million people. At the beginning of the twentieth century, Houston and Dallas were small towns equivalent to the size of Youngstown, Ohio, whereas New Orleans was the nation's biggest port city with a population more than three times as large as that of Houston and Dallas combined. As Figure I.2 shows, the demographic trajectories of Houston, Dallas, and New Orleans continue to diverge. As of 2010, it is evident how the populations of these two cities have dramatically increased over the past century in contrast to New Orleans, whose population either stagnated or diminished to a significant degree as the century progressed.

Combined with population loss, low population density has also compromised the city's ability to deliver adequate services. As shown in Figure I.3, New Orleans has maintained low population density relative to other postindustrial cities that have decreased substantially in size. Compared to the small, densely populated cities in the Northeast and Midwest, New Orleans has a large, extensive land area and is more sparsely populated than its northern counterparts (Figure I.3). The population density in New Orleans proper increased somewhat until the 1960s, then started decreasing as the city began expanding its territory to the east of the Industrial Canal and developed suburban-style residential housing in New Orleans East. However, the residential development in Eastern New Orleans eventually coincided with the city's population decrease and contributed to lowering the population density.

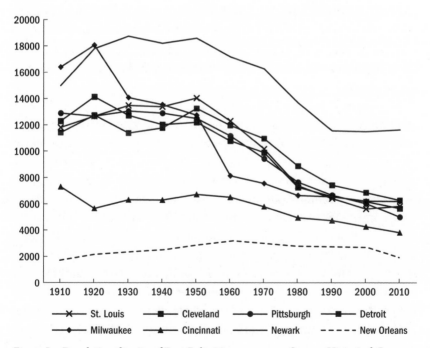

Figure I.3. Population density of Rust Belt cities, 1910–2010. Source: Historical Census Data. Compiled by author.

The broad sketch of demographic shrinkage reveals the difficulty in managing the city's territory with limited resources. The sparse distribution of its urban population places a heavy burden on the city government because of the high cost of public service provisions per person. Basic services such as public transportation, fixing streetlights, and repairing potholes become arduous tasks if people are spread out. In addition to this lower quality of services, vacant and abandoned properties spread throughout the city proper also invite crime and drive down home prices. Compared to, say, New York City, which experienced a sharp fiscal crisis in the 1970s but resuscitated itself through austerity programs,[40] the economic decline in New Orleans was more persistent and fundamentally undermined the city's ability to govern and respond effectively to the aftermath of Hurricane Katrina.

Research Design and Data

This book employs a single-case-study framework, defined as "the intensive study of a single unit wherever the aim is to shed light on a question pertaining to a broader class of units."[41] I chose to study New Orleans as a meaningful case for urban resilience because it permits us to reevaluate the utility of community civic capacity in dealing with various challenges facing a contemporary city.

Of course, there is a trade-off between studying multiple cases and studying a single case. To investigate the relationship between civic capacity and natural disasters, many studies tend to engage multiple cases and employ a comparative framework. Some studies compare societal responses to various disaster types such as tsunamis, earthquakes, and hurricanes to demonstrate that civil society, regardless of government type, contributes to overcoming the crisis.[42] This "method of agreement" finds commonalities on the study variable across the cases with varying general characteristics.[43] Others employ a neighborhood comparison strategy, whereby neighborhoods under similar distressed conditions are compared to examine various manifestations of their social capital and their different outcomes.[44] As a "method of difference," this approach ties the outcome with the study variable when other conditions are similar.

In comparing civic capacity across various disaster types and neighborhoods, these comparative case studies commonly affirm the positive role of civic engagement in substituting for a meager governmental response. The analytic framework of these comparative case analyses is implicitly based on the quantitative logic, which holds everything constant except the variable of interest.[45] For example, as criteria for quasi-statistical control, Sacheffer and Kashdan make clear that all three cases they use—the San Francisco earthquakes, the Great Chicago Fire, and Hurricane Katrina in New Orleans—are major disasters of similarly great impact on population in an urban area.[46] Without the presence of a centralized disaster response agency such as FEMA, they further argue, the first two cities—San Francisco and Chicago—achieved successful recovery with the active participation of multiple private actors. On the other hand, in the case of New Orleans, where the centralized Federal Emergency Management Agency (FEMA) was present, governmental intervention slowed down the recovery process and increased the cost of reconstruction to a significant degree.

While these studies elucidate the significance of civic engagement, the comparative studies tend to overlook the politicized aspect of civic actions, which can be observed more easily by comparing within-units in a single case. Furthermore, the historical conditions of a disaster site are one of the most crucial variables in assessing the success or failure of disaster response, and yet the comparative case study design takes this local variance as one of the "control" considerations. This is a potentially weak design because few cases have decidedly different or similar characteristics.[47] The strength and capacity of local actors, thus, tends to be omitted in the analysis and makes the result dubious.

Therefore, increasing the number of cases would compromise the depth and breadth of description because "[t]he more cases one has, the less intensively each one is studied."[48] This does not mean that comparing multiple cases prevents us from providing a thick description, giving us only a cursory examination of each case; rather, it means that we are bound to tone down certain characteristics that we could otherwise delve into more deeply in exchange for ensuring generalizability and comparability across cases. For example, if I intend to frame natural disasters more broadly and compare New Orleans with cities that experienced similar yet different kinds of natural hazards—such as earthquakes and citywide fires[49]—or urban crises such as those of September 11, 2001,[50] I cannot fully incorporate the ecological conditions such as sea-level rise and land subsidence that are central to analyzing the pros and cons of civic power. These geographic factors are too important to serve merely as background conditions or an exogenous shock because they contributed to defining, shaping, and activating the collective interests of residents across neighborhoods in a way that is quite distinct from what other types of disasters and crises would produce. For example, the modern history of urban development in New Orleans is tightly associated with the geographically uneven distribution of vulnerabilities, whereby the city's disadvantaged population had little choice but to settle in the low-lying, disaster-prone part of the city. Many homeowners in these communities, who had lived on their properties for generations, necessarily developed a strong sense of attachment to their communities and expressed a strong desire to return thereto after a disaster.[51] In addition to the strong emotional ties to the site, compensatory programs from the federal disaster relief system—however meager and inefficient they might be—further justified the option to rebuild, generating a repetitive cycle of loss and recovery.[52] In this context, people's engagement, while helpful during the recovery process, contributed to the reproduction of vulnerabilities and inequalities. Analyzing the historical construction of preferences and actions of disaster victims, therefore, allows us to simultaneously consider the potential and pitfalls of civic engagement in the context of natural disasters.

For these reasons, I opted for a single-case study and leverage the advantage of rich analysis and description on one subject. Within a single-case-study framework, I employ a mixed-methods strategy that incorporates both quantitative and qualitative logic into exploring the main inquiry of the book—whether resilient communities lead to building a resilient city. The mixed-methods approach has several advantages for a single-case study.[53] In this book, the mixed-methods approach affords us an opportunity to examine how the similar motivations in each community, that is, post-disaster reconstruction, may be associated with the uneven outcomes and growing disparities at the city level.

Furthermore, a mixed methodology also accommodates the diversity of data sources I gathered—administrative records, historical documents, census statistics, field notes, interview transcripts, and so on—as well as the multiple analytic techniques used in each chapter. Within a single-case-study research design, I support my argument by drawing on multiple sources of data and employing a mixed-method strategy: a type of analysis based on multiple techniques and types of data.[54] To this end, I accessed various data sources. To trace the interaction between civic actors and various levels of governments, chapter 2 relies on archival sources, including government documents, as well as local and national newspapers, such as the *Times-Picayune*, the *States-Item*, and the *New York Times*. To demonstrate how civic activism took shape during the post-Katrina period, chapters 3 and 4 are based on quantitative analyses of citywide civic capacity and reconstruction. An ideal data set for civic capacity would include data in each neighborhood that surveys the membership of each civic-oriented organization, their financial health, and their leadership structure *before* Katrina. Unfortunately, a comprehensive citywide data set on New Orleans civic resources before and after Katrina is not readily available. To overcome this limitation and estimate the strength of civic capacity, I rely on several pre-Katrina datasets, including the local directory of all civic organizations, demographic and socioeconomic indicators from Census 2000, and election data from the Louisiana secretary of state.[55] Taken together, these data sets show what collective resources had been available before the catastrophe. The pre-Katrina socioeconomic and electoral information is then analyzed alongside post-Katrina recovery data at various time periods, which were gathered from a nonprofit organization (New Orleans Data Center) as well as from the city government. Not only do these chapters elucidate the isolated effect of pre-Katrina civic capacity on post-Katrina recovery in each neighborhood; they also analyze the broad consequences of such an effect. In so doing, these chapters employ spatial methods that use statistical techniques and mapping software to present spatial interactions and connections among the city's neighborhoods. The spatial lag regression used in chapter 3, for example, allows us to examine the interaction (or lack thereof) among communities in the repopulation process, which has an important implication in connecting community resilience with urban resilience. Chapter 4 also engages in spatial analysis by mapping the differential patterns of repopulation and reconstruction across the city and highlighting the mismatch between slow repopulation and active reconstruction in flood-damaged areas.

Chapter 5 uses a mix of interview and observational data I collected during my two rounds of fieldwork in 2008 and 2010. During my stay,

I attended public meetings and interviewed city officials, key community organizers, and residents in two adjacent neighborhoods: Broadmoor and Freret. These neighborhoods are by no means representative of all communities, and yet I selected them because they embody the tension between community and urban resilience. In addition to interviewing key figures in these neighborhoods, I attended neighborhood meetings, master-plan meetings in each planning district, and public city council meetings. This chapter alone is based on twenty semistructured interviews with people in various positions of disaster recovery, transcripts from ten public meetings at the neighborhood, district, and city levels, as well as historical and statistical data on the neighborhood history.

Plan of the Book

Chapter 1 discusses key theoretical issues surrounding civic capacity and urban resilience. After defining resilience and identifying the nature of the problem, I explain why communities' civic strength may lead to vulnerable resilience in the city and how legitimate government coercion can help coordinate the varying community interests.

After the theoretical and conceptual discussions, the rest of the chapter is organized chronologically to document the pre-Katrina as well as the short- and long-term trajectories of post-Katrina civic engagement. Chapter 2 builds a historical narrative on how New Orleans's civic actors influenced policies and politics around emergency management at the federal, state, and local levels. This chapter focuses on the ways in which citizen requests have influenced the federal, state, and local governments. This has been done in two ways. First, civic actors urged the federal government to pursue structural solutions by constructing levees and drainage systems around flood-prone areas. To government officials and residents alike, disasters were considered infrequent disruptions from which the city of New Orleans had to be protected, and the protection was mainly provided by the federal government's engineering and insurance programs. The expanding protection instilled an elevated sense of security in residents and justified rebuilding in vulnerable regions. Second, because of the federal protection, the Louisiana and New Orleans governments developed policies that minimize investment in long-term hazard mitigation for the sake of economic development.

Chapter 3 addresses how civic engagement affects the physical rebuilding of a broken city. Based on the data set of more than five thousand post-disaster building permit applications submitted during the early period of recovery, this chapter examines the ways in which civic capacity influenced the process of property reconstruction after Katrina. I find that high levels of local political participation led to a greater number of building permit approvals as well as faster issuance of permits. While affirming the positive aspect of civic capacity on service distribution, the findings also reflect the dilemma of reconstruction because the physical rebuilding occurred in a haphazard pattern without reference to the long-term, coherent planning. The strength of civic power revealed the lack of local government capacity to enforce strict building regulations, leaving the city no less vulnerable to natural hazards than it had been before Katrina.

Chapter 4 is key to showing the long-term consequences of the civic-oriented recovery, in terms of widening the racial and social disparities across the city. In this chapter, I investigate the relationship between community civic structure and the patterns of repopulation after Katrina. Using a novel data set on the repopulation of entire New Orleans neighborhoods for ten years, I find that structural conditions based on civic organizations such as churches, schools, and childcare centers lead to two disparate patterns of recovery in the long run. In a high-lying location, civic structure facilitates repopulation and reduces vulnerabilities in a way that was expected. However, in low-lying neighborhoods, civic-oriented repopulation is much slower than in high-lying communities, and active civic performances increase social vulnerabilities by attracting low-income, minority populations. This, I argue, creates a two-tiered city with an enlarging gap between the city's safe and vulnerable areas.

Chapter 5 expands on the idea of community resilience and shows how communities have grown to be self-reliant but have done so through limited engagement with cognate communities or city government. Using both archival data and direct observation of the post-Katrina rebuilding process, I describe the processes in which the ideas of community self-reliance, prevalent before Katrina, have become equated with the moral trait of resilience in the post-disaster period. I illustrate this argument by examining community development in Broadmoor and Freret. Initiated by community development corporations and active neighborhood organizations, reconstruction in these neighborhoods was more extensive than what their socioeconomic conditions would have predicted. Simultaneously, however, civically oriented recovery transformed these neighborhoods in subtle yet powerful ways, such as by privileging stable homeowners over poor renters and by inviting new economic opportunities at the expense of existing local businesses.

In the conclusion, I discuss the implication of resilience building in the domestic context, especially with regard to what cities can learn from the New Orleans experience. In revitalizing urban areas, the New Orleans case demonstrates that encouraging physical restoration and expansion alone is not the best strategy for building long-term resilience. Rather, it warrants caution against equating resilience with the physical growth of a city, especially for those cities that have experienced depopulation and degeneration. Rethinking resilience in conjunction with decline, therefore, leads to policy suggestions that we allocate more resources for post-crisis resilience in a realistic, rather than hopeful, assessment of a city's future, and that we communicate about available policy options thoroughly with local communities.

1

Resilient Communities in a Vulnerable City

Eighty miles south of New Orleans lies Isle de Jean Charles, a small island that is home to two American tribes, the Biloxi-Chitimacha-Choctaw and the United Houma Nation. Since 1955, a series of hurricanes and constant wetland erosion have washed away 98 percent of the island. Rising water has also encroached upon Island Road, the only highway connecting the island with inland Louisiana. Although the tribes are worried about losing their historic habitation, most of them are feeling the threats from nature and preparing to leave the island. In response, the federal government allocated $46 million to relocate the island's sixty residents and help them form a new community in a safer area. This is part of the Department of Housing and Urban Development's (HUD's) $1 billion National Disaster Resilience Competition (NDRC), a national program intended to reward state and local governments that present proposals to mitigate extreme weather events and make communities more resilient.[1]

Since two massive natural disasters—Hurricane Katrina in 2005 and then Superstorm Sandy in 2013—devastated one of America's most culturally rich and economically vibrant areas, the term "resilience" has quickly entered into the parlance of national and local decision-makers. Originally used to describe a rebound of a plunging national economy, resilience is now discussed more frequently to define the human capacity to withstand the adverse effects of extreme events, from natural disasters to terrorist attacks. The private sector has also begun responding to impending crises in cities. In parallel with the Obama administration's NDRC, the Rockefeller Foundation launched the 100 Resilient Cities initiative, which provides funding for each selected international city to create a comprehensive resilience strategy led by a chief resilience officer. In this mega-philanthropic project, New Orleans has played a leading role and serves as a successful case of urban resilience. As the board members of the foundation put it, New Orleans "is the birthplace of resilience" and serves as a "model" for other cities, proving that people's undying will and commitment can save a city from a dire situation like Hurricane Katrina. The efforts to integrate resilience planning into urban governance began in New Orleans, then stretched to the East Coast after Hurricane Sandy struck the region as experts suggested various ways to "climate-proof" the city.[2] With strong backing from the federal government, New York City's government held a design competition, Rebuild by Design, to incorporate innovative urban design proposals into that city's resilience planning. The pursuit of resilience continues to hold sway—to the extent that some people complained that the mayor spent too much energy on ensuring "long-term resilience" at the expense of delaying compensation for disaster victims. In fact, none of the twenty thousand homeowners who had applied to have their houses rebuilt had received federal grants as of 2014.[3]

Despite the growing popularity of resilience planning and the frequent usage of the related terms "communities," "networks," and "partnership," a nuanced discussion is surprisingly scant when it comes to how a community is defined and how communities can promote resilience. Nowhere in the proposal for NDRC is there a clear definition of that term, for example, even though the word "community" appears thirty-six times in the seven-page document. As it turns out, "communities" can encompass a wide range of jurisdictions in this nationally held competition, and can be defined as whole states, counties/parishes, cities, or even US territories.[4] These units are different from what we commonly think of as communities. They might be larger in size than a single neighborhood but are generally understood as much smaller geographic units than states, cities, or counties. These political units are not as intimate as neighborhoods either. As social and economic units, neighborhoods instill a more distinct sense of community than a city, county, or state can invoke. People in Isle de Jean Charles, for example, are reluctant to leave because the island is their community and represents their culture, history, and communal livelihood. Likewise, many felt the same way in the Lower Ninth Ward in New Orleans, where multiple generations of African Americans had raised families, owned homes, and built their community. Nested within the city, the Lower Ninth was home to middle-class Black families who were denied access to the city's higher ground. For them, it was not just a submerged land that they lost, but the distinctive social and historical reference points and experiences that had sustained them.

This chapter draws upon this spatial scale of communities and explores the reasons why resilient individual communities may not always make for a resilient city. I explain why the two competing notions of resilience create a tension between the goals of communities on the one hand and a city government on the other, and further discuss what we can expect when local communities prevail. New Orleans's experience is a case in which the gap between the spatial scale of a community and of a city is palpable. With discrete goals and constraints between respective neighborhoods and the city as a whole, it shows why civic-oriented neighborhood recovery alone was unable to completely address the complexities of urban crises. Without properly defining what "resilience" means and how the strategies of resilience may differ depending on the spatial scope of the area at hand, we may miss this gap and end up making a vague and underdeveloped argument that community civic capacity promotes urban resilience, or even identify the former with the latter. This argument is tautological because, in large part, the very definition of civic capacity already entails a certain amount of resilience. To the extent that resilience means regaining the rhythm of a previous period, a high rate of civic participation will likely foster communal resilience most of the time. As I will show in this chapter, however, achieving forward-focused urban resilience requires more progressive and complex strategies that merit equitable and balanced development. In this sense, neighborhood resilience cannot completely replace or represent urban resilience, and distinguishing the two is an important step toward understanding the limits of community civic capacity.

Defining Urban Resilience

In disaster contexts, "resilience" largely refers to a process of recovering from damage and restoring a functional state to at least pre-disaster levels.[5] At the individual level, being resilient refers to an ability to survive a crisis, cope with its aftermath both physically and mentally, and return to the pre-crisis state. A resilient individual is, therefore, one who overcomes the adversities of a disaster and reclaims her health, property, and life in general. Community resilience is built on a similar connotation. Aldrich discusses the concept of resilience as the capacity to adapt to disruption and crisis at the neighborhood level, defining it as a "neighborhood's capacity to weather crises such as disasters and engage in effective and efficient recovery through coordinated efforts and cooperative activities."[6] However, "community" and "urban resilience" are frequently used interchangeably, often without a clear distinction across different geographic scales. For example, Aldrich and Meyer define "community resilience" as "the collective ability of a neighborhood or a geographically defined area to deal with stressors and efficiently resume the rhythms of daily life through cooperation following shocks."[7] Likewise, the Rockefeller Foundation's centennial project on urban resilience defines it as the "[ability to make] people, communities, and systems better prepared to withstand catastrophic events—both natural and manmade—and able to bounce back more quickly and emerge stronger from these shocks and stresses."[8]

Since most studies on resilience draw upon community (or neighborhood) boundaries, these studies tend to treat neighborhoods as units of analysis to validate the positive effect of civic resources. When communities with high and low levels of civic capacity are compared, civically active communities appear to show a greater level of resilience than their less civic counterparts. In *Heat Wave*, for example, Eric Klinenberg compared two spatially adjacent neighborhoods in Chicago—Black North Lawndale and Latino South Lawndale—and concluded that while similarly exposed to high heat, South Lawndale had many fewer casualties than North Lawndale because of the strong civic ties among the Latino residents.[9] This controlled comparison served as strong evidence to support policies that can enhance mutual trust and collective efficacy among community members to mitigate disasters' negative impacts, such as time banking, focus group meetings, and social events.[10] The argument then goes so far as to suggest that strengthening the social structure of the at-risk area can be more efficient than spending resources on physical infrastructure, such as levees and housing elevation.[11]

Although counting how many people died or returned to their neighborhood may correctly identify community civic resources as a main cause of success for achieving community-level resilience, it cannot address the question about how a variegated recovery pattern may affect the resilience of an entire city. Although extensive reconstruction in some civically active communities in New Orleans may have benefitted the individual residents of those communities, these community-wide reconstructions may actually increase the cost of protection and sustainability for the overall city if such reconstruction occurs in the city's high-risk areas. In that instance, all city dwellers who are directly or indirectly affected by natural disasters—especially those occupying the risky parts of the city—must bear the cost of increased risks.

In this sense, urban resilience goes beyond the traditional notions of community-led recovery that focuses on speedy repopulation and extensive reconstruction in the damaged areas. Instead, urban resilience is defined more broadly as the *city*'s ability to distribute resources to reduce vulnerability, adapt to external risks, and maintain its economic vitality.[12] While community resilience focused primarily on restoring the "dry infrastructure" in the affected neighborhoods—the personal properties, commercial establishments, and social institutions that had been encroached upon by the hurricane—urban or regional resilience in the context of climate change engages a greater number of spatial units and tends to entail broader and more complex challenges, particularly with regards to reducing and adapting to ecological vulnerabilities. Here, ecological vulnerabilities refer to the degree to which a collection of individuals, or communities, is exposed and sensitized to external stressors such as environmental change, natural hazards, and adverse social conditions (such as gentrification or urban violence).[13]

Given the ecological aspect of resilience, therefore, it would be too restrictive to associate resilience with revitalization and redevelopment driven primarily by marketized interventions. Scholars have rightly pointed out that post-crisis, resilience-oriented projects are often driven by market forces and only exacerbate and perpetuate the preexisting inequalities within the city.[14] The privatized mode of resilience building, it is further criticized, glosses over the politicized outcomes of such resilience, which are only selectively enjoyed by a certain group of residents in the city.[15] While resilience should not be equated with privatized revitalization alone, I pay further attention to the potential consequences when *civic* (and individual) motivations at the community level are concomitantly aligned with the dynamic of expansion and redevelopment.

As we will examine in later chapters, successful civic interventions tend to involve the familiar logic of reconstruction, rebuilding, and repopulation, albeit in a more empowering and equitable fashion. While the civic-oriented recovery is by no means identical with the neoliberal mode of reconstruction in its scope and intention, civic and privatized approaches may not fully replace the void created by the absence of centralized, authoritative measures that are critical to achieving long-term ecological resilience in times of crisis. Therefore, the primary focus of the book lies in capturing the patterns of reproduction and continuation of vulnerabilities caused by pursuing revitalization for all facets of a locale, along with the uneven distribution of the benefits of privatized redevelopment.

Operationally, reducing environmental vulnerabilities and adapting to existing risks require fundamental changes in preexisting policy arrangements, mainly in terms of limiting previously available options and imposing stricter regulations. For example, after a catastrophic hurricane or rainfall, riverfront development is generally curtailed and monitored, and more stringent building elevation requirements are enforced to prevent the area from being submerged or flooded again. For earthquakes, seismic resiliency design and restrictions on the degree of swaying (called drift by engineers) become important criteria for helping to withstand shocks and preventing extensive damages. These coercive strategies bring about clashes between various stakeholders, and often encounter resistance from those whose livelihood is directly and disproportionately affected. Compared to community resilience, therefore, it is important to understand that cultivating resilience at a larger spatial scale is more likely to be contentious than consensual, thus requiring a greater level of coordination.

However, despite (or because of) the important differences between them, it is often difficult to extend people's perception of resilience beyond the community level to a larger spatial scale. People seldom recognize a distinction between the two and tend to pay closer attention to their surrounding communities than to the larger geographic unit. Even though they are located close to the coast and exposed to vulnerabilities, for example, residents' concerns about flooding often reach only so far as their properties and proximate communities are concerned, and not to consideration of the city or county in which they reside. Permanent, entrenched risks do not register easily in people's minds, and there is a great deal of optimism once people restore their own pre-disaster liveli-hood. Ten years after Katrina hit the city, New Orleanians gave highly positive views about the future of the city. In a tenth anniversary public opinion poll, 70 percent of the residents of New Orleans said that the city is going in the right direction.[16] And a limited scope of risk percep-tion does not just exist in New Orleans but can be found in many coastal communities. In a survey of residents in a coastal county in Maryland, a team of researchers found that the risk perception on sea-level rise was only salient at the smaller scales of neighborhood and household, but not at the larger community scales such as county. When asked whether sea-level rise was a risk to their own home, neighborhood, or county, those who are exposed to the risk of flooding said sea-level rise is indeed a risk to their own home and neighborhood—but not to their county.[17]

In sum, the concept of and strategies for community resilience are different and should be divorced from those for urban and regional re-silience. The conceptual distinction suggests that the greater the spatial scale becomes, the more complex the approaches are to achieving resil-ience. Especially for the cities confronting crises, urban resilience not only entails efforts to restore and rebuild what has been destroyed but also includes decisions to identify problems and implement long-term strategies for a sustainable, efficient urban system. The process can often be contentious and complex, as multiple interests and distributive deci-sions are involved. Therefore, reconciling and coordinating various civic demands becomes a significant task at the city level, and this is especially so when people's perceptions on resilience are set at a community scale and there is no agreement on what is best for the larger spatial unit in which their respective communities are located. In this context, consid-ering the spatial context of civic activism is an important benchmark for parsing out the relationship between civic capacity and resilience. De-pending on where and when it takes place, active civic participation may have nuanced effects on accomplishing optimal outcomes for the city.

Resilience as Adaptation: Shrinkage in the Age of Climate Change

Although some New Orleanians imagined a "bigger and better" city right after the hurricane, such a promise seemed hard to fulfill given the continued population decrease and chronic revenue shortage.[18] Resorting to market-based strategies alone, such as promoting tourism and business, encouraging downtown development, and privatizing city services, would not likely address the long-standing patterns of sinking and shrinking in the city that were documented in the introduction. The climatic and economic crises pose real and ongoing challenges that require a careful and comprehensive overhaul of city policies, not a false promise of economic expansion.[19]

Urban resilience strategies may well embrace, rather than fight, geographic constraints while making the city more manageable, and the "soft" or nonstructural approaches to curtail settlements in low-lying areas would ultimately make the city more compact than its pre-Katrina size. Reducing settlements in geographically low-lying areas is also called "managed coastal retreat."[20] Compared to the "hard" techniques that protect and fight against rising water (such as building levees and canals), managed coastal retreat refers to a strategy of shifting development away from vulnerable areas along the coast to provide room for the water, protect the shoreline, and adapt to potential sea-level rise.[21] Instead of armoring the community with dams and walls, a managed retreat aims to relocate people and properties from the threatened area. For example, the local government can enforce strict regulations on buildings in hazardous areas to make it difficult and costly to build a structure in such locations or, if built at all, to ensure the safety of those buildings. Furthermore, the federal government can design a public insurance program that places a high premium on the properties in flood-prone areas and thus discourages property development in those areas.[22] The most drastic measure would be relocation, which means moving people and properties away from the high-risk areas.[23] FEMA's Hazard Mitigation Grant Program (HMGP), for example, has been financing buyout programs that help state or local governments defray the cost of purchasing properties located in high-risk areas.

Although a relatively new idea, retreat is already happening in some communities that have experienced both the direct and indirect impacts of rising sea levels. In some cases, retreat is embedded in market-based activities. Real estate sales in coastal areas have slowed down over time,

suggesting that people are becoming more reluctant to risk their investment in flood-prone areas. In Miami-Dade County in Florida, for example, the most flood-prone areas experienced about an 8 percent drop in
home sales, compared to a 2.6 percent increase at the national level.[24] In
other cases, residents in coastal regions are requesting to sell their properties and relocate to a dry area. After Hurricane Sandy, a neighborhood
in Staten Island organized to request buyouts for their damaged homes
instead of rebuilding.[25] After experiencing repetitive flooding throughout their lifetimes, people in North Carolina are facing a "wrenching decision" to leave behind their beloved communities and find new homes
in dry areas.[26] Mostly inhabited by low- to middle-income households,
people in these flood-prone communities are beginning to weigh the
costs and benefits of protecting properties on vulnerable terrain.

Retreating from hazardous areas is closely related to the economic
idea of compact cities.[27] Also referred to as rightsizing, planned shrinkage, or smart decline, the compact city approach aims at adjusting the
size of the city according to a realistic assessment of a city's financial
capacity so that the city government can sustain itself.[28] In the United
States, an increasing number of cities have embraced shrinkage as part
of their long-term planning strategies. Youngstown, Ohio, and Buffalo,
New York, are two of the well-known examples among depopulated
cities that have actively engaged with adapting to a smaller population.
Indeed, the compact city approach requires a fundamental shift from
the conventional, growth-oriented strategies to prioritizing and target-
ing development in certain areas but not all over the city.[29] Although the
empirical evidence in support of compactness remains inconclusive,[30]
scholars and practitioners generally agree that the compact city approach is a desirable strategy for enhancing sustainability and resilience
in a declining, depopulated region.[31]

Contrary to popular belief, this "shrinking strategy" does not rely
solely on private market incentives such as abandoning unused land and
vacant properties and leaving each neighborhood to fend for itself. Even
when a city is losing its population and has a high vacancy rate, it cannot
simply close its operations like a shopping mall. Depopulation leads to
decreased population density, which happens in irregular forms across
the city and therefore creates inefficient service delivery and raises con-

cerns for safety. Therefore, it is important to track settlement patterns and adjust service delivery and investment accordingly. In this sense, the compact city framework still seeks to maximize the advantages of the city as a densely developed urban form by reducing empty, unused space, saving energy, and increasing social and economic interactions within the proximate distance.[32]

Imagining a Smaller City

The idea of clustering redevelopment did briefly appear in the city's series of planning efforts after Katrina, though it was ultimately rejected by residents. Convened on September 30, 2005, the Bring New Orleans Back Commission (BNOBC) was the first citywide organization that sought to implement a shrinkage plan. Chaired by Joseph Canizaro and consisting of members from the national research group Urban Land Institute, BNOBC published a blueprint for New Orleans covering four main areas: flood and stormwater protection, transit and transportation, parks and open space, and neighborhood rebuilding plans. In this proposal, the committee suggested that open space and parks could serve multiple functions to provide amenities and work as an internal stormwater management system. To create more open space, BNOBC proposed a long-term plan to identify and acquire properties at their pre-Katrina market value and allotted $12 billion as an estimated cost of citywide acquisition.

Idealistic as it may sound, the proposal did acknowledge that the city needs a new approach that incorporates the city's real challenges, such as population decline and revenue shortage, and urged that neighborhoods "require sufficient population to support the equitable and efficient provision of public facilities and services." In other words, the proposal reflected the planners' view that redevelopment must occur within the constraints of the region, which, in the case of New Orleans, concerned continued economic decline. Restricting neighborhood recovery, therefore, was part of the BNOBC's larger plan to build higher levees and make the city more compactly redesigned and neighborhoods better connected to one another than in pre-Katrina state. Retrospectively, professionals in and out of the city gave sympathetic opinions to the general approach of BNOBC. As two urban planners in New Orleans put it:

Could city officials and residents have developed a citywide restructuring plan in these circumstances? BNOBC Land Use Committee members had rational reasons to propose restricted redevelopment. The strategic shrinkage would allow the city to guide redevelopment, target limited resources, maintain or increase density, and potentially reduce public service costs.[33]

Although adjusting the size of the city might have addressed the geographic and economic problems tied to continued sinking and population loss, implementing these ideas would have required a tremendous amount of coordination among residents and their representative bodies.

Despite the idealistic promises of retreat and rightsizing, the logistical processes necessary for a retreat from the coast and to shrink the city were highly contentious and unpopular among most residents. In New Orleans, plans that aimed at restricting recovery were met with harsh criticism. Contrary to popular belief, the BNOBC panelists had not singled out any one neighborhood for removal in proposing the new plan. Still, residents and media interpreted the commission's maps as a plan to diminish a significant part of the city's physical footprint. Residents in the neighborhoods where BNOBC suggested building parks and greenspace—such as Broadmoor, Gentilly, the Lower Ninth Ward, and New Orleans East—were particularly incensed. City council members responded to this angst by approving a resolution on December 15, 2005, that would allow residents from every part of New Orleans to return and recover if they wished.[34] The legislative body's support for equal treatment of neighborhoods constituted the cornerstone of the city's recovery plan. Five years later, in a public meeting in District E—which included most flooded sections, such as the Lower Ninth Ward and Holy Cross—Jackie Clarkson, then city councilmember-at-large, responded to citizens' complaints about slow recovery as follows:

I have to tell you this. Immediately after Katrina, when they, whoever they may be, were talking about shrinking the footprint . . . I stood in front the microphone at a press conference, publicly, side by side with Ms. [Cynthia] Willard-Lewis [council member for District E], and fought to not shrink one inch of the city. I not only said, "it is not proper, not necessary and we would not stand for it." I also said, "it is unconstitutional and violates property rights and I will fight it all the way up to the Congress. So this master plan has nothing, nothing to do with shrinking land; it has everything to do with bringing all these ideas."[35]

Indeed, the backlash was palpable. Not only did the city's least politically connected groups resist territorial shrinkage as an inequitable plan to dislocate already disadvantaged people, citizens also opposed the idea of rightsizing because they wanted to preserve the character and culture of their existing communities and the city.

In parallel with confronting the idea of reducing the city's size, residents also became active and vocal about restoring damaged properties and recovering the physical and social infrastructure in their respective communities by creating grassroots organizations, organizing neighborhood protests, and even running for local office. Tensions escalated. Some found hope in the "regeneration" of derelict neighborhoods like the Lower Ninth Ward, claiming that the low-lying, storm-devastated neighborhood was growing slowly but would regain the vitality that had once prevailed. Although "[e]mptiness still dominates the landscape once filled with homes," a news article reported, "clusters of rebuilt houses and new construction are not hard to find."[36] Territorial contraction was not a popular option among politicians either. When the Urban Land Institute published a proposal to temporarily ban development in the city's highly flooded areas, residents and their political representatives immediately opposed it.[37] During his campaign to defeat then-mayor Ray Nagin, Mitch Landrieu directly addressed the issue by saying, "Some people want to shrink our city. I won't let them. That only shrinks our future."[38]

Community and political actions were so powerful as to eventually thwart the city's plan, providing the active communities with momentum for redeveloping each and every corner of the city.[39] These civic demands against shrinkage were reflected in the final version of the city's Plan for the 21st Century, referred to as the Master Plan, which was adopted in 2010 and went through an amendment process from 2016 to 2018. The Master Plan promulgates that there is to be no shrinkage in the size of the city. The first goal of the Future Land Use Map, which is part of the Master Plan, states that there will be "no change in the overall existing footprint of the city."[40] Other goals include preserving neighborhood residential character and promoting mixed-use land use designations for flexible site development.

The fierce opposition to shrinkage and the ultimate grassroots victory serves as a vantage point from which to view the relationship between resistant civic action and urban resilience. So far, the ecological history of New Orleans has been framed as triumphant resistance against the city's inherent weaknesses. In fact, the city's rich cultural narratives, commercial advantages, and urbanization patterns have been inseparable from its topographical conditions. However, as Colten (2005) reminds us, the celebrated history of New Orleans's metropolitan development was also tied up with accommodating its geological vulnerabilities. These include heavy precipitation and recurring floods as well as continued land subsidence and poor drainage. To the extent that economic and climatic challenges are present and will continue to affect the region, what happened in New Orleans raises the question about why and how civic resistance gained momentum and eventually prevailed. In the following section, I explain why active engagement at the community level does not just imply a sentimental response to the loss of place but rather signals a rational reaction by community members, especially those living in marginalized neighborhoods. The lived experiences of vulnerability and inequity, I argue, further justify a concerted reaction by the community in favor of protecting marginalized neighborhoods, despite the possibility that such an action is likely to expose the residents to greater risks and damage.

Why Strong Communities Generate Vulnerable Resilience

Although the property buyout program is considered a beneficial and safe way to manage coastal hazards, it is also the most difficult policy to implement because of the myriad legal, political, and economic issues that involve properties in high-risk areas.[41] Perhaps because of this, coastal regions have actually had lower rates of property acquisition than high-risk areas of inland states. Since 2003, FEMA has paid only $417 million to property owners nationwide who are willing to sell their homes and remove themselves from a hazardous area. This is because individuals in coastal regions do not always opt for voluntary buyouts. Of the ten biggest disaster buyouts in the nation since 2003, only four coastal states made the list, namely New Jersey, New York,

North Carolina, and Virginia—the rest of the buyouts were located inland.[42] New Orleans, or Louisiana, did not make the list.

To explain why some communities may refuse to retreat, let us consider how individuals and communities view the costs and benefits of their future actions. Their calculations often involve two decisions. First, each individual can immediately return and restore his or her own property after a disaster. Alternatively, the individual could wait and follow the consensus. In most cases, people choose the former because it maximizes their immediate benefits against the uncertain future. As political scientist Elinor Ostrom explains:

> Individuals [and communities] attribute less value to benefits that they expect to receive in the distant future, and more value to those expected in the immediate future. In other words, individuals discount future benefits—how severely depends on several factors. Time horizons are affected by whether or not individuals [in communities] expect that they or their children will be present to reap these benefits, as well as by opportunities they may have for more rapid returns in other settings. . . . Discount rates are affected by the levels of physical and economic security faced by appropriators [communities] . . . [and] are also affected by the general norms shared by the individuals living in a particular society, or even a local community, regarding the relative importance of the future as compared with the present.[43]

As Ostrom opines, individuals and communities tend to discount future benefits for immediate gains, and disasters tend to truncate the time horizon even further in favor of short-term benefits. For many residents, it is too abstract to register the fact that since 1930 coastal Louisiana has lost land mass the area of the state of Delaware, or that it will lose more. They would rather disregard this data and rebuild their homes as quickly as possible. After extraordinary events, the future gain from following a long-term plan, such as retreating from the high-risk areas, is often perceived as too small or uncertain to consider.

Consequently, the primary reaction of affected people is often to protect and rebuild their immediate surroundings, such as their properties and built environment, and this can be better achieved by mobilizing the collective resources that the members of a neighborhood have developed rather than by doing it individually. Small in population and homogeneous in their socioeconomic status, neighborhoods are optimal geographic units to serve this purpose.[44] Unless long-term goals are firmly established and enforced reliably by a local government with support from superordinate governments, individuals will focus on rehabilitating their own properties, and neighborhood-based organizations will rally around the efforts to redevelop the communities.

On the other hand, relocation encourages individualized actions. It is mainly done through voluntarily selling off one's property, and communities rarely organize themselves to vacate their neighborhoods altogether. As legal experts Benjamin Means and Susan Kuo stated, "[i]n communities with high levels of social capital, individuals are more likely to invest in recovery because they believe their neighbors will, too. Buyouts send the opposite signal—that the neighbors will not return—and so buyout programs could be understood to create a kind of 'antisocial capital.'"[45] According to Means and Kuo, buyout programs by definition encourage antisocial activities. The main concern of the homeowners interested in joining a buyout program would be how much money his or her home would be appraised for compensation, and participating in neighborhood recovery activities would do little to raise their home value because in buyouts home values are determined at pre-disaster values. In contrast, if residents hope to stay in the neighborhood, improving the community conditions becomes much more important for home values, and the residents are more likely to organize to revive their community. In this sense, conditions considered essential to forming tight-knit communities—such as high rates of homeownership, residential stability, and the social bonds that result from such long tenure—may discourage residents from relocating.

In other words, a "sense of community"—the collective memory about the history, experience, and legacy of a community—plays a paradoxical role in shaping a collective opinion in favor of staying in a risky area rather than opting out of it. Furthermore, this tendency is likely to be more intensified among the poor and disadvantaged compared to those who "vote with their feet," that is, those who move out of their neighborhood soon after a disaster or who do not rally to convince others to move out together. With low property values, poor families cannot afford to move to a better location on the compensation from selling off their properties, so they are likely to choose to stay and organize themselves around revitalizing their current neighborhood. For them, neighborhoods are more than economic entities, and the social meaning of community becomes more salient when the residents face a decision that not only affects themselves but also those in their community.

In other words, the place attachment and resultant collective actions may reveal something deeper than civic spiritedness when these sentiments are intertwined with spatial inequality and socioeconomic disadvantages. This was a particularly important point in New Orleans, where the socioeconomically disadvantaged communities also occupied the city's most geographically vulnerable areas. For people living in these communities, moving out of their old community was hardly a viable option because they could not expect to acquire a property in the city's safer areas for their current home's value. Residential stability and the relatively high rates of homeownership in the communities of color, such as the Lower Ninth Ward, serve as impetus for civic action but had little to do with raising property values. Also, it is important to note that the city's income inequality had already been high, and there had been a substantial wage gap between White and Black residents. Using the Gini index, a representative measure of income inequality, a 2017 study shows that New Orleans's had been consistently higher than the national average since it was first measured in 1979 and until 2014. Accordingly, Black and Latino households tend to face greater housing burdens,[46] which means that in these households, renters and homeowners alike spend a larger percentage of their income on housing than their White counterparts. Facing these adverse economic conditions, the best possible strategy for the residents is to protect and revitalize their existing neighborhoods. In this sense, an emotional attachment may be an important factor but not the core reason why disaster victims demand to return and rebuild. Rather, the unique cultural and historic asset that is a neighborhood, built over time, may have further justified the residents' decisions to return to and stay in their communities despite the clear economic cost of staying in high-risk areas.

Because of strong bonds and resistant action, communities with a high level of civic capacity tend to rebuild faster and host a larger population, and stories of New Orleans's recovery mainly document this success.[47] Engaged citizens can collectively pressure the city government for better service through various means, such as lobbying, lawsuits, and protests.[48] When the New Orleans city government requested devastated communities to prove viability as a community, residents in Eastover, a politically active African American community (58 percent of the residents voted in the 2002 mayoral election), quickly turned to their homeowners' association to hire a professional planner and create a blueprint for revival, and continued rebuilding damaged houses.[49] Likewise, the Vietnamese American community of Village de l'Est waged a successful protest against the city government's plan to site a landfill nearby.[50] Second, these residents can articulate their demands in a more sophisticated manner by virtue of community social capital. When filing building permit applications, for example, residents can exchange information "about bureaucratic procedures and upcoming application deadlines,"[51] introduce competent contractors, and contact government officials to request faster processing.

In addition to involved citizenship, everyday organizations—churches, neighborhood associations, and schools—can serve as the basis of civic activism in emergent situations.[52] Local organizations provide physical assets of space for rescue and reunion, as large buildings such as churches and schools often serve as emergency shelters immediately after a storm.[53] Also, local organizations provide space for mobilizing and organizing collective action. In these communal spaces, people hold meetings, exchange information on housing reconstruction, and distribute resident directories. Saint Matthias Catholic Church in Broadmoor provided meeting space after Katrina, and residents gathered and held meetings in other churches including Broadmoor Presbyterian Church and the Episcopal Church of the Annunciation. In Freret, a neighborhood meeting was held in a classroom at the neighborhood's Samuel J. Green Charter School because the neighborhood association did not have a designated building of its own. In Village de l'Est, the Catholic church quickly became the focal site for neighborhood organizing, and was where the Vietnamese residents shared information about post-Katrina recovery plans and discussed plans for their community.

The upside of these neighborhood actions may, however, become an obstacle for building long-term resilience. Because of the strong impetus to rebuild, it is not likely that people will voluntarily remove themselves from high-risk areas. Since these rebuilding activities are based mostly in neighborhoods, civic inequality may lead directly to neighborhood inequality. In the recovery-planning process, certain community-based organizations in New Orleans circumvented government-offered plans and came up with their own master plan; their demands often clashed with the city government's ability to meet them, to the point where some neighborhoods made unrealistic suggestions that could not possibly be executed.[54] During the recovery activities, the gap between civically active communities and inactive communities widened, making community boundaries more pronounced than before Katrina. In other words, the uneven distribution of civic capacity can distort resource allocation in such a way that services and goods are more likely to be diverted to civically active communities, even when these communities are not the priority for redevelopment purposes. Furthermore, in a situation where cooperation is difficult among communities, the positive effects of community social capital are hard to diffuse across neighboring communities. Instead of cooperating with each other, neighborhoods may compete for scarce resources and reinforce community boundaries rather than transcend them.

When civic actions are performed within neighborhood boundaries, it is challenging to expand this community-based civic capacity to a citywide civic capacity. While community civic capacity is a prerequisite for building a citywide civic sphere, civically active communities do not always succeed in creating a civically vibrant city. Transitioning from "bonding social capital," which refers to the cohesiveness within a smaller community, often based in residents' neighborhoods, to "bridging social capital," which means crosscutting ties among those small communities, does not happen automatically. In their study of eight neighborhoods in Arizona, Larsen and colleagues found that people show a varying degree of attention to citywide issues, and those without sufficient resources tend to focus more on their immediate networks than on the issues beyond the area where they have bonding social capital.[55] Poor individuals, or their collective networks, had a hard time extending their concerns to a broader scope of communities. In other words, "The main problem for poor communities may not be a relative deficit in social capital, but that their social assets have greater obstacles to overcome, and are constantly under assault."[66]

In disaster situations where many communities are deprived of critical resources regardless of their previous economic conditions, bridging different community interests and concerns can be even more challenging than in ordinary situations. Although citywide civic coalitions play a crucial role in coordinating resources among disparate communities, preexisting socioeconomic disparities coupled with disaster-specific emergencies may further lower the possibility of creating a truly citywide civic sphere. Resource-deprived communities have little means or motivation to form a coalescing bond with communities that have different socioeconomic conditions, even when the members of the disadvantaged communities have a high level of civic bonding among themselves. While a tight-knit church group in a poor community may help the community members gather together and share information about public assistance, the church group may not be so politically effective as to influence the public agenda to rehabilitate the region where the neighborhood is located. On the other hand, residents and communities with a higher socioeconomic background may voice more concerns at the city level than their poor counterparts, which is likely to further isolate the disadvantaged communities in terms of agenda setting, resource allocation, and distribution. In this regard, increased civic capacity at the neighborhood level does not always boost civic capacity *beyond* the neighborhood.

Conclusion

This chapter examined why community-based recovery is not sufficient for building overall citywide resilience and may lead to undesirable consequences in the long run. In particular, this chapter builds an argument of why spatial scale yields different motivations and strategies for building resilience. As expressed through social networks, engagement, and participation of community members, civic capacity at the community level is regarded as an important asset for disaster recovery. An egocentric social network, for example, is beneficial to individuals' survival, recovery, and rebuilding after disaster. People with dense social ties are better positioned to overcome difficulties during and after natural disasters.[57] In contrast, people in isolation—the poor and the elderly in particular—are more vulnerable to the harmful effects of disaster, as previously shown in the disproportionate death of African Americans and the elderly during Chicago's heat wave in 1995.[58]

Scaling up from this familiar discussion of civic capacity, however, requires further scrutiny. It begins with acknowledging that the effects of civic capacity are not uniform but vary considerably from community to community, and such a variation imposes a challenge to urban governance—especially when civic inequality is intertwined with geographic inequality. As we shall see in the following chapters, the reach of civic capacity is spatially bounded. Given the limited scope of risk perception, the scale of community remains localized, and so do the effects of community resilience.

All in all, these suggestions call for a paradigmatic shift from viewing cities' underlying challenges as unexpected crises to embracing them as inherent vulnerabilities that can be wisely managed through legitimate coercion by a durable regime—a sustained coalition of political, economic, and civic actors in the city. Despite its appeal, however, there exist structural constraints that prevent local governments and civic actors from investing in long-term resilience in favor of economic development. The next chapter identifies these challenges, focusing on how the federalist structure is embedded in the city's pursuit of economic development and protection against natural hazards.

2

Federalism and the Construction of Protection from Betsy to Katrina

[T]he Army Engineers' plans, with our proposed revisions,
in conjunction with Governor John McKeithen's plans for a
levee across the Gulf Coast line of Louisiana should forever
eliminate any danger of hurricane flooding to the populated
areas of Louisiana.
—Kenneth LeSieur, chairman of the Citizens Committee for
Hurricane Flood Control, November 24, 1965[1]

In a letter addressed to the Army Corps of Engineers, Kenneth LeSieur, chairman of the Citizens Committee for Hurricane Flood Control, made several suggestions for fortifying the region's flood protection structures, one of which included elevating the height of the levees. His committee suggested constructing a new levee and raising the existing levees to thirty feet from their current sixteen feet. LeSieur concluded, on behalf of the committee, that "surges from storms and hurricanes should not be allowed to enter the canals in the developed areas of the city," and for this purpose "levees of sufficient height would not be practical."[2]

LeSieur's wishful thinking of 1965 did not prove right; the levee breach flooded about 80 percent of the city forty years after the release of the report. The failure of levees incensed residents to the extent that one of the active residents founded a grassroots organization called *Levees.org*, which aims to promote the idea that the cause of Katrina's massive flood damage was levee breach. Established by former marketing director Sandy Rosenthal and her son in 2006, *Levees.org* has been active in educating citizens about the faults of the federal levee system and boasted 900,000 website views as of September 2015.[3] Their mission statement captures the core message: "The catastrophic flooding of metro New Orleans was due to the failure of the levees and floodwalls. . . . Primary responsibility for the failure of the levees and floodwalls lies with the

US Army Corps of Engineers."[4] As the name of the organization clearly suggests, this civic association was founded to focus exclusively on levees and floodwalls, to raise awareness about the systematic failure of the levees during Katrina and to urge federal action toward a stringent review of the levee board for its decisions, which it believes led to the undue damage caused by Katrina.

Citizens such as LeSieur and Rosenthal firmly believe that levee construction is key to protecting New Orleans from hurricane flooding. In fact, the birth of the city itself was dependent upon the existence of both natural and human-made levees. Since the arrival of the early French settlers in the early eighteenth century, levees have served as the primary device to protect the low-lying city from serial flooding and inundation, and they represent the ways in which people have fought with nature to build their urban life.[5] The territorial expansion from the small quadrant of the Vieux Carré to a city of nearly 350 square miles was made possible by the construction of levees, canals, and drainage systems that kept the land dry. The contemporary definition of resilience as adapting to nature's impending hazards has yet to be adopted there, and conquering and resisting natural forces was the prominent factor that shaped the Crescent City.

The collective historical memory of insulating the city from water still looms large, as people remain optimistic about the capacity of levees. When asked whether levees would hold if a hurricane of Katrina's magnitude were to land on the Gulf Coast again, most of the respondents (53 percent) said that the levees would hold, compared to a smaller group who were skeptical about the capacity of levees to withhold the next hurricane (36 percent). Furthermore, most citizens of New Orleans felt that for the past ten years, more improvements have been made in repairing the city's structural protective measures than anything else. Eighty-two percent of the public perceived "a lot" or "some" progress on repairing levees, pumps, and floodwalls, while fewer people recognized visible improvement in the city's economy (75 percent), education (59 percent), or public safety (35 percent).[6] Given the public preference for and confidence in structural solutions, it is not surprising to see why citizens like LeSieur and Rosenthal, fifty years apart, called for a federal action to build safer and taller floodwalls.

In neither Betsy nor Katrina did these federal engineering projects fully prevent the floodwater from inundating communities. However, as the poll shows, the robustness of the continued effort to shore up the city largely reflects how people measure the city's post-Katrina resilience.

Why do citizens prefer levees, and what are the consequences of supporting and continuing to build structural protections? This chapter shows that the strong confidence in structural protection served as the building block upon which flood victims garnered their civic strength to return and rebuild their homes and communities. In other words, federal protection is an important precondition to pursuing community resilience, which aims at maintaining the physical size of the city and restoring the neighborhoods to their pre-Katrina states. This preference, and the policy measures that follow from it, speak to the broader context of how government disaster policies developed at the federal, state, and local levels have continued to encourage redevelopment in hazardous areas.

In this sense, civic actors—performing as individual citizens, interest groups, and voters—have played a subtle yet profound role in shaping disaster-related policies from Betsy to Katrina. Facing threats from the water, people have negotiated protection in various forms, including by filing lawsuits, sending petitions, and pressuring local representatives and federal agents. All so that their properties and livelihoods would be protected under federal tutelage. Local civic actors, therefore, were active participants in, rather than passive observers of, planning the current bifurcated structure for disaster mitigation, whereby the federal government provides structural and individualized protection on the one hand, and state and local governments continue to pursue economic development policies on the other. These agencies give little attention, however, to the region's high susceptibility to natural hazards. Furthermore, this dual structure undermines the capacity and incentive of lower-level governments to design long-term resilience strategies against natural hazards, which could be achieved mainly through regulatory measures such as strengthening land-use regulations, enforcing strict building codes, and ultimately curtailing property development in vulnerable areas. Established throughout the latter half of the twentieth century, this political context provided tacit support for community-oriented resilience projects after Katrina, many of which were made possible through federal grants and collaboration with the city government. The federal responsibility to provide adequate protection also constituted an important legal ground for a series of law-suits following Katrina, which sought financial compensation from the federal government for the damaged properties in flood-prone areas.

Hurricanes Betsy and Katrina marked an important juncture in this trajectory because the impact of local actors' engagement in these di-sasters spread beyond the region to influence national discussions.[7] Far from being dormant or passive recipients of government ideas, civic actors eagerly navigated pathways that would enable them to sustain and protect their properties from external interventions. This is neither to say that these actions were the major cause for the massive damage nor that the government is not accountable for the devastating failure to predict, protect, and engage with hurricanes. Instead, this chapter sug-gests that although seemingly independent, the political responses and civic reactions to disasters are mutually constitutive events. However dysfunctional it may look, the bifurcated mode of the federal policies—individually targeted relief grants on the one hand and levee recon-struction spending on the other—is not a policy arrangement arrived at arbitrarily so much as a cumulative result of past disaster policies that reflect the interests of both civic and political actors, including home-owners, city administrators, and federal agents.

Perhaps it may be helpful to recall Ostrom's claim from chapter 1, which states that individuals tend to favor immediate benefits over distant ones, and that this tendency is reinforced by the uncertainty inherent in a disaster situation. The present chapter harkens back to this insight and shows that federalism, as a political structure, tends to satisfy individuals' immediate benefits at the expense of pursuing long-term goals at the city level. Citizens wanted to maximize the height of the levees while paying as little tax as possible, and also while receiving little regulation against building on the coastline. When the federal government suggested an extensive protection plan that may have violated private property rights and increased the tax burden, citizens contested it and changed its course. This historical trajectory made the current suggestion to shrink the city all the more undesirable among residents and city politicians, as shrinkage would have meant an abrupt departure from past programs and would have required heavy-handed intervention by the subnational governments in what are potentially "development" issues, such as land use and zoning. The following section elaborates on how the current federalist structure may conflict with taking preemptive measures for urban resilience.

Promoting Urban Resilience under Federalism

Federalism can be considered a weak system for mitigating disasters not because it has too much power but too little to regulate local development. As an administrative structure, federalism operates as a system of intergovernmental coordination in which natural disaster management is a local government function rather than a federal responsibility. In principle, it is expected that subnational governments develop disaster management programs to accommodate different types of hazards, and the federal government ensures maximum flexibility and autonomy in administering localized programs in the event of an emergency. The idea of a swift and efficient emergency response at the state and local level presupposes that the governments that are geographically proximate to disaster sites do a better job than the federal could of collecting knowledge, experience, and resources about the disasters, thereby preventing future occurrences.[8]

In practice, however, government responsibilities do not increase in a linear manner as the geographic proximity increases between a governmental jurisdiction and a disaster site. Instead, federalism has created a complex set of incentives for federal, state, and local governments. Preparing for an emergency—defined as a rare and unpredictable event—conveys second-degree importance, and state and local government authorities would therefore rarely risk their political or economic fortunes to help prevent one.[9] In general, hazard mitigation does *not* constitute a priority within the agendas of state and local governments, even when the probability is high. The aversion to disaster prevention is also greater for local governments than state governments.[10] As Peterson argues in *City Limits*, cities seek to maximize their development potential in order to attract human, physical, and financial capital and to foster competitiveness against their suburban counterparts or cities in other regions (1980). Compared with the federal government, which has an authoritative control over human migration across national borders, local governments do not have the power to regulate the mobility of citizens and businesses between states or regions,[11] which generates the following motivations: "Local governments are more concerned about operating efficiently in order to protect their economic base, while the domestic policy structure of the national government is more concerned about achieving a balance between developmental and redistributive objectives."[12] Due to the autonomous and competitive nature of subnational governments under federalism, state and local governments are incentivized to invest in developmental policies while the federal government is more likely to engage in regressive policies to help the poor and the disadvantaged. Over time, the discrete focuses on redistributive and developmental policies become entrenched, with the federal government increasingly concentrating upon the former, and state and local governments upon the latter.[13]

To the extent that we accept Peterson's logic, the mismatch between what the federal government can do and what it should do is apparent in disaster management. Patrick Roberts captures this inconsistency and claims that the federal government has a limited capacity to respond to disasters due to the complexity of the federal bureaucracy and legal constraints within federalism. The federal government, according to him, is bound to provide *ex post*, rather than *ex ante*, assistance:

> [T]he federal government's increasingly bold claims and heightened public expectations are disproportionate to the ability of the federal government to prevent or reduce the damage caused by disaster. Most of the authority over zoning, development, and land use, all of which contribute to disaster losses, is in the hands of state and local governments and private citizens. . . . And cities control one important aspect of disaster vulnerability, which is land. Unfortunately, if cities can find someone to certify valuable but vulnerable land as safe, they will likely develop it, no matter the risk.[14]

This logic partly explains why New Orleans was ill-prepared for promoting disaster-related policies, and why citizens had to fill the gap *after* the disaster devastated the city. Even if the cost burden of the disaster ultimately fell heavily upon the shoulders of its citizens, it would have been difficult, if not impossible, under the existing political framework to induce the local governments and citizens to voluntarily curtail development in order to prepare for an event that is too uncertain and rare to compromise development.[15] Underestimating the cyclical impact of hurricanes and floods in the delta area, government and civic actors focused on finding short-term fixes for a long-standing problem.

Mitigating Disasters at the Federal Level

Constructing Structural Protection

Federal involvement with flood control in Southeastern Louisiana has a long history. Federal assistance with levee construction dates back to the mid-nineteenth century, when a privately maintained levee breached and displaced thousands of residents along the Mississippi River. In response to the increasing risk of levee breach and flooding, the federal government passed the Swamp Land Acts of 1849 and transferred federal swampland to Louisiana in order to subsidize levee construction with profits from the sale of the land.[16] The federal involvement continued to grow during the nineteenth century, after major military actions during the Civil War once again destroyed the levees, but the State Board of Levee Commissioners showed little progress in repairing the broken floodwalls. Congress thus passed legislation to create the Mississippi River Commission in 1879, which was responsible for designing a levee system in collaboration with the Army Corps of Engineers. Since then, the Army Corps of Engineers has focused exclusively on levee construction by actively adopting a "levees only" policy.[17]

Because of continued federal assistance with levee construction, individual landowners and private developers began to lose the incentive to protect themselves from possible floods.[18] Residential development in the floodplain flourished during the storm-free period between 1910 and 1940—and then another storm hit the region in 1947. To accommodate expanding development in the metropolitan area, the Corps of Engineers continued to work on raising the levees surrounding the Jefferson and Orleans Parishes. Their effort, however, proved insufficient; Hurricane Betsy hit the city and killed seventy-five people in 1965. Realizing the limitation of the existing levees, Congress passed the Flood Control Act in the same year and authorized the Army Corps of Engineers to assume full responsibility for a project named the Lake Pontchartrain and Vicinity Hurricane Protection Project (LPVHPP).[19] The LPVHPP consisted largely of two options. First, the high-level option essentially suggested raising the height of existing levees to withstand future hurricanes of greater magnitude. According to plans for the original lakefront, levees were to measure nine to thirteen feet high depending on the topography of the area directly in front of the levees; this option was intended to elevate these levees to between sixteen and eighteen feet, if properly constructed. In contrast, the second option, a barrier option, planned to erect floodgates in order to focus on managing the quantity of floodwater flowing into the city. This option would involve fortifying, but not necessarily raising, levees around the lakefront, building flood channels along the Inner Harbor Navigation Canal (the Industrial Canal), and constructing control structures such as barriers and flood-control gates located at The Rigolets and Chef Menteur Pass areas.[20] That these control structures would be closed during a hurricane and would be able to prevent storm surges from entering the Industrial Canal from Lake Pontchartrain in the first place was the reason given for not raising the height of the levees.[21]

The Corps favored the barrier option because it attempted to address a fundamental problem, namely the ability to control the amount of water flowing into the city. Studies had concluded that the project design would have to address the closure of natural channels that connect the waters of the Gulf of Mexico with Lake Pontchartrain, so that the wind from hurricanes could not thrust storm surges into the city of New Orleans.[22] Practically speaking, the barrier option would also circumvent the difficulties of negotiating the government's taking of private land near the levees. Still, in pursuing the barrier option, the Corps soon faced opposition from citizens who would be directly or indirectly paying the cost of the strengthened prevention system. For one, landowners near the levee area demanded high prices for their parcel property, accelerating the cost for compensation and delaying construction indefinitely. As local interests often impeded necessary rights-of-way for constructing floodwalls, the local levee board and government gave priority to other projects over the Corps plans.[23] The escalating costs of negotiation with civic activists and compensation for property owners later became the major reason that the Corps withdrew the barrier plan and switched to the high-level project.

Collective Contestation: Save Our Wetlands v. Early Rush

The growing discontent surrounding the Corps's barrier method manifested in a formal lawsuit, *Save Our Wetlands v. Early Rush*, in 1976. According to the newly passed National Environment Policy Act (NEPA) requirements in 1970, the Corps had to submit an Environmental Impact Statement (EIS) to report the effects of the LPVHPP on the ecosystem. A coalition of local fishermen and a local environmentalist group charged the Corps for failing to properly address the effects of hurricane barriers on shellfish and finfish populations, and for neglecting the procedures required by the newly passed NEPA regulation. In 1977, the federal district court enjoined the LPVHPP, requiring the Corps to suspend the project until an adequate assessment could be made. Now, the Corps faced oppositions from inside and out. On the one hand, the federal court ordered the Corps to resubmit its EIS to fully address the barriers' effect on marine life.[24] After NEPA passed, federal agencies were required to consider the environmental impacts of their projects and reasonable alternatives to their project. On the other hand, the barrier project had been facing fierce opposition from local citizens and representatives who did not want to pay a high price for a project that might endanger the economic vitality of their region. A spokesperson of the League of Women Voters, for example, testified in a public hearing in 1978 that the Corps had not fully considered the taxpayer burden in financing the barrier project, and voters in New Orleans had already opposed the plan. At the hearing, the Republican house representative of Louisiana's First District, Robert Livingston, presented an informal poll, where many respondents (38.5 percent) opposed the project and a substantial portion (23.6 percent) demanded the discontinuation until a proper impact statement could be made.[25]

Fearing an indefinite delay on the project, the Corps abandoned the barrier plan and chose to complete the high-level option even though elevating existing levees was acknowledged to be deficient for overall protection. After a period of reevaluation and preparation by the Corps, the official authorization for the plan was issued in 1985. Although the Corps did not entirely "lose" the case, which would have meant abandoning the project altogether, the Corps had to adjust its plan to comply with the court order to be able to resume the project. In addition to

environmental litigation, difficulties with landowners and civic opposition leaders contributed to delays of the levee construction project.
Because of updated data, threats of litigation, and feasibility studies, the
project continued to reinvent itself as a never-ending task with massive
budget increases. Twenty years into the project, having begun with a
projected budget of $85 million, the barrier project was in fact never fin-
ished. Until Katrina's landfall in 2005, that is, and it continued thereafter
with a budget that snowballed to $738 million.

Mailing Civic Discontent: Individual Actions against Levee Protection

Another stream of discontent came from a broader base. Local citizens
were reluctant to share the cost of shoreline improvement in exchange
for diffuse, uncertain benefits. Some residents on the barrier side of Lake
Borgne, for example, worried about the negative effects of closed barriers on the potential for economic development in their region. Still
others questioned the justifiability of a tax burden for local taxpayers in
transforming wetlands into development areas and thus endangering
the environment around Lake Pontchartrain.[26]

The concerns about development potential and additional financial
burden led some individuals to engage directly in civic actions against
the federal government. David P. Levy, an army veteran and the CEO of
Balehi Marine, a shipbuilding company, was one of the most outspoken
critics of the Corps's LPVHPP. He argued that constructing high dams
around Lake Pontchartrain would undermine "the pleasure of sailing,
fishing, and shipbuilding industries," as well as ruin the region's ecology
and reverse the course of flooding to neighboring Saint Bernard Parish
and New Orleans East.[27] His strong opposition to the barrier plan was
based on the historical record of hurricanes and flooding in the area,
which had not occurred around Lake Pontchartrain and were caused by
other factors, such as a windstorm and the failure of the pumping system. In one of his many letters addressed to the Corps, on April, 5, 1976,
Levy made the following claims:

> Every probable path a hurricane could take has been experienced since
> [Bienville founded the city in 1715]. . . . The areas north of the lake do

not need levees or BARRIER protection. There is no history of hurricane flooding here; the people do not want it, and the building codes are being updated to ensure that future construction will be sufficiently high.[28]

He criticized the simulated study of the Standard Project Hurricane (SPH), in which a hypothetical hurricane was used to gauge the potential height of flooding and the extent of damage it could cause. Roughly equivalent to a fast-moving Category 3 storm, the SPH was weaker than real-life Hurricane Katrina. However, arguing that "an earthquake is more probable than anything close to" what the Corps had simulated, Levy denounced the overprotection of lakefront areas as damaging to navigational and developmental prospects as well as endangering for ecological conditions around the lake. In addition to voicing his own view, Levy also made it clear how unpopular the barrier plan was among the voters, who had rejected its funding three times, including in a 1974 referendum that approved $3 million for the Orleans Levee Board on the condition that the money would not be spent on the barrier plan.

In defense of the numerous formal complaints including Levy's, the Corps made two points. One was based on a cost-benefit analysis, which found that the high-level plan would be costlier than the barrier plan. The projected cost of the high-level plan amounted to $100 million, while the cost for the barrier plan was estimated at $64,703,000. Not only was the barrier plan cheaper, it also protected a more extensive area than what the high-level plan would cover. The partial coverage of protection in the high-level plan was the second point of the Corps defense for the barrier plan. As the high-level plan elevated the levees and yet would not lower the overall height of the floodwater, the Corps argued, it would only protect leveed areas. The goal of the barrier option, however, was to lower the overall height of the floodwater by controlling the amount of water, and thus serve to extend the coverage of protection more so than the high-level plan.[29]

The erection of tall, massive levees around the riverfront served various purposes. First, it sent a symbolic message to citizens that disaster prevention was a national responsibility and best achieved through structural protection. The visual image of seemingly impenetrable levees generated a "false sense of security"[30] among the public. Building floodwalls around the floodplain provided residents with feelings of safety from external harm without inflicting direct costs on their private properties. Armoring flood-prone areas thus led to a vicious cycle: the safer the levees that the Corps tried to build, the greater the sense of security became among the citizens of New Orleans, who did not then realize the urgency of retreating from the coastline.[31] Second, the coastal armoring strategy was politically convenient, as levee construction and drainage improvement projects tend to concentrate the responsibility of hazard mitigation on the Corps. As a federal agency, the Corps bears the responsibility for engineering protective and preventive measures for potential disasters, although in fact multiple actors—landowners, developers, and city government authorities alike—must be involved in successful prevention efforts. When the levee construction failed, it became convenient and politically gratifying to blame a single agency— that is, the Corps—rather than to find fault with many of those whose seemingly benign actions constituted part of the escalating cost of the disaster.

Individual Relief and Mitigated Blight in Post-Disaster Recovery

In addition to structural protection, the federal government also provided individualized protection by directly distributing emergency and recovery aid to disaster victims. With the Stafford Disaster Relief and Emergency Assistance Act of 1988, the president's role was expanded during major disasters—it fell to that office to declare a federal disaster, which would then provide emergency-relief funding to state and local governments through FEMA. Like the logic that constructing a visible protection measure is more appealing to the public than restricting development activities, immediate cash relief and rebuilding assistance is more palatable than spending on mitigation projects such as house elevation. As a redistributive good,[32] federal assistance to disaster recovery is important for political reasons because of voter myopia, as voters tend to exchange their electoral support with individual-based relief spending but not with collective projects for disaster mitigation.[33] Voters do not support disaster-preparedness spending even in the form of particularistic distribution, only favoring relief spending when it is distributed toward individual clients. Knowing the direct benefits of post-disaster aid, politicians target local constituents with it in anticipation of electoral support. Presidents use disaster declarations to distribute federal funds directly, thus securing electoral support.[34] This matters particularly in battleground states such as Florida, where a marginal increase in vote counts can cast a significant impact on election outcomes. For example, FEMA hurricane aid award distribution in Florida in 2003 had a direct effect on increasing the Republican turnout and helped raise the vote share of the incumbent, President Bush, in the 2004 election.[35]

After Katrina, the federal government spent most of its disaster-related funding on repairing destroyed public facilities and providing cash assistance to individuals. The individualized assistance by the federal government disappointed the cash-strapped city government, which had anticipated a more extensive scale of financial support for long-term reconstruction of the city. This point was raised by a city official I met during my fieldwork in 2010, when I asked questions about the difficulties he and his colleagues had in the aftermath of Katrina. Among several difficulties, the financial problem was listed as the most important issue. With the city's "tax base being wiped out" and therefore the "revenue stream cut off," the city government had anticipated an outpouring of support from the federal government for reconstruction. However, according to the official, the bulk of federal assistance was directed toward immediate disaster relief rather than the reconstruction of the city:

> Yes, we did get some federal assistance, like the community disaster money [Community Development Block Grant]. There were some federal appropriations that were made, but the vast bulk of federal appropriations that were made to the city were not for the actual reconstruction. They were for, kind of, immediate post-storm relief . . . or rescue operations, to rescue people from the rooftops of their homes. Yes, a lot of money was spent there, but actually the amount of money that was directly given to reconstruction purpose was much smaller. . . . So money, it was definitely an issue, and then I think there was also more expectations of national NGO support. And there was definitely some of that, but not to the extent that many of us expected.[36]

As he mentioned, much of the federal grant was used in repairing publicly owned infrastructure and on rescue and relief missions. FEMA allocated

61 percent of the grant (about $12 billion) to repairing, replacing, and restoring public facilities—including roads, bridges, and schools—and to eligible private nonprofit organizations as well as healthcare facilities. Another 30 percent of the grant covered individual recovery, subsidizing rents, and lodging expenses for temporary housing, down payments for replacement homes, and repair costs for damaged houses.[37]

Compared to the immediate relief and repair of public facilities, a much smaller amount of the federal grant went to building preventive measures for future hazards. Only 9 percent of the total funding covered mitigation efforts through the HMGP, which provides state and local governments, tribal organizations, and nonprofit organizations with funding to implement long-term mitigation measures following a disaster.[38] Individual homeowners may receive funding through state and local governments and spend it to fortify their houses, in which the most common mitigation measure is home elevation and flood-proofing.[39]

Individual mitigation efforts through HMGP, however, have shown a mixed record. One unintended consequence was "mitigated blight," whereby storm-damaged houses were funded and raised to mitigate future hazards and yet remained abandoned because of unfixed damages such as broken windows and destroyed roofs. After Katrina, FEMA committed $1.2 billion to the state for a housing elevation project. The project was largely unsuccessful, partly because of the lack of accountability in the contracting process, which led to a low completion rate. Furthermore, insufficient efforts were made to fix the damages to other parts of homes, leaving units uninhabitable and blighted despite the completed elevation.[40] As of 2012, the *Times-Picayune* reported that as many as eighty properties had been found to produce mitigated blight, whereby the recipients of the HMGP had elevated their houses with the elevation grant and yet did not repair the rest of the house with a Road Home grant, leaving units blighted and empty.[41] It is unclear whether the homeowners abandoned their houses intentionally or due to lack of additional funding. Whatever the intent was, the misuse of federal grants resulted in the collective detriment of neighborhood blight and increased the residents' vulnerability. Because different agencies may subsidize elevation and damage repairs, a house could be elevated and yet remain inhabitable because the interior or exterior of the house remained unrepaired. Furthermore, local inspectors tended to issue a certificate of occupancy to such half-restored properties to let the grantees receive the final payment of the federal grant. Because of this unsatisfactory performance, FEMA cut the funding from $1.2 billion to $750 million and spent the rest in housing projects in Northern Louisiana.[42]

Emergency Preparation at the State Level: The Case of Louisiana

Shrinking Tax Base by Popular Demand: Homestead Exemption

Compared to the federal government's targeted and direct involvement with levee construction and individual disaster relief, state and local governments exerted an indirect but more profound influence on shaping the economic and social vulnerabilities around New Orleans communities. With few incentives to invest in disaster prevention, the Louisiana and New Orleans governments further exacerbated the potential for future catastrophe by maximizing economic development opportunities through market-based approaches such as tax cuts, budget reductions, and property development.

The state's homestead exemption created a significant hurdle and undermined the city's governing power by increasing volatility to its financial structure. Enacted in 1934 to encourage homeownership, the homestead exemption increased from $20,000 to $75,000 in 1980 and has placed substantial strain on the financial capacity of municipal governments. Unlike most cities, New Orleans's fiscal budget does not rely on property tax as its primary revenue stream because of Louisiana's homestead exemption. In Louisiana, the first $75,000 of the value of the property is exempt from taxation if the property is the owner's primary residence. In other words, this legislation allows properties valued below $75,000 to be exempted from paying property tax, and about 68 percent of owner-occupied residences in New Orleans fall into this category.[43] In 1996, 65 percent of all properties were exempt from property taxation, which led to a $265.3 million loss in tax revenue for New Orleans.

Despite political efforts to lower the exemption or even to eliminate the policy altogether, the homestead exemption has been popular, receiving strong support from voters and their political allies. After defeating three-term governor Edwin Edwards, the newly elected governor, Charles "Buddy" Roemer, pushed a series of tax reforms including the reduction of exemption exclusion down to $25,000.[44] To diversify the economy from natural resources extraction, Roemer proposed securing revenue through less volatile sources such as property tax and shifting some of the tax burden from businesses to individuals. Not surprisingly, this proposal garnered little favor with voters. The local newspaper highlighted the contention between Roemer and Lawrence Chehardy, a tax assessor in Jefferson Parish:

> [Chehardy] has come to symbolize the belief of many Louisianans that homeowners should pay little or no tax on their personal residences. If the homestead exemption is lowered by two-thirds as Roemer suggests, only the first $25,000 of the value of each owner-occupied home would be tax-free.[45]

Interestingly, the base of support for the homestead exemption not only included affluent voters but also the region's poor citizens. In addition to fierce opposition by homeowner-voters and their elected officials, the lower homestead exemption also concerned Black legislators who represented low-income urban districts. Representatives of the poor districts feared that the increased tax burden of landlords would ultimately translate into higher rents and negatively affect renters in urban areas. Consequently, Roemer failed to achieve his reform proposal. Historically a populist government,[46] the Louisiana legislature defeated his proposal, and the voters once again voted against the watered-down version of the proposal in the state's constitutional referendum, by 55 percent to 45 percent.[47] Out of all fifty states, Louisiana has the lowest percentage of property taxes on owner-occupied housing as a percentage of median home value, amounting to 0.14 percent, less than a tenth of the 1.76 percent in Texas.[48]

Homestead exemption yielded both economic and political consequences. First, because of the hierarchical tax structure between state and local governments, the latter competed against each other in using their limited taxing power and depended heavily on state authorities beyond their stated limits. Not only did the homestead exemption strain the city's fiscal power by wiping out the city's tax base,[49] it also invited a new form of political corruption. The haphazard tax assessment system produced inconsistent valuations for similar-priced properties, causing confusion and raising questions of accountability and fairness among taxpayers. More seriously, tax assessors tended to undervalue properties of constituents in anticipation of electoral support. Undervaluation happened mainly on properties with high market value, serving middle- to-upper-class homeowners in affluent areas of the city, including the Garden District, Uptown, and the French Quarter. Furthermore, not only did assessors apply less-rigorous criteria to certain homeowners, but the city bureaucracy was too understaffed and resource-deprived to accurately evaluate residential property values every four years as stipulated in the original legislation. The *Times-Picayune* special report on property taxes from 2004 shows how the homestead exemption practices are associated with the distortion in the tax revenue system. The report found huge discrepancies between market value and valuation, as shown in Table 2.1. Not surprisingly, the greater difference between sales value and valuation exists for more affluent areas, such as Districts 1, 2, and 4. In District 4, for example, the difference between average market value and tax valuation is over 100 percent, which means that market value is more than twice as high as the values assessed for tax purposes. District 4 also happens to be the richest district, with its average home value being the highest among the seven districts investigated. Differences are present in other districts as well, where the home values are underassessed from 50 percent to almost 100 percent.[50]

Furthermore, the homestead exemption cast a far-reaching impact on financing emergency management and recovery. Louisiana's "tax base has been narrowed significantly by giving extensive and generous tax exemptions and tax credits," and homestead exemption undermined the state's property tax base.[51] The reduced tax base exacerbated the budget problem after Katrina, when the property tax assessment fell by one-third from the previous year in New Orleans. Thus, the city government raised the tax rate by an equal amount to substitute for the decline in taxable property values. Furthermore, the homestead exemption made the property tax base highly volatile and encouraged businesses to be involved in post-disaster financing. Due to the generous exemption ($75,000), income-producing properties accounted for as high as 90 percent of the property tax base, meaning that businesses with nonexempted properties were responsible for paying the largest share of property taxes.

TABLE 2.1. Average sales value, valuation, and the percentage of underassessment by Tax Assessment District, 2003. Source: *Times-Picayune*. Compiled by author.

	1st (Warehouse District, Mid-City, Lower Garden District)	2nd (French Quarter, Mid-City, Lakeview)	3rd (Eastern New Orleans, Gentilly, Ninth Ward)	4th (Garden District, Central City)	5th (Algiers)	6th (Uptown)	7th (Carrollton, Hollygrove, Lakeview)
Market sales value (dollars)	211,762	258,061	141,756	334,537	172,321	312,120	221,382
Valuation (dollars)	106,967	145,758	91,868	154,868	120,747	184,885	131,806
Difference from valuation (percent)	98	77	54	116	43	69	68

Opposition came from these businesses when the post-disaster budget problems arose and forced tax rate increases. Two business-funded nonprofit groups, the Bureau of Governmental Research and the Public Affairs Research Council of Louisiana, suggested filing for bankruptcy—a proposal that would shift the cost burden from tax-paying businesses to existing bondholders.[52] In their joint report, these research organizations used the language of economic development to advocate the idea of municipal bankruptcy in Orleans Parish, stating that "[f]or a devastated community, continuing to shoulder pre-Katrina debt loads and obligations may interfere with the community's ability to create the conditions needed for recovery. In that context, bankruptcy is a legitimate line of inquiry and should be evaluated."[53] Concerned with the property sales increase, these organizations further suggested using the federal disaster relief grant through the tax credit program and paying the cost of unfunded federal mandates such as unemployment compensation.[54] In addition to the push for municipal bankruptcy, diverting the use of the disaster relief grant to finance redistributive programs such as unemployment assistance reveals the structural deficiency of the state and local governments, who then invest in nondevelopment issues as little as possible. Local stakeholders, voters, and businesses alike sought to buttress the homestead exemption even when the region's financial prospects looked bleak, and the urge to maintain minimal taxation levels was not abated after Katrina. When the affected area incurred financial distress that pointed to the necessity of a potential tax increase, suggestions were made to pay for the disaster without affecting the existing system, which was justified under the rationale of promoting economic development.

Hazardous Development: Coastal Restoration without Emergency Preparedness

The strained economic conditions in the state of Louisiana, from various causes including the tax exemption laws, had a direct effect on shrinking the size of an already modest emergency preparedness budget. During the 2011–12 fiscal year, the Louisiana government consolidated the Governor's Office of Homeland Security and Emergency Preparedness (GOHSEP) with the Louisiana State Police and the Office of Juvenile Justice, under the rationale that such consolidation would reduce overlapping jurisdictions and save approximately $1.2 million and sixteen positions.[55] As fewer state budget funds were allocated toward GOHSEP, the state government tried to compensate for the loss by claiming a larger proportion of the federal grant and funneling a smaller amount to local government agencies. Of the $5.4 million federal grant in 2013, Louisiana allocated only $1.9 million to the state's sixty-four parishes while reserving the remaining $3.5 million for the state government. Initially, it was proposed that the federal grant be divided in half between the state and local governments, but Governor Bobby Jindal vetoed that legislation and distributed 80 percent of the fund to the GOHSEP.[56]

In contrast to the shrunken intergovernmental transfer and overall reduction in emergency response capacity, Louisiana has reaffirmed its will to focus on the coastal restoration of the Gulf region. In her speech at a 2012 Water Challenge, a nonprofit event held during New Orleans Entrepreneur Week, Senator Mary Landrieu rejected suggestions that residents move away from the coast to reduce the risk of flooding—just as her brother, Mitch Landrieu, had criticized the idea of shrinking the city's footprint in his mayoral race. Citing the example of the Netherlands, Senator Landrieu argued that Louisiana should not back away from continued economic development because of coastal erosion. She said, "Sixty percent of the country is below sea level, they're backed up against the North Sea and have no place to move. But everyone's feet stay dry and they're protected against storms."[57] However, what she did not address in this analogy was the collective consensus and financial commitment by the Dutch to build and sustain a massive protection system—this does not match the political preference of Louisianans. After a devastating flood in 1953 that killed about two thousand people, the Netherlands constructed a flood control system called the Delta Works, which cost about $8 billion annually over a twenty-five-year period. The cost of protection in the Netherlands far exceeds the projected investment of $30 billion suggested after Katrina. Furthermore, the annual maintenance cost amounts to $500 million, a relatively large amount of money given the small size of the population (15.5 million).[58]

Demanding the federal government's financial support from the fine paid by British Petroleum (BP) after the company's oil spill incident in the Gulf of Mexico in 2010, Landrieu called for greater awareness and extensive research about the coast and its promising future. Although the theme was coastal restoration, her remark had an undertone of promising coastal development and job growth instead of shoreline protection. She emphasized the importance of the state to the national economy as a supplier of oil and gas since the 1940s and as a major producer of seafood for the rest of the nation. She also promised local contractors access to coastal restoration work. To finance the initiative, the state planned to draw upon its revenue surpluses, federal appropriations, and the revenue from leasing the Outer Continental Shelf to oil and gas development by the Coastal Protection and Restoration Authority.[59]

In a sense, the disparity between the underinvestment in emergency preparedness and the pitch for coastal restoration as a strategy for economic development mirrors the state's conservative political ideology. A Gallup poll from 2014 marks Louisiana as one of the most conservative states in the nation, where 45 percent of its population consider themselves conservative, compared to 15 percent who consider themselves liberal.[60] On the one hand, the preference for "smaller" government justifies the contraction of fiscal budget and the reduced assistance for disaster preparedness. On the other hand, Louisianans still support government spending on policy areas supporting economic development.

In the 2014 Louisiana Survey, most respondents supported smaller government only for select issues. Sixty-eight percent of the respondents said they supported government spending on economic development, and 69 percent were in favor of spending on road and mass transit projects. In contrast, only 22 percent of the respondents agreed with more spending on welfare and assistance to the poor.[61] The strong preference for economic development without big government continues to hold sway at the state and local level, which resulted in an underinvestment in disaster mitigation and the continued development in coastal areas.

Weak Foundations: Ex Post Building Code Adoption in Louisiana

Upon Katrina's arrival, the local government's penchant for economic development with minimal government intervention became most evident in insufficient regulation on land use and building structures. Land use is one of the few functions where local governments have greater authority than state or federal governments, and there has been a wide consensus to enforce stricter building codes in disaster-prone areas *ex post* major hurricanes, because enforcing strict building codes contributes to preventing catastrophic damage substantially.[62] The federal government does not have a legal authority to force state governments to adopt (nor enforce) building codes, and likewise, state governments also have a limited power to regulate city governments. As a result, the degree to which subnational governments enforce building codes varies significantly. For example, in states such as California, state building code adoption is mandatory, while states like Mississippi and Alabama do not have statewide building codes that regulate all construction activities within their states.[63]

Louisiana only adopted statewide building codes after Katrina. Following the hurricane, Louisiana adopted the Uniform Construction Code in 2005, and yet the state does not have the legal authority to regulate building codes in the city of New Orleans due to the Home Rule Charter. State construction code states:

> In the enforcement of any provision of the construction code provided for in this Part, if any provision of this Part conflicts with the provisions of a home rule charter pertaining to the powers, functions, and duties

of local governments or the structure and organization or the particular distribution and redistribution of the powers and functions of such local government, the provisions of such home rule charter shall supersede the conflicting provisions of this Part.[64]

As will be discussed in chapter 5, people's strong will to come back and rebuild, coupled with the loose legal arrangement between Louisiana and New Orleans, spurred the redevelopment of most flooded areas as the recovery progressed. Returnees have built or repaired their properties without elevating their houses, and the city government faced huge resistance and criticism when the then-mayor Ray Nagin suggested a building permit moratorium in places that would likely incur severe damage if there were to be a storm like Hurricane Katrina again.

In general, high elevation standards are not desirable for the private sector.[65] Although disaster prevention may contribute to localities' development potential in the long run, natural disasters occur only rarely and unexpectedly. Therefore, building regulation, especially with regard to disaster preparedness, is not a primary concern for state and local governments that aim to maximize their economic development potential. Strict building regulation means increased cost of housing construction and thus sends a negative signal to commercial developers, as the existence of disaster-related building codes confirm the belief that there is a possibility for natural hazards in an area and therefore dampens development potential. The burden of stringent building codes is especially great in urban areas. Stringent building codes were found to increase construction costs for both single-family and multifamily housing in urban areas, reducing the competitive advantage vis-à-vis their suburban counterparts.[66] In other words, strong building codes and land-use regulation ensures safety and represents local government's administrative capacity, and yet some cities are reluctant to enforce these regulations because they do not want to stifle local economic development. The city of New Orleans also maintained a weak regulatory regime, which ultimately undermined the city's regulatory authority over residents. Because the city did not have a well-functioning building department, residents relied on community leaders who could provide necessary resources for rebuilding. This, in turn, further compromised the process of building citywide resilience because the city government lacked both the capacity and legitimacy for long-term, comprehensive planning. While this happened, community representatives were able to build support from their residents.

The process of building code adoption at the local government level is byzantine at best, and many local bureaucracies lack the capability to implement and enforce strict codes. Usually, jurisdictions adopt one of the model codes developed by an association of interested groups,[67] and the capacity of local administration affects the degree to which building regulation is enforced. In fiscally strapped states like Louisiana, Mississippi, and Alabama, there has been much difficulty in establishing and maintaining departments for building inspection. None of these three states even had statewide building codes before Katrina.[68] As of 2010, only seven municipalities out of eighty-two in Mississippi enforced flood and wind requirements recommended by the International Building Code,[69] and it took roughly a decade after Katrina for Mississippi to enact statewide building codes—it did in 2014. And yet, the state cannot mandate or enforce the codes if local jurisdictions opt out of the requirement. Similarly, Alabama adopted statewide building codes in 2012 but does not enforce them throughout all municipalities.

In rebuilding flooded areas, the federal government has constantly suggested "recommendations" for better protection and prevention, but it has hardly gone beyond that. Recommendations include an adoption of updated building codes and provision of guidelines to reduce biological and chemical hazards in repair and reconstruction. For example, upon the arrival of Hurricanes Katrina and Rita, FEMA issued Advisory Base Flood Elevations (ABFEs) that adjusted the existing Base Flood Elevation (BFE) levels to reflect changes in floodplain conditions. ABFEs are significantly higher than their precedent BFEs and their scope is more extensive than what the Special Flood Hazard Areas used to encompass. Local enforcement of these federal recommendations, however, did not meet expectations due to the lack of personnel in building inspection and people's resistance to the stronger (and thus costlier) regulations on rebuilding.

The case of Mandeville, Louisiana shows how difficult it is to comply with federal regulations while maintaining a potential for economic development. This small town was praised for strictly enforcing code regulations and even setting a higher standard than the federal recommendation. After Katrina, the American Planning Association (APA) contacted several communities to participate in a Planning Assistance Team program. The APA wanted to help incorporate the Old Mandeville Redevelopment Strategy into the city's newly drafted Comprehensive Land-Use Regulation Ordinance (CLURO).[70] Furthermore, FEMA reported the town of Mandeville as one of the "Mitigation Best Practice" cases.[71] An NFIP member since 1979, Mandeville had adopted a BFE for new construction. Moreover, in 1993, the city voted to raise the building standard to one foot higher than the BFE in return for a 30 percent reduction in flood insurance. Not only were high building standards in place, building officials also strictly enforced the standards. The FEMA report started and ended with building inspector and floodplain manager Wayne Berggren's firm declaration that there would not be any exceptions to the rule. However, Mr. Berggren's determination did not last long, as the financial burdens from flood mitigation—a risk that is preventive at best—compromised a potential for economic development in the area. In May 2012, the city of Mandeville adopted new federal flood elevations, which reduced them by one to four feet from the previous elevations. The city appealed to FEMA to implement lower elevations to save homeowners' high insurance payments and promote greater economic development.[72]

Although highly effective, regulating hazard risks at the local level through building codes and land use has been difficult to implement. When Katrina came ashore, few people pointed out how development in hazardous areas aggravated the chance for destruction. Compared to the Corps of Engineers, which is directly responsible for constructing levees and floodwalls (and for the failure thereof), the responsibilities of land-use regulation and building codes enforcement are diffused to many different agencies, making it difficult to find a single authority to be held accountable. Therefore, compared to the wealth of criticism against the Corps, there were fewer discussions on how land and buildings should have been built to minimize the damage.

Internalizing Risk at the Local Level: Sustained Vulnerabilities in New Orleans

Thus far, I have shown how federal and state policies have steered disaster mitigation in particular directions and how civic capacity has influenced it both directly and indirectly. Directly, civic groups and individuals pressured the federal government to increase spending on structural protection and immediate disaster relief—at the expense of other preventive measures. Indirectly, voters favored economic development policies with minimal tax burdens, which motivated politicians to underinvest in emergency preparedness and to facilitate coastal development. At the federal and state levels, disaster-related policies, or the lack thereof, were largely a response to intermittent citizen demands, which were often made by individuals, small groups, or a large group of voters. The relationship between government and civic actors at the local level is less responsive to citizen demands but transpires in a more sustained and interactive way. The growth-oriented style of New Orleans city politics directly affected territorial development in the city's low-lying areas and encouraged the construction of less-safe buildings. As urban historian Lewis Mumford put it, "the law of urban growth, as dictated by the capitalist economy, meant the inexorable wiping out of all the natural features that delight and fortify the human soul in its daily rounds."[73] When Hurricane Betsy hit in 1965, the city government did little to overhaul the city's infrastructure but instead relied on federal assistance, leading to the creation of the NFIP. Civic organizations, dismayed by the meager reaction from the city government, sought to negotiate with federal agencies.

Recipe for Disaster: Accelerated Development amid Growing Poverty

Despite population and economic decline since the 1970s, New Orleans continued to allow developers to construct commercial properties until the mid-1980s, culminating in the World's Fair in 1984. Much of its downtown commercial development occurred between 1975 and 1985, especially in the old downtown areas such as the Central Business District (CBD) and the Warehouse District. The city government adopted the Growth Management Program (GMP) in 1975, in which city administrators and private developers agreed to concentrate commercial development into areas where high-intensity land use had already been happening, but not in the districts with historic significance. Furthermore, a special tax district called the Downtown Development District (DDD) was designated in the CBD area to collect a special property tax and spend it within the District. Accordingly, private developers continued to build high-rise buildings and concentrate many of the city's financial resources into the CBD, to the detriment of nearby residential neighborhoods.[74] Due to the corporate-centered revitalization programs such as the GMP and DDD, New Orleans witnessed a significant building boom during this period, only to experience a steep economic decline afterward. Downtown development ignored financial and geographic constraints and harbored underlying sources of vulnerability in the coming decades. After the World's Fair in 1984 and the implementation of the GMP in 1975, the local economy showed downturn due to rising unemployment, diminishing revenue, and vacant offices.

However, investing in the downtown area continued after the halcyon days were over in the mid-1980s; politicians and business leaders believed that investing in the CBD was still the best way to revitalize the declining city. This time, however, the focus shifted to tourism rather than residential property construction, and many public resources were allocated to promoting tourist and retail activities in the downtown area. As a result, the number of tourists, for example, increased from 6.5 million in 1975 to 11 million in 1989. New Orleans also became a major venue for conventions, hosting 1,360 events in 1989 with a million delegates, about a twofold increase from 764 in 1976.[75]

New Orleans's shift to focus on the tourism industry unsettled the economic bases of its residents in fundamental ways. As a group, hospitality workers—janitors, cleaners, bellmen, and front desk workers—had not been successful in amassing collective negotiating power and remained a fragmented labor force. The failure to organize persists, so workers remain unable to collectively negotiate their pay and benefits. In Las Vegas, by contrast, another city heavily reliant on the hospitality business, about 17 percent of all workers and nearly all the hotels are unionized, whereas less than 5 percent of the hospitality workforce and only two hotels—Loews and Harrah's—are unionized in New Orleans. As employment in the tourist industry is highly sensitive to various factors, from general economic fluctuations to context-specific conditions such as weather and holidays, the job security of low-income workers was equally volatile, and the absence of union representation weakened their leverage in wage and benefit negotiations. The unstable status of working-class New Orleanians, most of whom were Black, contrasted with the middle- to upper-class

Whites', who not only dominated the discourse on urban development but also occupied the city's safest areas on higher grounds.[76]

Increasing economic instability accompanied parallel social vulnerabilities. The promoted image of the French Quarter as a vibrant, entertaining urban space masked the true reality of the larger city, where a growing Black population lived in poverty exacerbated by the White flight of the 1960s. Throughout the last half of the twentieth century, more than a quarter of the city's population was living below the poverty level, which placed New Orleans among the top ten high-poverty cities during this period.[77] In 1970, for example, New Orleans ranked first in poverty rate of persons, at 26.8 percent, while other postindustrial cities (except for Newark, New Jersey [22.5 percent], and Saint Louis, Missouri [20.3 percent]) had less than 20 percent. By 2000, only Newark had a higher poverty level (28.4 percent) than New Orleans (27.9 percent) among the declining cities. In the Central City neighborhood, the number of persons living under the poverty level rarely changed while the total population decreased, widening the gap from its surrounding metropolitan areas. From 1970 to 1990, the poverty rate of central New Orleans was more than twice as high as that outside the city.[78]

As the city government continued to pursue territorial expansion in the city's vulnerable areas, it did not cultivate a sufficient bureaucratic and institutional capacity to oversee, regulate, or control the pace of development. Except for such established communities as the thriving French Quarter and affluent Garden District, many parts of the city remained marginalized from core resources such as public transportation, crime prevention, and basic maintenance. The limited access to public transit left residents isolated within immediate social boundaries, which generated tragic consequences in the wake of Hurricane Katrina. The police department's limited manpower resulted in a reduced ability to provide adequate surveillance in certain parts of the city, which in turn rendered these parts crime-riddled, especially the sparsely populated eastern trenches. Inhabiting a city with one of the highest crime rates, New Orleanians living in the marginalized sections of Central City and Eastern New Orleans were perennially exposed to the dangers of homicide, burglary, and robbery.

Along with economic and social insecurities, housing construction practices contributed to augmenting the cost of damages. Few houses during the post–World War II period had been built on elevated ground because of the nationwide trend for building on inexpensive concrete slabs that could be poured directly on the ground. This practice ran contrary to a two-hundred-year-old habit that had persisted until World War II, whereby residents used to elevate floor bases when building houses. Improved floodwalls and drainage systems augmented optimism for this cheap and speedy construction method, and yet the city government did not enforce strict building regulations on nonelevated housings. To make matters worse, the hasty construction practice in the low-lying areas coincided with suburban-style housing patterns of lower density and extensive land use. Contrary to new cities in the South, New Orleans had maintained a dense residential pattern that was more like northern cities', and yet the topography of concentrated housing began to dissipate as new land developments took shape in the eastern part of the city and as people began to move out from the city core. Private developers continued to pursue housing developments but did so without consideration for the geological and engineering conditions best for housing construction.[79]

Federalizing Disaster: Hurricane Betsy and the Creation of a National Flood Insurance Program

The subnational governments' efforts to share the fiscal burdens of disaster management with the superordinate government culminated in the actual arrival of a disaster. On September 9, 1965, Hurricane Betsy came ashore at more than 150 miles an hour. In the face of this Category 4 storm, the city experienced a collapse of its infrastructure: 80 percent of the city lost electrical power, and two hundred thousand telephones went out of service. Mayor Victor Schiro, Senator Russell Long, and Representatives T. Hale Boggs and F. Edward Hébert had maintained a close relationship with President Lyndon B. Johnson and successfully persuaded him to visit the flooded city immediately. Upon his arrival at New Orleans airport on September 10, Johnson promised federal assistance for the area and made the following remarks:

> I have ordered that all red tape be cut. Our assistance will be given the highest priority. The Department of Agriculture is already providing

emergency food at food stations such as we visited. They've been set up by the Red Cross and the help of other local agencies. Troops from Fort Polk have called into action to prevent starvation and to protect life and property. The Small Business Administration, under the direction of Gene Foley, will tomorrow morning begin processing the first long-term loans in New Orleans. The Corps of Engineers is at work tonight, opening levees and dikes and removing debris. But we're ready to do much more. Within the hour, Governor McKeithen asked us to declare Louisiana a disaster area. We will so declare it tonight.[80]

Having made the hurricane a national disaster, Mayor Schiro positioned himself as a middleman between the federal government and disaster victims and would deliver everything from food to money.

Despite disapproval from state officials including Senator Long and Representative Hébert, Schiro went to Washington to request a loan program that included a grant of $5,000 for the disaster victims. His efforts to federalize the disaster became successful when President Johnson asked Long to cooperate with Schiro and promised presidential support. As a result, they proposed a "forgiveness bill" (s.2591), whereby homeowners, businessmen, and farmers would receive forgiveness for up to $5,000 for the repairs of their residential and commercial structures through Small Business Administration loans.[81] Although the chance to pass the legislation was slim due to its high cost of over $24 million, Schiro continued to pursue the agenda by asking constituents to pressure their representatives and by meeting with state officials to plead his case.

Schiro's plan to strike a deal with the federal government was largely successful. Because of his campaign in both Washington, DC, and New Orleans, the Southeast Hurricane Disaster Relief Act (H.R. 11539) was signed by President Johnson in 1965, just two days after Schiro's re-election. The new bill was a contracted version of the original terms that Schiro had proposed—it allowed forgiveness of $1,800, instead of $5,000, if the borrowers paid the first $500 on SBA loans. More importantly, the Relief Act became the harbinger of subsidized federal flood insurance, as the Act requested the Federal Housing Administration to study the feasibility of the federal flood insurance program. Because of this study, Congress passed the National Flood Insurance Act in 1968 and established the NFIP. The NFIP offers federally subsidized flood insurance to property owners in participating communities under the condition that the insured follow the federal floodplain management regulations.[82] Although the NFIP was established to encourage the participation of the flood-prone communities, the initial participation rate was quite low.[83] Later, in 1973, the Flood Disaster Protection Act (FDPA) was passed to further strengthen the protection of properties in flood-prone areas. While subnational jurisdictions participated voluntarily in the NFIP, the purchase of flood insurance became mandatory under the FDPA for the homeowners and home buyers whose properties were located on a floodplain map.

Despite its initial intentions, the NFIP produced substantial financial exposure to the federal government, much of which was incurred by the claims from Hurricane Katrina and Hurricane Sandy. As of December 31, 2014, FEMA owed the Treasury $23 billion and was included on the US Government Accountability Office's (GAO) high-risk list along with Medicare and Medicaid.[84] Although the Biggert-Waters Flood Insurance Reform Act was passed in 2012 to alleviate the deficit, the effort has been offset by the passage of the Homeowner Flood Insurance Affordability Act of 2014 (HFIAA), which resumed some premium subsidies and halted premium rate increases proposed by the Biggert-Waters Act.[85]

Not only was it clear that the mayor himself had sought to secure federal assistance, victims of Hurricane Betsy also attempted to negotiate directly with the federal government because the city government provided little compensation to help reconstruct damaged areas. In contrast to the mayor's visible efforts to appeal to the president, he did not pay equal attention to the individual victims of the hurricane. Residents in Desire and the Lower Ninth Ward, whose communities had been severely flooded, deplored the powerlessness and neglect of the mayor and the city council and instead pleaded to Congress.[86] Thanks to the federal government's War on Poverty, civic organizers could lobby federal bureaucrats through local administrators, and they eventually succeeded in securing millions of dollars for street repair and drainage improvement.[87] Furthermore, it was through this process that neighborhood civic associations shifted their focus from traditional, church-based community organizing to a "growth-oriented" approach. In the Lower Ninth Ward, for example, the newly founded Lower Ninth Ward

Neighborhood Council replaced the traditional Ninth Ward Civic Improvement League, and the Neighborhood Council successfully lobbied HUD in turning around the state legislation that had ceased urban renewal funding since the 1950s.[88]

Failure to Regulate Vulnerable Properties: The Passage and Repeal of the Biggert-Waters Act

Although the major avenue for federal flood prevention lay in levee construction, the federal government also passed several pieces of legislation to curtail floodplain development and encourage retreat from vulnerable locations. The most notable action was the passage of the Biggert-Waters Flood Insurance Reform Act in 2012. Passed with bipartisan support, the Act was part of the Resources and Ecosystems Sustainability, Tourist Opportunities, and Revived Economies of the Gulf Coast States Act (the RESTORE Act) that would divert penalties collected from the 2010 BP oil spill in the Gulf Coast. Intended to restore the financial solvency of the NFIP by increasing the insurance premiums of policy holders based on updated hazard risk information, the Biggert-Waters Act stipulated that properties with repeated flood damage could no longer receive coverage, and that the premiums on existing properties would be recalculated according to an updated flood-risk map.[89] Not surprisingly, Senator Mary Landrieu was one of the biggest opponents of the Act. On May 9, 2013, Landrieu introduced a bill to delay flood insurance premium increases, speaking on the Senate Floor:

> Flood insurance is not just about business and commerce; it is about culture; it is about a way of life; it is about preserving coastal communities; it is about being resilient in storms. We must make the flood insurance program resilient without endangering the financial future of our coastal residents.

Arguing that the Biggert-Waters Act placed an undue burden on middle-class homeowners in coastal communities, Landrieu emphasized the importance of spreading out the cost of flood insurance to all states rather than concentrating it into a few flood-prone states. Along with the support from fellow legislators in flood-prone states, including fellow

Democrats Senator Chuck Schumer of New York and Robert Menendez of New Jersey, Landrieu's bill was eventually realized when Congress passed HFIAA in 2014, which repeals and modifies some provisions of the Biggert-Waters Act. The HFIAA reversed the following major rate increases proposed by the Biggert-Waters Act. First, the HFIAA places limits on yearly premium increases for individual policy holders to not exceed 18 percent per year. Second, it reinstates the "grandfathered" provision that prevents rate increases for properties that had complied with previous Flood Insurance Rate Maps (FIRMs) but were subject to higher rates under the updated FIRM. Third, property owners who purchased homes in flood-risk areas would also be refunded the increased amount of insurance incurred by the change of ownership. Legislators from Louisiana were major supporters of the HFIAA. In the Senate, Landrieu and David Vitter, also of Louisiana, sponsored the Act, and in the House, Michael Grimm, a Republican from New York, and Bill Cassidy, a Republican from Baton Rouge, sponsored the legislation with cosponsors including two Louisiana representatives, Steven Scalise, a Republican from Jefferson, and Cedric Richmond, a Democrat from New Orleans.[90]

The passage and subsequent repeal of the Biggert-Waters Act demonstrate the difficulty with and resistance to the federal government's efforts to impose nonstructural restriction in flood-prone areas. As a federally subsidized program, the NFIP made a tacit agreement between the government and communities, whereby the former provides subsidized insurance while the latter was mandated to adopt land-use laws that restrict development in high-risk areas.[91] So long as state and local interests in protecting coastal communities remain a priority, the federal government cannot leverage its lawmaking power in flood mitigation.

Compensating Vulnerable Properties: Saint Bernard Parish v. United States

While the NFIP and the repeal of the Biggert-Waters Act demonstrated the difficulties with regulating private properties through insurance premiums, the federal government was also forced to assume direct financial liability for post-Katrina damages. On May 1, 2015, Judge Susan Braden of the US Court of Federal Claims ruled in *St. Bernard*

Parish v. United States that the federal government was liable for the property loss in Saint Bernard Parish and the Lower Ninth Ward of New Orleans during Katrina. In this long-standing dispute, the plaintiffs— Saint Bernard Parish, nine individuals, and eight businesses—argued that the Army Corps of Engineers "constructed, expanded, operated and failed to maintain" the Mississippi River–Gulf Outlet (MRGO).[92] Completed in 1968, the MRGO is a seventy-six-mile-long navigational channel built through virgin coastal wetlands. Over time, the MRGO had increased salinity and had gradually eroded its banks, expanding its width to 1,970 feet and 27,000 acres of wetland. The widened channel weakened the capacity of the levees, according to the plaintiffs, caus- ing storm surges to crest the levees and inundate Saint Bernard Parish and the Lower Ninth Ward. The mismanagement led to the "temporary taking" of property values in Saint Bernard Parish during Katrina and subsequent hurricanes Rita, Gustav, and Ike, meaning that the land and buildings were inaccessible for weeks and months after the disasters. This, they further argued, violated the Fifth Amendment to the US Con- stitution, which forbids the government's taking of properties without just compensation.[93]

The 2015 decision upheld a previous ruling in 2009 by Judge Stan- wood Duval Jr. of the Federal District Court, who had written that "the negligence of the Corps, in this instance by failing to maintain the MR- GO properly, was not policy, but insouciance, myopia and shortsighted- ness."[94] Both decisions rested on the fundamental principle established in the takings clause, which states that the government must protect individual properties and provide compensation when it cannot. How- ever, in 2018, the Federal Circuit Court of Appeals reversed the finding of the Federal Claims Court, stating that the plaintiffs presented no evi- dence of the causal association between the MRGO and the storm surge that damaged their properties. The Federal Court's final decision made clear that the government's liability only applies to the cases whereby it engaged in affirmative acts, such as releasing water from a government- constructed dam, or operating the dam to cause flooding on the plain- tiff's property.[95] The plaintiff's petition to the Supreme Court was denied on Jan 07, 2019, and the case was closed.

Although the Federal Appeals Court eventually reversed the initial decision, the significance of *St. Bernard Parish v. United States* goes further than the final verdict. The case reflects citizens' general view that the range of the federal government's liability extends to include the inadvertent management of federal infrastructure. To the victims of the hurricane, the government is not only liable for deliberate decisions to harm private land and property, such as releasing water from a dam, it is also not immune from the failure to act against possible harm.[96] Legal scholars such as John Echeverria have expressed concerns over the Claims Court's rejection of the long-term signs of climate risks, such as sea-level rise, land subsidence, and land loss as the major causes of massive flooding. Although many factors may have contributed to escalating the magnitude and duration of flooding, the Claims Court pointed out that the MRGO was the "principal cause" of the flooding, narrowed the scope of causation to structural matters, and applied the takings clause to a case where the causal chain is more diffuse than straightforward.[97]

Conclusion

As an agent of change, disasters are important because "disaster policy rarely changes without them, and disasters shape people and places in ways that would not have occurred without a catastrophic event."[98] This chapter sheds light on how civic actions and inactions have been intertwined with the government during, between, and after the nation's two biggest disasters. Lacking the legal power to enforce authoritative measures such as eminent domain or relocation of private properties, the federal government often relies on more politically palatable options such as fortifying levees and building canals, which turned out to be ineffective at mitigating a disaster of Katrina's magnitude.

Furthermore, the bulk of the federal funding was distributed as cash assistance to individual recipients *after* the disaster, as direct disaster relief was more politically visible to politicians and immediately economically beneficial to disaster victims than place-based infrastructural spending on mitigation. For state and local governments, incentives to invest in disaster mitigation were even weaker than for the federal government, as economic development became the dominant political issue for elites and citizens alike. Disaster mitigation, in this sense, seemed too distant a goal to achieve immediate economic benefits. Constantly facing the pressure for budget reform, elected officials reduced prospective spending on emergency preparedness. The retrenchment occurred while levee construction continued in the region, which local communities believed was a federal responsibility and supported as a necessary and sufficient way to protect their communities from storm surges.

Whereas the federal government has been obligated to provide structural solutions to protect disaster-prone areas, the state and local governments continued to pursue economic development at the expense of devising nonstructural methods of long-term disaster mitigation. Louisiana and New Orleans negotiated with the federal government to secure financial support, mainly through levee construction and individualized programs in disaster relief and flood insurance. Within the dual structure, civic actors got involved in the government's disaster prevention efforts both directly and indirectly. Directly, they intermittently employed legal and political means to fortify levee and drainage facilities, requiring a greater protection of coastal communities through armoring the shoreline. Indirectly, civic actors supported policies that minimized their tax burdens and maximized opportunities for territorial expansion and real estate development. Despite, or because of, the high visibility of federal policies on disaster mitigation, residents were more critical of the federal government than they were of the state and local governments.[99]

In the process of making natural disasters a federal responsibility, state and local governments have largely bailed themselves out of protecting citizens. Believing in a small government, Louisiana and New Orleans pursued economic growth and prosperity without a far-sighted vision for assessing and reducing future hazard risks. The decisions that came in the process of economic expansion and development, such as minimizing building regulations, freezing property tax rates, and expanding HUD projects in hazardous areas, carved a lasting imprint on the norms and preferences of civic actors. As the subnational governments had pursued a laissez-faire approach to economic development during ordinary times, citizens showed considerable resistance to any regulatory actions on their reconstruction efforts when an extraordinary event disrupted their lives.

This is not to say that state and local governments are inherently constrained and unable to innovate on policies that address long-term challenges. Some state and local governments do innovate, and the potential for local experimentation is indeed one of the advantages that federalism can offer. In managing perpetual disasters, however, it is difficult to form a wide public consensus around the need to curtail development and promote adaptability. Politicians have a hard time making such an argument given that citizens prefer a minimum burden out of their own pockets. This conclusion is somewhat ironic given that federalism is designed to encourage local innovation and autonomy.[100] In New Orleans, public opinion did not welcome the political will to slow down the pace of recovery, not to mention to restrict rebuilding in hazardous areas.

3

Rebuilding the City

Reconstruction and the Paradox of Participation

Post-storm, they have ten. There are ten. And this is for the
entire Parish of New Orleans. Can you imagine trying to
maintain an entire parish, post-Katrina, with all this?
—Jason Abate, March 10, 2010

During my interview with Jason Abate, the chief of staff for the then-
councilwoman Stacy Head in the city's District B, he became somewhat
agitated while he was speaking about the significant reduction of manpower in the maintenance division of the Department of Public Works.
According to him, it had previously employed about eighty people, but
after Katrina, its size had been reduced to ten. As quoted in the epigraph
to this chapter, the task of rebuilding the post-disaster city was frustrating due to the substantial reduction in city government staff. As early as
October 4, 2005, about a month after the hurricane struck the city, then-
mayor Ray Nagin announced that the city government would lay off
about half of its employees, three thousand in total.[1] The budget cuts led
to the retrenchment of the department that was responsible for repairing roads, buildings, and streets. Indeed, Katrina did not just breach
the levee but also destroyed the city's physical infrastructure, leaving
nearly 1.2 million housing units damaged and about three million homes
without power.[2] With only ten people in the workforce, it was almost
impossible for the maintenance division to respond to the massive
devastation after Katrina. Abate further explained how the shortage of
dedicated workforce could complicate even a simple task such as digging
a drainage trench:

> Like two weeks ago, I was with the superintendent, a public works
> field superintendent. A constituent had a flooded front yard, and what

needed to be done was a little ditch, trench needed to be dug, maybe about one hundred feet to the drain basin. As he said, "I can dig that trench for you, I just got my ditch machine out of the repairer's fix. But I can't pick it up . . . [b]ecause my front-end loader is in the repair shop, and the money that was given by FEMA to repair, the city pushed that to somewhere else. . . . Very simple task for a maintenance division, but to dig that ditch, we have to pull guys off from other shifts because I've only got ten."[3]

The shortage of workers was a significant burden on city government as it tried to oversee and regulate where and how rebuilding would happen. The number of service requests for fixing damaged buildings and restoring electricity skyrocketed, further constraining the city's already-low capacity to fulfill requests. The number of building permit applications filed to demolish, rebuild, and repair broken facilities soared.[4] Six months after Katrina, more than thirteen thousand building permits were issued by the city government, and the total number of building permits almost tripled after another six months, reaching more than thirty-eight thousand permits issued.[5] Due to the devastating effects of the hurricane, the city government sought to streamline "the process for obtaining permits to repair or demolish and reconstruct housing in the city"[6] without compromising safety. Despite that promise, the permit-issuing process was nothing but chaos. As evidenced by the city official's lamenting remarks, the drastic contraction of human resources in the city government, combined with the avalanche of building permit applications, meant delays to what would have been a simple and straightforward task in ordinary times.

Equally troublesome was the hasty delivery of government-authorized services. In principle, building permit approval should be strictly based on the level of a project's compliance with the city's building codes; after a permit is issued, building inspectors should carefully review whether the repaired or newly constructed unit does in fact comply with building codes. In practice, however, the shortage of building inspectors made it difficult to manage the surge of building that followed the physical devastation in New Orleans. For example, there were only fifteen building inspectors as of November 2006, making it impossible to count the number of returnees or to follow up with proper inspection and surveillance.[7] The then-director of the Department of Safety and Permits, Mike Centineo, remarked that he did not have a reliable estimate of the number of units that were being reconstructed after the storm and mentioned the reduced workforce as the primary reason for the oversight.[8]

Indeed, the total number of permit applications—including for repairs, additions, and demolition of physical structures, as well as electrical and commercial permits—reflects the chaotic nature of post-Katrina recovery. Before Katrina, the department received about 440 permit applications in an average month. In the post-Katrina period, the number of total permit applications went through the roof to reach three thousand applications in December 2005. Though it abated somewhat in early 2006, the total number of permit applications remained high, and was still over one thousand per month by May 2008. With the reduction of staff members in the building department, the high number of permit applications supports the journalistic accounts that the degree of workload may have been quite intense throughout the recovery period.

The consequence of such carelessness in the initial permit issuance process can be more severe than a bureaucratic mishap because rebuilding has a lasting impact on the city's sustainability. A lax process sends a strong signal to people that they can build their homes without having to spend too much money on flood-proofing. Recognizing the inconsistency in code enforcement, many homeowners had already expressed their intention to bypass home elevation requirements, even in those areas encroached upon by nine to ten feet of water.[9] After the storm, FEMA published a map that marked the required elevation levels for new and rebuilt houses, a height at which a house could withstand a hundred-year flood. A house is designated as new construction and subject to the federal regulation if the assessed damage exceeds 50 percent of the entire house. The new construction, in turn, must comply with the newly published map's height requirements, accordingly. If the damage is assessed at less than 50 percent, the house is qualified as a repair and need not abide by the new federal regulation. To avoid the cost associated with the elevation required by FEMA, hundreds of homeowners appealed to City Hall to lower their damage estimates to below 50 percent. City officials were criticized for accepting more than

90 percent of those appeals without strict code enforcement, which allowed for haphazard and fraudulent redevelopment in flood-prone areas.[10] This resulted in what experts worry was a hasty issuance of building permits for repairs, which may have rendered the city vulnerable again to future disasters.[11]

The collective consequences of the expeditious rebuilding practices are, therefore, greater than the sum of the risks that individual property owners are willing to undertake. As long as the chance of natural disasters remains high in New Orleans, rebuilding in vulnerable areas without proper mitigation measures will only escalate the cost of the next disaster. Indeed, some have raised concerns about the unfair burdens on federal taxpayers for subsidizing the increasing costs of rebuilding in coastal communities. Thirteen hundred residents of Dauphin Island in Alabama, for example, have paid $9.3 million in insurance premiums since 1988 and received $72.2 million for their damaged homes. In this case, the federal subsidy encouraged risk-taking behaviors of property owners in coastal communities. Similarly, if damaged areas are rebuilt too quickly, the risk of future damages will increase, the argument goes, and so will the amount of public assistance for disaster relief.[12]

This chapter investigates how residents' civic capacity influenced the allocation of city services across New Orleans after Hurricane Katrina. Post-Katrina building permit distribution serves as a unique laboratory to examine how distressed cities allocate their services when pressured by citizens, and whether the civic-oriented distributive pattern is conducive to enhancing urban resilience. Identifying permit locations provides us with a sense of where recovery occurred immediately after Katrina. Moreover, the uneven pace of permit processing shows how effectively and equitably city services are distributed across communities. Citizens exploited the weaknesses caused by explosive service demands and a short labor supply in the building permit division. I will show how people's civic capacity has significant bearings on how much and how fast rebuilding occurs, and how the power of civic participation affects the degree and speed of recovery across the city in crisis. Evidence from these quantitative analyses further suggests that fast, extensive rebuilding, while more likely to occur in civically active areas, does not always overlap with the city's resilient geography.

Building Permit Explosion and Moratorium in Post-Katrina New Orleans

Due to the immediate need to recover people's homes, the city's planning efforts to regulate reconstruction widened the chasm between public desire and government expectation. The most visible example was the short-lived building moratorium proposal by the city's recovery commission. In January 2006, the BNOBC, established by Ray Nagin with planning experts from the Urban Land Institute, proposed that the city enforce a building permit moratorium. In this proposal, the BNOBC recommended that the city cease issuing building permits for four months and create a Crescent City Rebuilding Authority that could seize properties through eminent domain in the city's most damaged neighborhoods.[13] The proposal was based on an evaluation showing that the wetland that used to protect the city from water continues to shrink, and that levees are not the safest measure in case of future hurricanes as strong as Katrina.[14] The moratorium also reflected a concern that land-use and building regulations, rather than structural protection, should serve as a long-term solution for environmental hazards.[15] Thus far, building codes had not been strongly enforced in much of the city's housing stock. As a scholar pointed out, "[m]easures such as building codes are still largely irrelevant to the older and lowest sections of the city. . . . The [Orleans] Parish . . . while forced by the FEMA lawsuit to manage land use more effectively for flood protection, has petitioned the Corps of Engineers to fill more than 2000 acres of wetlands . . . further reducing floodwater retention capacity."[16]

Despite its proactive intent, the building moratorium proposal faced a huge backlash in and out of the city and was ultimately rescinded. City council members, who had maintained a sour relationship with the mayor, held a press conference and chastised him, with one of the members dismissing the proposal as "a blatant violation of property rights."[17] Homeowners of severely flooded neighborhoods such as Lakeview, the Lower Ninth Ward, and Village de l'Est expressed their anger and frustration in public meetings, accusing Joseph Canizaro, the central figure at BNOBC and the sculptor of the proposed master plan, of taking a heavy-handed approach to reshaping the city by taking their homes. "I don't think that it's right that you take our properties.

Over my dead body," said one resident in the public meeting.[18] "Our neighborhood is ready to come home. Don't get in our way and prevent us from doing that. Help us cut the red tape," said another homeowner in Lakeview, one of the city's most severely flooded neighborhoods.[19] For the homeowners eager to rebuild their broken homes, shrinking the city's footprint via suspending reconstruction was not morally acceptable because it seemed to them that the government authorities were placing unfair restrictions on those who had been most affected by the storm. Furthermore, the building moratorium divided the already deep racial gap between Blacks and Whites. Given the residential history of New Orleans, it was hard to separate racial issues from selective rebuilding.[20] Whereas most of the poor Black population inhabited the city's low-lying areas such as the Lower Ninth Ward and public housing projects, Whites occupied relatively high grounds that avoided flooding, such as Uptown and the Garden District. Naturally, the decision to halt reconstruction confirmed the widely held belief that the city was deliberately trying to dislocate the Black population. As a result, the building moratorium quickly became a politically charged issue, and city council members and the local chapter of NAACP, for example, showed their intent to fight against it.[21]

In addition to being politically charged, progressive civic leaders and academics also argued that the building moratorium favored business elites over disaster victims. Although a smaller footprint does not directly benefit the stakeholders in the real estate business, the moratorium and an idea of concentrated development was believed to be a "land grab" that would benefit property developers by raising the exchange value of high-lying communities at the expense of closed disadvantaged neighborhoods.[22] For this reason, some argued that it would be inappropriate to apply moratoria for an economic development purpose if the compensation for displaced residents is delayed.[23]

The politicization and rejection of what could have become "sensible planning strategies" led to a paradoxical consequence.[24] Although the objection to the moratorium was based on the popular idea that everyone deserves the right to return and rebuild, what followed was a privatized, laissez faire–style reconstruction that relied on philanthropic generosity and donor preference and ultimately led to patchwork reconstruction across the city. Brad Pitt's Make It Right Foundation (MIR), for example, was launched in the Lower Ninth Ward to realize the progressive ideal of equitable recovery. Collaborating with national architectural firms, MIR embarked on a large-scale social experiment that employed innovative design and environmentally conscious building practice, and built about one hundred homes in the neighborhood.[25] While MIR's project sheltered the city's most vulnerable population, the housing complexes were still built amid the fundamental civic problems that had beset the neighborhood: depopulation, sustained poverty, and neighborhood decay.[26] The slow pace of repopulation did not serve to accommodate the ambitious scope of the philanthropic housing projects. Only 37 percent of the pre-Katrina population returned to the Lower Ninth Ward after ten years, while the city as a whole regained almost 90 percent of its residents.[27] Perhaps except for the many churches that still occupy the area, the Lower Ninth Ward is institutionally vacant. As of August 2015, there was only one grocery store in the Lower Ninth Ward, and it takes three bus changes to get to the next-closest grocery store, Walmart, which is located across the city.[28]

Reconstruction and Urban Service Provision in Post-Katrina New Orleans

Given that reconstruction is only possible with government-authorized building permits, looking at the ways in which these permits were distributed addresses a series of questions on post-Katrina reconstruction. First, the most vexing question has been whether rebuilding occurred at a fast rate in the city's affluent communities and more slowly in poor neighborhoods. If they suffer the same amount of damage, do affluent communities still fare better than their poorer counterparts? Then, to what extent does the civic capacity of a given community play a role in widening the disparity? By comparing the speed and extent of permit issuance between communities, we can gain insight into the equitability of the rebuilding process at the neighborhood level. Second, the permit issuance process allows us to evaluate whether civic engagement affected the bureaucratic protocols of the building department. In theory, building permits should only be issued to the applications that meet its technical requirements, and yet the post-Katrina experience suggests that pressure from local residents may have intervened in the permit issuance process. This is related to the third question about the equitability of post-Katrina reconstruction. If we can conclude that permits were issued in a fair and efficient manner, then we would expect to observe no significant relationship between civic participation on the one hand and permit issuance on the other. Furthermore, in consideration of the long-term sustainability of the city, fewer permits should have been expected for the high-risk areas, regardless of how active the residents were in those communities.

Analytic Approach

With these questions in mind, I examine which factors are associated with the speed and volume of building permit issuance. In examining permit applications, I consider two dimensions. First, the total number of building permits per census tract measures the degree of reconstruction, as a high number of building permits indicates a greater extent of recovery in the area. To calculate the total number of active permits in a census tract, I geocoded the locations of each active permit and aggregated their frequency by census tract. In addition to the number of building permits, I also examine the duration until permit issuance for each application, which measures the speed with which a permit decision is made. I calculate the duration until permit issuance with the number of days until the permit decision (active or pending) is reached. The median turnaround time in the dataset is five days, which roughly corresponds to the average working days needed to complete residential building permits by the Department of Safety and Permits (two to five days).[29]

Reconstruction

To gauge the degree of reconstruction, I use new residential and commercial building permit applications filed with the Department of Safety and Permits from November 2005 through June 2008. Among the various types of building permits available, I focus mainly on new construction permits to track where people—especially homeowners whose houses were severely damaged and who thus needed new construction permits—resettled after Katrina. Repairing or demolishing properties also played a part in recovery activities, but these activities are less burdensome than building a new property. It takes a much shorter time to issue a repair permit for work involving simple renovation. For example, permit applications for kitchen remodeling or repair work after a disaster are reviewed by permit analysts and can be issued on the same day. However, "if plans are required for your job—such as new construction or structural work—a building permit will not be issued until after a plan review is completed. This review ensures compliance with the Building, Electrical, and Mechanical Codes of the city."[30] Given the difficulties associated with mitigating future hazards—for example, meeting more stringent flood regulations—most new residential construction demonstrates the extent to which people are willing to invest their resources in their properties.

I also examine where new commercial permits were distributed across the city to complement and contrast with residential permit applications. Commercial permits enable us to look at whether new commercial developments match pacing with residential reconstruction and whether business owners and homeowners make similar locational decisions.

Civic Capacity

Several previous studies on disaster recovery have suggested voting turnout as a proxy for the civic capacity of a community.[31] Using voting as a proxy for civic capacity highlights the competency of neighborhood residents, as the act of voting entails using knowledge and skills to carry out complex tasks. Figuring out how to file a residential permit requires a similar kind of competency, as residents must be able to estimate the extent, cost, and process of reconstruction and express it in the permit application.

To measure the strength and resilience of community civic engagement, I use election turnout as a primary indicator of civic capacity before Katrina. Turnout is defined as the proportion of votes cast divided by the total number of registered voters in each area within New Orleans Parish. The heightened interest and civic competence of locals may explain why civic capacity matters in the distribution of urban services like building permits. Local political participation is a representation of civic capacity, a belief that individuals can influence the political system as well as an ability to carry the belief into participatory action.[32] Voting in local elections is one of the methods through which citizens express their interest in local governance, with a belief that their votes can affect administrative decision-making.[33] Local elections generally have lower turnout than presidential elections, but those who vote have a very high level of interest and involvement in local affairs. These voters are likely to be the "stakeholders" in their community and to have high rates of education, income, and homeownership.[34] Therefore, if turnout indicates potential demands for better services rather than the deliverability of electoral success, we will observe an isolated effect of political participation that is independent from political support for a candidate.

I use separate variables for local and national elections to highlight that local turnout captures the strength of community political engagement more accurately than national turnout. Existing studies do not make a clear distinction between political participation at national and local levels, often using the former as an indicator of civic engagement.[35] However, local elections have different characteristics from national elections, and voters turn out for different reasons. For instance, candidates' and voters' race and ethnic identities play a crucial role in local elections,[36] whereas these factors are less salient in national elections, where partisanship and interest in national issues drive votes. Furthermore, the voting population in the latter is skewed toward people with more affluent and educated backgrounds and greater knowledge in local affairs.[37] Therefore, I expect that local turnout will have a more positive relationship with building permit issuance than turnout for a presidential election.

Civic capacity as expressed through local voting also means a high level of citizen competence, i.e., knowledge and skills to carry out complex tasks. Well-informed and engaged citizen constituents have greater demands for urban services, and the city government is more likely to respond to high-turnout areas by competent and prompt requests from the demand side. In other words, "[m]ore demands yield more services."[38] Active communities can thus stimulate demands for greater access to urban services. This is particularly relevant in a post-disaster context when people have dire needs to reconstruct homes and communities, and when each community must compete for scarce resources.

Finally, active participation in local politics represents a voter's social attachment to his or her own community. Residents with limited mobility and sufficient resources tend to build up high levels of social capital with neighbors, and their active engagement in community affairs leads to greater political participation.[39] At times, the motivation behind active political participation can be also purely economic. People with higher income and their own home in a community are concerned with any political choices that may influence property values (such as taxation, land use, and zoning) and thus are more likely to participate in the decision-making process.[40] Since their property values are directly connected to the overall development of their community, they try to elect officials who can administer policies favorable to the interests of property owners. In both cases, social attachment to and economic investment in their community not only increases the level of interest in local political matters, but also enhances the civic competence of residents in dealing with local government.

More specifically, I use turnout data from two elections that were held before Katrina: (i) the presidential election on November 2, 2004, between George W. Bush and John Kerry; and (ii) the mayoral runoff on March 2, 2002, between Ray Nagin and Richard Pennington. Using pre-Katrina election data is necessary and beneficial for at least two reasons. First, it avoids confusion in the temporal order between independent and dependent variables. Although the 2006 mayoral race was closer on a timeline to Katrina, using data from this election is illogical because this election occurred after permit applications had already been submitted in 2005. Second, pre-disaster elections capture the resilience of civic competence better than post-disaster political events. In New Orleans, the 2002 election was a regular mayoral race with two Black candidates; however, the 2006 election between Nagin (African American) and Landrieu (White) was much more contested due to heightened racial, social, and economic tensions in the city and unprecedented nationwide attention to its results. Therefore, turnout for the 2006 election is a result of various external factors that are not associated with community civic competence only.

Following Cingranelli,[41] I match precinct-level data on registered voters and votes cast for each candidate with census tracts. There are 442 voting precincts in New Orleans, and I superimposed a precinct map onto the census tract map in the Geographic Information System (GIS). When the census tract and precinct boundaries did not perfectly coincide, I divided the precinct data among census tracts according to the proportion of the area covered by each census tract.

In a similar vein, I include community organizations as another source of civic competence (*commorg*) to complement the local turnout variable. In addition to voting as individuals, members of community-based organizations also influence government service delivery by expressing and mediating resident demands.[42] As will be mentioned in chapter 4, community-based organizations represent the interests of clients and engage in political negotiations with the city government to secure necessary social services for their neighborhood.[43] As a cumulative result of civic competence and participation, community organizations are expected to have a positive relationship with the quantity and speed of urban service delivery. To estimate the strength of community organizing, I first geocode churches, social service organizations, and neighborhood associations to calculate their frequency in each census tract. While voter turnout measures an overall level of civic competence, *candidate support* captures the intensity of support for a specific candidate, which I calculate with a ratio of Nagin support out of total votes cast in the runoff.

Other Factors

In my argument, geography plays an important role in adjudicating the utility of civic capacity on reconstruction. To make the city safer and more resilient, redevelopment is expected to be concentrated in the city's "safe" areas—those higher than sea level. In contrast, an area is considered vulnerable if located below sea level. *Vulnerability* is a binary variable that captures this dynamic and is coded 0 if the census tract is above sea level, and 1 if below sea level. Also, *flood* measures the peak height of floodwaters in the area. measured in meters. Both variables are point estimates, which is measured at the intersection of longitudinal and latitudinal coordinates. To approximate the regional average of elevation and flood levels, I randomly take five x- and y-coordinates in each census tract from United States Geological Survey (USGS) areal maps and calculate their mean value.[44]

I also include a set of measures that influence the complexity of each application and thus may delay or facilitate permit issuance. First, *Use* is coded as 1 if there is any change in the use of the building, and as 0 if no change is requested. *Fees* refers to the application fee charged for each permit, which is imposed based on the work to be performed.[45] *Double* is coded as 1 if the project is a two-family dwelling (as opposed to a single-family dwelling). *Balance* is coded as 1 if an applicant has not paid the application fee and has a remaining balance, which is positively associated with duration. *Plan* and *Sketch* are coded as 1 if the project is complicated enough to necessitate a construction plan and sketch, respectively, in the permit application. If plans are required, a more strenuous process is applied to review the plan to check if it complies with city building, electrical, and mechanical codes.[46]

In addition to the civic capacity variable, I use demographic, socio-economic, and geographic indicators from US Census data and the USGS. If the underclass hypothesis holds, then these indicators will have statistical significance throughout the analysis. *Percent Black* measures the proportion of African Americans among the total population. For economic conditions, *Poverty* is defined as the percentage of residents living below the poverty line designated by the Census Bureau, *Logincome* as the logarithm of median household income per census tract, and *Rent* as the percentage of rented dwellings. Furthermore, I control for the median year when homeowners moved into the unit (*Owner Tenure*) to control for housing mobility. Finally, I include a total number of permit applications (*Permtotal*). More new construction permits are likely to be granted active status in proportion to the number of other applications filed, such as repair and demolition permits, because if a new structure is built upon a damaged property, the old must be demolished first. Controlling for the total number of permit applications therefore enables us to know the extent to which new construction, which is costlier and takes a longer time than repairing existing structures, occurs relative to the overall recovery.

Mapping Reconstruction, 2005–2008

Tracking the number of new construction projects during the early period of recovery offers a first look at where post-Katrina reconstruction unfolded. Figure 3.1. shows the number of new construction permit applications by month from March 2005 to May 2008. In the months

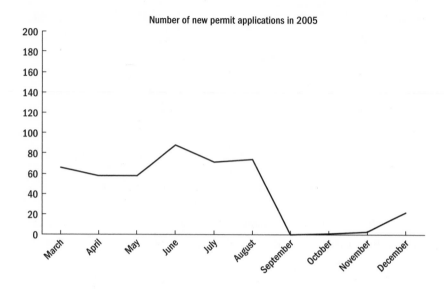

Number of new permit applications in 2005

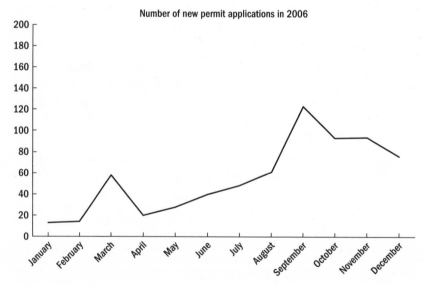

Number of new permit applications in 2006

before Katrina, there were about sixty-eight permit applications per month. After the hurricane, the pace of new construction was somewhat slow in the first few months after the disaster, as shown by the low number of new permit applications. The number of new construction permits returned to its pre-Katrina level about a year later and remained

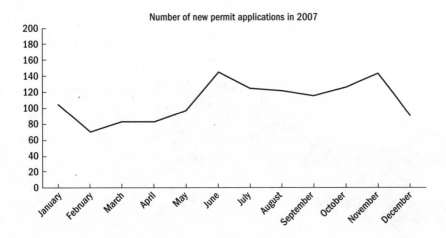

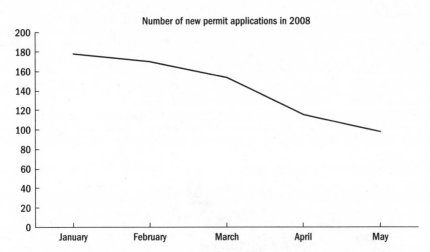

Figure 3.1.a–d. Number of new construction permit applications by month. Source: Think New Orleans and the Department of Safety and Permits.

high afterward, mounting to nearly two thousand new construction applications in February 2008, of which fewer than two hundred received permits.

To explore where new buildings were constructed, I mapped the building permits against flooding and repopulation maps. First, I compare post-Katrina residential permits and the height of floodwater in Figures 3.2.a and 3.2.c. In these maps, darker areas represent the higher

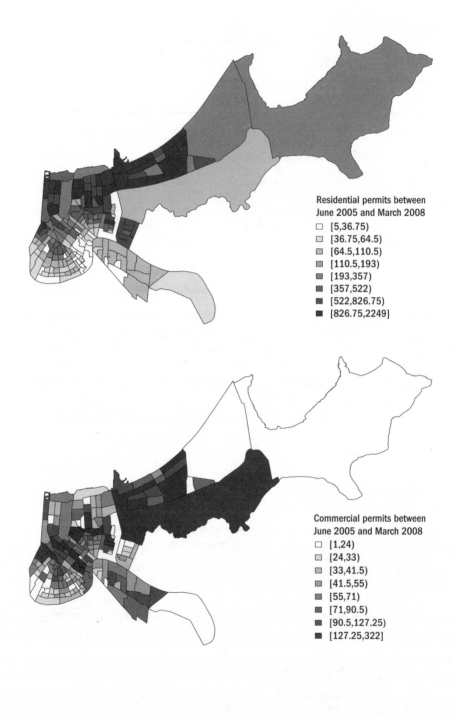

Residential permits between
June 2005 and March 2008
☐ [5,36.75)
☐ [36.75,64.5)
▨ [64.5,110.5)
▨ [110.5,193)
▨ [193,357)
■ [357,522)
■ [522,826.75)
■ [826.75,2249]

Commercial permits between
June 2005 and March 2008
☐ [1,24)
☐ [24,33)
▨ [33,41.5)
▨ [41.5,55)
▨ [55,71)
■ [71,90.5)
■ [90.5,127.25)
■ [127.25,322]

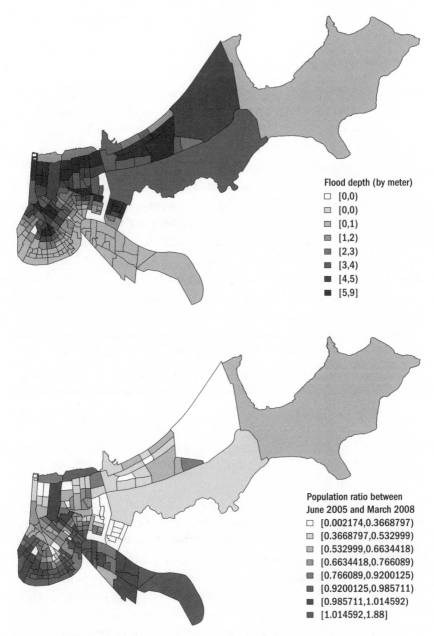

Flood depth (by meter)
☐ [0,0)
☐ [0,0)
▨ [0,1)
▨ [1,2)
▨ [2,3)
▨ [3,4)
■ [4,5)
■ [5,9]

Population ratio between June 2005 and March 2008
☐ [0.002174,0.3668797)
☐ [0.3668797,0.532999)
▨ [0.532999,0.6634418)
▨ [0.6634418,0.766089)
▨ [0.766089,0.9200125)
■ [0.9200125,0.985711)
■ [0.985711,1.014592)
■ [1.014592,1.88]

Figure 3.2.a–d. Patterns of recovery and damage in New Orleans by census tract, 2005–2008. Sources: the Department of Safety and Permits, Think New Orleans, United States Geological Survey, and Greater New Orleans Data Center. Compiled by author.

number of permits and the more severe flooding, respectively. The dark areas in the new permits and flooding maps largely match, suggesting that for the first three years, new construction appears to have occurred mainly in heavily flooded areas. Not all construction was done in flooded neighborhoods, however. In contrast with residential permits, commercial permits, presented in Figure 3.2.b, were concentrated in the city's central areas; there is less overlap between commercial permits and flood levels than with residential permits.

Despite these substantial reconstruction activities, however, fewer people have come back to the city's wet areas. Figure 3.2.d shows that heavily flooded areas have shown slower repopulation rates than areas with less or no flooding. Flood-damaged areas tend to attract far fewer people than they housed pre-Katrina, with the population rates remaining below 50 percent. In contrast, the high-lying, dry areas recovered most of, or even augmented, their pre-Katrina population in three years. In addition, the average response time to permit applications differs widely across communities, taking as little as one day to more than three hundred days (Figure 3.3). Some neighborhoods average faster turnaround times than others: for instance, in heavily damaged neighborhoods like the Lower Ninth Ward and Lakeview, the mean response time is about fifty-five days, whereas it is about half the time in Uptown Audubon (twenty-eight days) where Katrina produced little to no damage.

In sum, the temporal and spatial overviews teach us three things about the post-Katrina reconstruction. First, the number of building permit applications increased significantly after Katrina, far exceeding the average number of applications prior to the hurricane. New construction permits rose steadily after Katrina, suggesting that rebuilding activities, some of which continued long after Katrina, had devastated the building stock. The skyrocketing volume of permit applications also corroborates the chaotic situation described around the building moratorium discussed earlier in this chapter, making it possible to think that permit approval decisions may have been influenced by something other than technical compliance. Second, the new construction occurred unevenly across the city. Topography maps show that reconstruction, especially the rebuilding of residential buildings, was most prevalent in heavily flooded, low-lying communities. The gap between flooded and dry areas is quite large. The number of permits issued in less-flooded

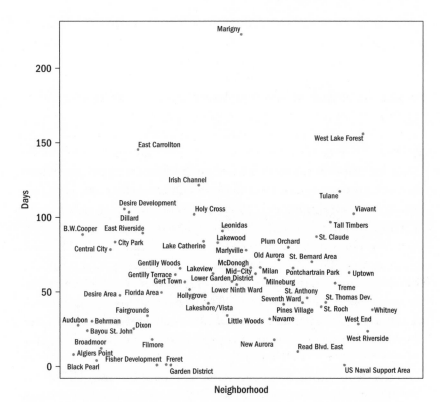

Figure 3.3. Average response time by neighborhood. Note: Dots indicate average days for processing an application by neighborhood. *X* axis denotes neighborhoods in an alphabetical order.

areas was usually lower than one hundred during the study period, whereas the number reached more than two thousand in heavily flooded areas. Third, the average response time to building permit applications varied considerably from neighborhood to neighborhood. An explanation should be made as to why such a variation exists and whether the community's civic capacity influences the variation.

Does Civic Capacity Increase the Number of Successful Permits?

To assess whether civic capacity guides these uneven patterns of new construction, we will need to see whether civic capacity is still a relevant factor after controlling for a set of community character-istics. Table 3.1 presents results from multivariate negative binomial regression (see the appendix for a methodological note).[47] To wit, civic capacity is positively associated with the increased number of permit applications in each area. A high level of political participation facili-tates the issuance of new construction permits, even after controlling for several socioeconomic factors as well as the likelihood of overall reconstruction happening in an area. Also, civic capacity had a ubiq-uitously strong effect across the city regardless of where a community is, facilitating residential rebuilding in vulnerable areas in an equally strong way as the safe areas. The relationship still holds after the fact that other recovery-related activities such as repair and demolition are accounted for, suggesting that civic capacity not only facilitates fixing small damages but also reconstructing heavily damaged or destroyed homes. As turnout increases by 10 percent, there is about an 18 per-cent increase in the number of residential permits. The two geographic variables—flood level and vulnerability—tell a lot about where new residential construction is most active across the city. With other con-ditions being equal, the number of permits is positively associated with the depth of the flood and vulnerability of the area. Consistent with the public's opposition to a building moratorium, rebuilding occurred in an extensive manner across the city's flood-prone areas. In the first three years of post-Katrina rebuilding, there were almost twice as many permits issued in areas that let in a high level of flood-water and/or were located below sea level as for the new construction in high-lying areas.

Some might claim that these results are somewhat expected, as civic capacity tends to boost reconstruction and rebuilding tends to happen more actively in areas that suffer from greater damage. This is quite con-sistent with the existing findings on post-Katrina recovery. However, it is important to question whether a similar pattern exists for other types of reconstruction, such as nonresidential structures whose reconstruction was related more to economic assessments than civic ties. In fact, greater damage in a neighborhood may have reduced, rather than elevated, the possibility for rebuilding nonresidential establishments since it was dif-ficult to predict whether the city, or the community, would regain a suf-ficient number of consumers. Therefore, if we were to conclude that civic

TABLE 3.1. Factors influencing the number of active residential and commercial permits for new construction.

	Residential Permits	Commercial Permits
Civic Competence		
Mayoral Turnout	1.674*	−1.560*
	(0.920)	(0.896)
Socioeconomic		
Black	1.537***	0.582**
	(0.246)	(0.240)
Rent	−1.856***	0.551
	(0.485)	(0.475)
Logincome	−0.123	−0.495*
	(0.279)	(0.274)
Poverty	−1.698**	−3.135***
	(0.756)	(0.742)
Owner Tenure	−0.014	0.002
	(0.010)	(0.009)
Permtotal	0.005**	−0.003
	(0.003)	(0.002)
Flood Risk		
Flood	0.125***	0.015
	(0.037)	(0.036)
Vulnerable	0.645**	0.343**
(1= below sea level)	(0.154)	(0.151)
Intercept	5.961*	9.877***
	(3.257)	(3.195)
AIC	2201.1	1781.4

engagement fosters recovery in heavily flooded areas, we need to examine whether civic capacity also facilitates nonresidential permit issuance.

To put these contemplations into a comparative perspective, I conduct the same analysis on commercial permits (Table 3.1, Column 2). When it comes to restoring commercial activities, civic capacity has an opposite effect than what we observe in residential permits. Higher turnout is associated with *fewer* commercial permits in an area, so that a 10 percent increase in turnout led to 15 percent fewer total commercial permits than areas with zero participation. Instead, economic conditions play a significant role in predicting whether businesses will come back to an area. While income level is not a significant factor for residential permits, it is strongly associated with the number of commercial permits, as more commercial permits tend to be issued in high-income areas. Likewise, poverty level is a significant predictor of the quantity of commercial permits. If half of the residents in an area are below the poverty level, the number of commercial permits drops by about 80 percent compared to an area without any residents below the poverty level.

Equally important is that, compared with residential permits, commercial reconstruction is not actively pursued in areas that experienced extensive flooding. Nor is land elevation as strong a predictor as in residential permits, as the size of the coefficient is only half of the coefficient in the residential permits model. In numerical terms, the number of residential permits in the city's vulnerable areas is nearly twice as large as the number of permits filed on a higher ground, while for commercial permits, the difference is only about 40 percent. Different dynamics exist between where residential and commercial reconstruction occurs, suggesting that people's residential choices depend on calculations other than business decisions. Residents directed their rebuilding efforts in areas with greater flooding and vulnerability, while business reconstruction was driven mainly by the economic conditions of a community—whether a neighborhood had a sufficient number of potential clients and a good environment for commercial activities.

The conflicting motivators behind residential and commercial reconstruction suggest that civic capacity may not be a panacea for neighborhood revitalization, as it facilitates certain types of recovery but not others. Heavy storm damage and geographic vulnerability does take a toll on neighborhood recovery when it is measured by the return of commercial facilities rather than housing. While it is welcome news that active civic participation is indicative of the strong will to come back and repair their damaged homes, it has a selective effect on people's decision to return—but not on the businesses that are also necessary for community redevelopment.

Does Civic Capacity Speed Up Permit Issuance?

If communities with a higher level of resident participation are likely to build more new properties, then does community civic capacity also reduce turnaround time? I examine whether and how various conditions may bring any change in delaying or facilitating average permit application durations (Table 3.2).[48]

As far as permit-specific conditions are concerned, most of the technical criteria are statistically significant (Models 1 and 2). Recall that in the event history analysis, negative coefficients mean that it takes more time until an observation receives any decision (see the appendix for more discussion). For example, it usually slows down the permitting process when a proposed project has a remaining balance or is complex—such as if it is large in scale and/or involves a structural change. Results support this intuition. If a project in a neighborhood proposes to change the land use from vacant to residential (i.e., use=1), then it slows down the process by 33 percent (Model 2). After all other conditions are considered, civic capacity measures are still significant and positively associated with the speed of permit issuance (Models 3 and 4). A 1 percent increase in local turnout increases the tendency toward permit issuance in that area by 3.81 percent. As a community adds one organization, there is a 2.02 percent increase in the probability of issuance for the permit application filed in that community.

However, neither of the other political participation measures—presidential election turnout or support for the mayor-elect—has a statistically significant relationship with the duration to permit issuance. In other words, engagement with political affairs alone does not explain why permit issuance is slow in one neighborhood but not in others. Instead, interest in *local* politics is a positive and consistent factor that can reduce permit issuance procedural timelines, and this effect is still robust after neighborhood-wide risk factors are accounted for (Model 4). To illustrate the effect of local turnout, Figure 3.4 graphically compares predicted survival probabilities of permit issuance in low- and high-turnout areas.[49] When turnout for a mayoral election is high, at 80 percent, the chances of delayed issuance are much lower than when a community has a low turnout of 20 percent. A building application filed in a high-turnout area has a greater chance of receiving a permit within a shorter

TABLE 3.2. Factors affecting the duration to permit issuance.

	Model 1	Model 2	Model 3	Model 4
Civic Competence				
Mayoral Turnout			4.524***	3.744***
			(0.778)	(1.190)
Presidential Turnout			−0.303	−0.051
			(0.210)	(0.656)
Nagin Support			0.563	1.157
			(0.669)	(1.040)
Commorg			0.013**	0.020**
			(0.005)	(0.010)
Technical Criteria				
Fees	−0.000***	−0.000***	−0.000***	−0.000***
	(0.000)	(0.000)	(0.000)	(0.000)
Double	−0.255***	−0.242***	−0.230***	−0.239***
	(0.080)	(0.081)	(0.080)	(0.082)
Use	−0.467**	−0.412*	−0.422*	−0.412*
	(0.245)	(0.247)	(0.246)	(0.248)
Balance	−0.674**	−0.673**	−0.642**	−0.627*
	(0.319)	(0.319)	(0.319)	(0.320)
Plan	−0.533***	−0.571***	−0.556***	−0.583***
	(0.068)	(0.069)	(0.069)	(0.070)
Sketch	−0.074	0.123*	0.087	0.126*
	(0.066)	(0.066)	(0.066)	(0.067)
Socioeconomic Conditions				
Black			0.627**	0.349
			(0.261)	(0.478)
Rent			0.386	0.746
			(0.287)	(0.587)
Poverty			1.143*	1.018
			(0.619)	(0.842)
Logincome			0.220	0.107
			(0.196)	(0.323)
Owner Tenure			0.001	0.003
			(0.006)	(0.009)
Flood Damage				
Flood			−0.027	−0.044
			(0.016)	(0.037)
Elevation			0.011	0.022
			(0.033)	(0.057)
Frailty	No	Yes	No	Yes
R-squared	0.075	0.148	0.099	0.159

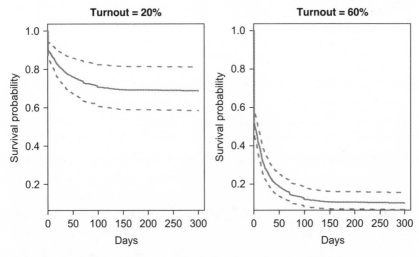

Figure 3.4. Predicted survival probability by low (20 percent) and high (60 percent) turnout. Note: The survival probability drops more sharply in a high-turnout area, indicating a greater chance of receiving approval within early days after application.

period. Permit applications in the higher-turnout area tend to receive a decision during within fifty days, while those in the low-turnout area are still likely to be waiting for approval within the same period. In sum, this study lends credence to the claim that civic capacity, expressed as turnout in local elections and being in possession of community resources, is a significant predictor of redevelopment after Katrina.

Fast Rebuilding and Slow Repopulation: The Paradox of Reconstruction in Vulnerable Areas

Findings from this chapter seem to suggest that civic capacity, represented by citizens' political engagement, is a generally strong facilitator of post-disaster reconstruction both in terms of quantity and quality of city services. Not only do civically active communities file more permits, they also enjoy a faster response from the city government. The good news is that residents can navigate bureaucratic labyrinths with ease if their community is rich with civic resources. For example, residents in cooperative communities are more likely to share information and knowledge about how to avoid contractor fraud and file thorough and compliant application forms that readily meet the technical requirements specified by the Department of Safety and Permits, which results in greater acceptance rates and quick processing.[50] Also, faster services can increase efficacy of and trust in city government. Although bureaucrats may not intend to favor applications from politically active communities, they are bound to be more attentive to well-documented applications. If we think of new property construction only as one part of recovery activities, facilitating the bureaucratic process through civic means is a promising way to mitigate some negative effects of a post-disaster situation.

This might also be bad news, however, because new construction does not only mean destroyed properties are being recovered, but it can also serve as a harbinger that people are putting energy toward redevelopment in what are still the city's most vulnerable regions. Recall that more permit applications were filed and processed in the city's flooded areas than in the dry areas. While this seems to be logical, the consequences of rebuilding flooded areas could be detrimental to residents, especially if these areas lie below sea level. The physical rebuilding of damaged properties makes a lasting imprint on the city's physical shape: once constructed, buildings will last for years. Unless carefully constructed, these buildings will likely be damaged by future storms again. Worse yet, once technical and civic factors are accounted for, geographic conditions matter little in terms of where and how fast reconstruction happens, and in some cases, more reconstruction happens in the worst-flooded communities.

The rebuilding of flooded communities strikes a sharp contrast with the slow repopulation trend in the same areas, which will be further discussed in the next chapter. As shown in the maps (Figure 3.2), repopulation is still slow and incomplete in flooded communities, although various reconstruction activities, including new construction and demolition, are in process. In the Lower Ninth Ward, for example, a strong push for rebuilding civic institutions in flooded communities led to the return of pre-Katrina organizations despite the sluggish repopulation of residents. Beginning with the reopening of an elementary program at Dr. Martin Luther King Jr. Charter School in 2007, a high school program also opened there in 2016 to replace a former high school that was closed after Katrina. Dr. Martin Luther King, Jr. Library and many churches still occupy the area, along with the newly opened Sanchez Multi-Service community center that features a health clinic and indoor pool. The reconstruction of civic facilities in this heavily damaged neighborhood is a testament to community resilience—it shows the willingness of residents to keep their neighborhood's vitality. And yet, the causal effect of these civic institutions—that is, whether they contribute to inviting more population into the area—remains unclear.[51] Furthermore, little has been discussed with respect to the possibility of future hazards and how these civic institutions may help mitigate, if not prevent, turmoil from the geographic vulnerabilities of the neighborhood.

If damaged communities do not regain enough population to sustain a healthy communal life, then those who rebuild their properties in the less-populated, high-risk areas will not be able to enjoy the public goods and services provided in more populated areas, such as frequent police patrol, more brightly lit streets, thriving businesses, and even block parties.

The interruption of core services was indeed one of the direst concerns among those who returned to and rebuilt in vulnerable areas. In a city council district meeting, a resident lamented the lack of infrastructure:

> The Lower Ninth Ward would be the last place for infrastructure. We [are] at the end down here. I don't see anything . . . Something has to be done . . . I mean we don't have a grocery, pharmacist, I am tired of paying for streetlights. I've been paying for streetlights since December, 2005. Thirty dollars a month. . . . I can't get a streetlight . . . this is ridiculous. This makes no sense. It's really nonsense.[52]

The sparse distribution of population and correspondingly limited services is part of what is called a "jack-o'-lantern" effect: a gap-toothed resettlement pattern in which inhabited houses are separated by vacant, abandoned lots. In the ten years following the storm, government and nonprofit sectors tried to reinvest in the neighborhoods that suffered most from housing blight and abandonment. As of 2015, the city still had more than 30,000 blighted properties, and revitalizing blighted neighborhoods has proven difficult if not impossible.[53] In the Lower Ninth

Ward, the New Orleans Redevelopment Authority (NORA) initiated a plan to subsidize developers to turn vacant parcels into affordable rentals and for-sale housing units, and yet the sparse population and lack of commercial establishments in the neighborhood sent mixed signals to potential renters and homebuyers.

In fact, the spreading out of unattended pockets is not only a problem for New Orleans; it also plagues Rust Belt cities such as Youngstown, Cleveland, and Detroit. With regard to addressing checkered residential patterns, various suggestions for remedy have been made including building light-rail systems. In an interview with a local magazine in Detroit, CNN journalist and Detroit native Miles O'Brien expressed hope that its light-rail project would cluster the city's dispersed population, saying "if you build it, they [people] will come."[54] As a host anchor of *Blueprint America*, a PBS documentary series on America's crumbling urban infrastructure, O'Brien observed the vivid urban decline in America's postindustrial cities and highlighted efforts to incorporate decline into resilient urban systems. Interestingly, a light-rail project was also part of BNOBC's post-Katrina master plan, although the proposal was vehemently rejected by residents. "Give me a break: We don't need a light-rail system. We're in the mud," said one resident from Lakeview when the city unveiled its plan to create a light-rail system along with a proposal to restrict rebuilding in heavily flooded areas.[55]

Taken together, the positive role of civic capacity, represented with participation in local elections, is intertwined with the paradoxical outcomes that characterize post-Katrina New Orleans. On the one hand, residents won the battle against a city government that tried to deter reconstruction by passing a building moratorium. When the city government apparently failed to deliver adequate services, residents were able to harness other civic resources and rebuilt their communities with little delay. On the other hand, however, this civic-initiated reconstruction generated an unplanned, haphazard urban fabric. Although stricter code regulation and inspection was called for to prevent a possible reoccurrence of damages on Katrina's scale,[56] the civic desire to build back presided over the deliberative process, leading to the extensive reconstruction of destroyed properties in both flooded and dry parts of the city. In this sense, the salience of civic competence and activism was in part activated by the city government's weak regulatory capacity. Instead of spearheading the reconstruction process, the city government failed to adjust its policies and coordinate the urges to rebuild as quickly as possible. Thus, permit application and approval occurred with little attention to the context or probability of future hurricanes and flooding, increasing the potential cost of service delivery and future disasters.

Conclusion

Heightened interest and the civic competence of residents explain why reconstruction has unfolded quickly despite the near absence of functioning bureaucracy in the city government. In an ordinary situation, requesting more and better services would pose little harm to the city's resilience. Rather, active citizen requests will enhance democratic governance and administrative efficiency. A well-paved road in a civically active neighborhood is still a public good, and if many communities receive improved services due to their engaged residents, it will ultimately help build a sound infrastructure for the entire city.

However ideal this situation may sound, the problem is that in emergent situations, such responsive government service may restack priorities in a way that aggravates the city's resilience in the long run. Particularly in regard to servicing building permit applications, yielding to civic demands has a direct effect on how the city is being reshaped while much of its territory needs some type of repair. In addition to nullifying the proposed building moratorium, residents' civic capacity also influenced the blueprint of reconstruction by increasing the number and the speed of permit issuance in all parts of the city. Communities that had actively participated in local affairs showed a greater willingness to rebuild, as shown by the large number of successful permit applications in those areas. Unfortunately, this civic activism does not occur within the city's more resilient geographic areas, allowing for a haphazard pattern of residential redevelopment in flood-prone neighborhoods. Taking away the right to rebuild poses a threat to the inalienable rights of property owners; however, protecting property rights comes with a hidden cost of increasing vulnerability for all.

4

Returning to the City

Community Civic Structure and Spatial Inequality

"Pontchartrain Park symbolized the opening of the American dream to Black folks in New Orleans," writes Wendell Pierce in his memoir *The Wind in the Reeds*.[1] A New Orleans native and Hollywood actor starring in highly acclaimed TV series such as *The Wire* and *Treme*, Pierce was dedicated to reviving his neighborhood. His parents, now in their eighties, have called it home since buying a house there in 1955. Indeed, Pontchartrain Park embodies a healthy, intimate community for African American homeowners like Pierce's parents. Developed in the 1950s, this subdivision was the first suburban-style community in New Orleans that was built for the city's growing number of middle-class Black families. Although far from being affluent, residents had stable jobs, tight family structures, and a strong political connection with the city's Black politicians. In Pontchartrain Park, they enjoy an eighteen-hole golf course, a ballpark, and a baseball stadium for family, friends, and neighbors—all located within the neighborhood. As Pierce mentioned, it is a realization of the American dream, especially for Black New Orleanians who had been denied equal residential opportunities to their White counterparts.

As a community of teachers, postal workers, and Black business owners, Pontchartrain Park is also known for its civic activities. Residents of Pontchartrain Park developed strong communal bonds around the local organizations by attending church services and participating in the neighborhood association,[2] the Pontchartrain Park Home Improvement Association, which focused on increasing homeownership, managing community amenities such as the golf course and tennis courts, and maintaining a unique neighborhood identity for middle-class Black families.[3] After Katrina surged over the levee and inundated the entire community, the neighborhood association reestablished itself as the Pontchartrain Park Community Development Corporation (CDC), and

Wendell Pierce chaired it. The main goal of the neighborhood association was to turn the flooded homes into new housing units, bring people back, and revive the community. Thanks to Pierce's national reputation, Pontchartrain Park gained wide support and attention from outside. With the help of philanthropic organizations like the Kresge Foundation and the Salvation Army, the Pontchartrain Park CDC could revive the American dream by building energy-efficient, green houses, providing financial assistance to homebuyers, and repairing the ravaged parks.

As Pontchartrain Park's neighborhood association demonstrates, community civic organizations can serve as a mobilizing structure to effect change when there is an opportunity to do so. Given that post-disaster recovery requires immediate intervention, everyday organizations that existed prior to Katrina assumed the responsibility to initiate various recovery activities.[4] In other words, the existing organizational structure was *appropriated* to trigger the collective action of community members.[5] Whether they knew it or not, residents employed organizational appropriation as a post-disaster recovery strategy, and people in Pontchartrain Park facilitated civic cooperation by repurposing the neighborhood association that was already in place.

This chapter examines the organizational dimension of civic capacity, which I refer to as community civic structure. Defined as a composite of organizational resources within geographic boundaries, community civic structure has an enduring presence and impact on community life. Everyday organizations—churches, neighborhood associations, and schools, for example—can be used for community building in emergent situations.[6] Local organizations' physical assets provide space for rescue and reunion, as large buildings such as churches and schools often serve as emergency shelters immediately after a storm.[7] They also offer a means to political action by donating space to mobilize and organize collectively—they're where people hold meetings, exchange information on housing reconstruction, and share resident information to bring people back. Pontchartrain Park's neighborhood association exemplifies the versatility of local organizations.

Another important asset of community civic structure is leadership. Leaders of these civic organizations serve broad clientele and represent the collective interests of the residents in an entire neighborhood rather than of members or homeowners in a specific area only. Wendell Pierce's leadership was a significant reason why residents sustained their support for their neighborhood. Community leaders, many of whom are homeowners in the neighborhood, add hierarchy, structure, and a sense of ownership in addressing community affairs. As an emphatic leader of the community, Father Vien Nguyen of Mary Queen of Vietnam Church spearheaded recovery efforts in his Vietnamese immigrant community in New Orleans East. He secured shelter, food, and electricity for the evacuees while working with governmental agencies and philanthropic institutions to solicit assistance for his community.[8] His leadership continued through the region's next disaster, the BP Deepwater Horizon oil spill in the Gulf of Mexico. From his New Orleans parish, he extended assistance to the larger ethnic community along the Gulf Coast and helped settle matters between Vietnamese fishermen and business and government officials, such as providing language assistance and legal advice.[9]

Still, evidence that links community civic structure with resilience outcomes is episodic. What remains unclear are the ways by which these everyday organizations, in aggregate, are related to various signs of urban resilience and vulnerability. While Broadmoor seems to signify a civic victory, Pontchartrain Park seems to defy generalizations about the link between organizational energy and recovery. Despite the heavy lifting by the community organization, Pontchartrain Park has been struggling to regain the glory of its past. Each building received 9 to 13 feet of water, leaving most of homes, schools, and churches in need of significant repairs. Although statistics report that the neighborhood has regained over 90 percent of its pre-Katrina households, the once-middle-class neighborhood looks very different now. While the neighborhood's poverty rate had hovered around 10 percent since the 1970s, it has grown exponentially since Katrina and had almost tripled to 28.6 percent in 2010. One out of every four houses remain empty, and the soaring vacancy rate has changed the community's landscape. Blighted and abandoned properties are peppered throughout the neighborhood. Only 3.5 percent of the housing stock was vacant as of 2000, but this rose to 24.4 percent a decade later. The neighborhood's effort to build new homes went sluggish, if not dormant. Only ten houses had been built after four years, and one resident simply boarded up his home. Frustrated with the slow process, donors from the Salvation Army rescinded its offer of $1.8 million for recovery and gave the money to other neighborhoods.

A close look at neighborhood recovery suggests that repopulation alone is insufficient to help the city regain rhythm and become more resilient than before. Rather, what we need to consider is how neighborhood repopulation has progressed over time—whether it happened evenly throughout the city or in an unequal manner and what role civic organizations played therein. Despite the many neighborhood activities, records show that post-Katrina New Orleans has become a more unequal city. Over the past ten years, for example, White neighborhoods have recovered above and beyond expectations, and yet Black neighborhoods, many of them located below sea level, have fallen behind.[10] Averaging out those differences does not paint a full picture of resilience in post-Katrina New Orleans, and examining community civic structure in this context can offer a more balanced view about its potential as well as its limits.

Geography is often a neglected area in discussions of the city's resilience, but the growing urban inequality is firmly entrenched in geography. Even if New Orleans did not officially shrink its footprint, some neighborhoods have become smaller and more vulnerable than their pre-Katrina shape. Here, spatial inequality does not just mean that the opportunities for better livelihoods are unevenly distributed across the city; rather, it also means that the shrinking neighborhoods are geophysically more vulnerable, as they are located below sea level. Areas of unplanned shrinkage present a sharp contrast with the city's bustling neighborhoods, where new restaurants, organic grocery stores, and entrepreneurs flocked to form younger, more vibrant communities. Separating these upward experiences from the struggles of residents in neighborhoods like Pontchartrain Park does little to portray a complete picture of the city's future from the standpoint of resilience.

Essentially, the coexistence of miracle and despair is what I show in this chapter. In post-Katrina New Orleans, social vulnerabilities are distributed unevenly across neighborhoods, and community civic structure is associated with this spatial inequality in three main ways. First, civic organizations contributed far more to repopulating the higher ground than low-lying neighborhoods. Although the difference was not so noticeable in the early period immediately following Katrina, it became wider as time went on. Second, despite the similar level of civic resources available before Katrina, community civic structure has had different impacts on reducing vulnerabilities across space. In low-lying areas, neighborhoods with dense civic structures have attracted *more* vulnerable populations, while the opposite happened in high-lying neighborhoods. Finally, community civic structure deepened the city's racialized geography; more Whites have occupied the city's safer areas and Black residents have settled in the low-lying parts of the city.

All in all, the present chapter reveals various ways in which different levels of resilience across communities end up accumulating vulnerabilities at a citywide level. Although many studies have captured snapshots of early recovery activities, the strong civic performance in some of the city's flooded neighborhoods does not tell the whole story of enduring urban resilience. Pierce's dedication to Pontchartrain Park is meaningful, but compared to other neighborhoods, its achievements to date are below average. And this comparison is important because urban inequality, after all, undermines urban resilience. This is especially true when the inequality manifests itself in spatial terms, reproducing greater susceptibilities to natural hazards and overall vulnerabilities. The whole story I propose in this chapter, therefore, is that despite the remarkable performance of some flooded neighborhoods in the early period of recovery, uneven development has expanded over time, and community civic structure has contributed to this growing spatial inequality. The early momentum in some neighborhoods, I argue, was an exception on the road to recovery rather than a rule. In the neighborhoods that are located below sea level and were exposed to heavy flooding, like Pontchartrain Park, recovery activities have ended up creating an even more precarious situation for the community. With evidence in this chapter, I raise caution against overstating the power of civic activism and argue that community civic capacity, although highlighted as the engine of recovery, ultimately helped create a two-tiered city that is divided by geography.

Data and Methodology

Measuring Community Resilience and Vulnerability

In this analysis, I consider three kinds of variables to measure resilience and vulnerability. First, I use repopulation as an indicator of recovery in each neighborhood. Repopulation is the core condition for disaster recovery and urban revitalization. Increased population means an expanded tax base, greater economic activities, and accumulation of human capital that can be utilized to promote further development. As a shrinking city, New Orleans has long suffered population loss, abandonment, and blight, and these problems worsened as Hurricane Katrina forced almost all residents (96 percent) to evacuate, among whom nearly 40 percent were displaced.[11] I measure repopulation with the ratio between counts of pre- and post-Katrina residential addresses that were actively receiving mail at the time of data collection, available before (in 2005) and after (2008–2015) Katrina.[12]

Second, I measure the degree of social vulnerabilities in each neighborhood with four indicators—percentage of people living in poverty (*Poverty*), percentage of households without a vehicle (*No vehicle*), housing vacancy rate (*Vacant*), and percentage of elderly population living alone (*Alone*). I compare these indicators in 2000 (*Pre-Katrina*) and in 2010 (*Post-Katrina*) and calculate the changes between the two periods. The higher the value is, the greater the vulnerability has become over the past ten years. These measures demonstrate the degree to which a community is exposed to potential vulnerabilities against natural hazards. Even if a neighborhood has regained population at its pre-Katrina level, for example, the neighborhood might have become more vulnerable if the demographic has since changed to older, less mobile individuals with fewer economic resources. Thus, juxtaposing repopulation with the measures of social vulnerabilities provides us with a more thorough map of post-Katrina recovery.

Third, I compare the percentages of Black to White populations before and after Katrina. It has been reported that post-Katrina New Orleans has become a whiter city, and the assessment of the city's post-Katrina state is racially polarized.[13] Indeed, the city's Black population has decreased from 66.7 percent to 59.6 percent while the proportion of Whites grew from 26.6 to 30.5 percent. This racial transformation is particularly noteworthy given the decreasing share of the White racial group across the country in the same period (from 69.1 to 63.7 percent). The changing racial demography in New Orleans defies this national trend, and I examine where the racial change is most prominent within the city's geography.

Measuring Community Civic Structure

Civic structure is defined as a set of organizations or associations whose main function is to enhance the sociability of members and to serve members or residents in a community by achieving explicit goals while also having requisite management structures to fulfill them. This category includes churches, schools, neighborhood associations, childcare centers, and social service organizations. For instance, a neighborhood association is formed to enhance the residents' quality of life, and it has a hierarchical organizational structure to serve this purpose.[14]

To estimate the extent of civic structure in each community, I calculated the density of civic organizations in each neighborhood by counting the number of civic organizations per one hundred active residential addresses. Organizational density is certainly not a perfect measure to gauge the civic strength of a neighborhood, for the mere presence of organizations does not always ensure active participation on the part of residents. However, just as the size of our own social network is measured by a number of friends or frequency of contacts and discussions,[15] organizational density captures the scope of *potential* civic capacity. The Sampson study, which focused on Chicago neighborhoods' collective civic actions, reveals that the organizational structure of urban communities is a conceptually and empirically distinct element of civic capacity from aggregate civic memberships such as voting and volunteering.[16] One of its important findings is that community institutional resources, measured as a density of nonprofit organizations, prompt collective social action, while civic participation at the individual level—group membership, social ties, and so forth—do not have a significant effect. Furthermore, the nature of civic events has changed from the "sixties-style" protests to more hybrid activities, which make public claims through civic forms of behavior rather than combative political actions. Organizational infrastructure, separate from interpersonal ties, matters for facilitating collective civic engagement.

Furthermore, organizational density allows us to estimate and compare the level of social resources across *all* communities. To my knowledge, no citywide survey had been conducted with regard to the extent of civic participation before Katrina, and the official records of local organizations are the best source of data to produce the comparable measure of community civic structure. To calculate the number of various organizations, I accessed the local directory from the New Orleans Public Library and used a Geographic Information System (GIS) to geocode the addresses of various types of local organizations, identify their locations, and calculate the frequency of organizations in each census tract.

Geography

As I did in chapter 3, I use geographic variables to capture New Orleans's geographic vulnerability; these account for nearly half of the city's territory. Naturally, the concentration of at-risk populations and properties takes a high toll in the low-lying neighborhoods. I base my analysis on this geographic division and include a dummy variable for vulnerability, where below-sea-level neighborhoods are assigned a 1 and above-sea-level neighborhoods are given the variable of 0.[17] The vulnerability measure will serve as an interacting variable to examine whether the effect of civic structure varies by geography. Furthermore, I control for the flood level of each unit to capture the degree of damage caused by the storm.

Finally, as in the previous chapter, I control for the factors that may correlate with our main independent variable: civic organizational density. First, I use *Percent Black* to measure the racial composition and estimate the socioeconomic level of each unit with four indicators. *Log-income* measures the log of the median household income in a census tract. *Education* measures the percentage of high school graduates, and *Unemployment* is the percentage of unemployed adults in a census tract. *Rent* is the ratio between renter-occupied housing and total occupied housing. It includes renter-occupied and owner-occupied housing but excludes vacant housing units.

Methodology

The standard Ordinary Least Squares (OLS) regression rests on the assumption that every unit is independent and thus no interactions exist between units. However, as Sampson mentioned,[18] this assumption is most likely to be violated in geographic contexts because, as geographer

Waldo Tobler's first law of geography states, "everything is related to everything else, but near things are more related than distant things."[19] In other words, we can expect more similar outcomes among neighborhoods sharing borders than among those that are distant from each other. OLS, on the other hand, predicts that each neighborhood outcome is independent from another.

Since it is possible that there is spatial interaction among neighborhood units, I first run spatial regression to check whether the unit independence assumption holds. Results show that spatial diffusion among neighborhoods existed in the early period of recovery and yet disappeared as time went on. Therefore, I use OLS regression for the following analyses (for detailed methodological discussion, see the appendix).

The Civic Structure of the City

What does community civic structure look like in New Orleans neighborhoods, especially in relation to their racial and economic conditions? Does it follow the conventional image of an "urban ghetto," where communities not only have low income but also suffer from few organizational resources? These questions are important because some might argue that disadvantaged neighborhoods had slower repopulation rates because their social organization is inherently different from other neighborhoods. These neighborhoods, one might argue, already have few organizational resources because they are occupied by unemployed, poor minority residents who do not have the capacity to build the same level of social structure as their wealthier, more stable counterparts. In other words, there could be a strong correlation between community civic structure and neighborhood racial and economic backgrounds, which can confound the isolated impact of civic capacity. Comparing community civic structure tests this claim. Counting the number of churches, schools, and neighborhood associations is not merely a fact-checking enterprise but an important step to probe whether vulnerable areas, such as neighborhoods below sea level and/or poor Black communities, had a comparable civic structure to the city's safer, more affluent areas. The multivariate analysis of community civic structure reveals that the city's poor, Black neighborhoods enjoyed as much civic vibrancy as rich, White neighborhoods. Table 4.1 shows the extent to which a set of socioeconomic variables is associated with the number of primary and ancillary civic organizations.[20] Contrary to popular expectation, more primary civic organizations—churches, neighborhood associations, schools, and childcare centers—are likely to be located in low-income areas, while racial conditions, represented by *Percent Black*, do not predict the density of primary civic organizations (Table 4.1, Column 1). This finding is not driven by the predominance of churches, which tend to be concentrated in Black neighborhoods. The results do not change much when the same variables are regressed on the civic structure without including churches (Table 4.1, Column 2). Rather, the primary civic structure without the churches still shows a similar pattern and is negatively correlated with income even after socioeconomic conditions such as race and income are controlled for.[21]

When the sum of organizations is disaggregated by each organizational category, we still do not find evidence in support of a deinstitutionalized urban ghetto.[22] Results show that while there are no consistent patterns, some organizations are even more likely to be present in disadvantaged neighborhoods than others. Most decidedly, more churches are in predominantly Black communities with low-average levels of education (Table 4.1, Column 4). Furthermore, the number of churches is positively correlated with the proportion of vacant housing units, which implies that churches still maintain their presence in areas experiencing blight. A greater number of social service organizations are found in lower-income areas with higher rates of renters but not necessarily with many blighted properties (Table 4.1, Column 5). The number of neighborhood associations is associated with the needs of a community, as more associations tend to exist in areas with high vacancy and unemployment rates (Table 4.1, Column 6). Schools are negatively associated with percent Black and income, making it difficult to posit a definitive relationship with neighborhood disadvantages. If anything, schools tend to be located in moderate-income areas with fewer Black people (Table 4.1, Column 7). Finally, childcare centers are more frequently found in "stable" Black communities. Their presence is strongly correlated with the percentage of Black residents in an area, and the signs of economic instability, such as unemployment and rental units, are negatively associated (Table 4.1, Column 8).[23]

TABLE 4.1. Factors affecting the number of primary and ancillary social organizations.

	Primary Social Organizations	Primary Social Organizations (No Churches)	Ancillary Social Organizations	Church	Social Service Organization	Neighborhood Association	School	Childcare Center
Percent Black	0.004	−0.401	−0.445	0.510*	−0.313	−0.120	−0.676*	1.768***
	(0.233)	(0.268)	(0.389)	(0.295)	(0.650)	(0.524)	(0.359)	(0.638)
Logincome	−0.433**	−0.438*	−0.470	−0.419	−1.400**	0.420	−0.563*	−0.575
	(0.215)	(0.250)	(0.355)	(0.271)	(0.610)	(0.424)	(0.335)	(0.529)
Education	−0.700	0.151	1.553	−1.481*	−0.344	1.783	1.030	−1.306
	(0.644)	(0.756)	(1.114)	(0.794)	(1.437)	(1.314)	(1.055)	(1.230)
Unemployment	−0.552	0.013	−3.265**	−1.357	−1.221	3.799***	0.130	−3.801**
	(0.721)	(0.843)	(1.305)	(0.914)	(1.606)	(1.001)	(1.168)	(1.928)
Rent	−0.060	0.283	2.157***	−0.369	2.252**	0.906	−0.190	−1.809**
	(0.372)	(0.439)	(0.623)	(0.464)	(1.010)	(0.752)	(0.592)	(0.868)
Vacancy	0.115	−1.161	1.302	1.355*	−4.189**	2.414*	−1.149*	−2.399
	(0.665)	(0.807)	(1.101)	(0.808)	(2.012)	(1.349)	(1.103)	(1.734)
Household	0.000***	0.000***	0.000***	0.000***	0.001	0.001***	0.000***	0.000**
	(0.000)	(0.000)	(0.000)	(0.000)	(0.001)	(0.000)	(0.000)	(0.000)
Intercept	6.616***	5.459**	4.156	6.136***	13.010**	−7.497*	5.606	6.785
	(2.227)	(2.600)	(3.688)	(2.797)	(6.209)	(4.405)	(3.473)	(5.750)
N	176	176	176	176	176	176	176	176

In sum, community civic structure in pre-Katrina New Orleans is not spatially concentrated only in select communities. This nonfinding is instructive, as it shows that the social structure of inner cities is more variegated and diverse than what we commonly assume. Some organizations are more likely to be present in disadvantaged neighborhoods than their affluent counterparts. For example, more churches are in predominantly Black communities with a low-average level of education, and a greater number of social service organizations are found in lower-income and rental areas. More neighborhood associations are located where the needs are great, such as high-vacancy areas with a high unemployment rate. This is somewhat contrary to the earlier findings in urban sociology,[24] which posits that socioeconomic disadvantage is closely tied with the paucity of organizational resources, which then leads to socially undesirable outcomes. New Orleans's community civic structure is another exception to this theory of social disorganization.[25] Although poor, these disadvantaged communities maintain rich organizational resources. Of course, this is not to say that disadvantaged neighborhoods are equally positioned with their affluent counterparts in terms of civic resources. Rather, what this means is that—at the very least—there exists a structural *basis* for civic organizing in both affluent and disadvantaged communities, with which residents can overcome their lack of material resources and public services (such as transportation).

The reason why the differences are smaller than expected may stem from both sides of the spectrum. On the one hand, affluent neighborhoods are becoming "less civic" because they do not feel the need to rely on civic resources to build rapport with neighbors or solve collective problems.[26] On the other hand, disadvantaged neighborhoods may have developed a distinct repertoire of civic resources not despite but because of a lack of resources. By the 1960s, Pontchartrain Park had become a neighborhood with numerous institutions that provided opportunities for participation and mobilization because of the city government's systematic racial discrimination against Blacks in and around the city. "Children of the Park," referring to the offspring of the first Black families to have settled in the neighborhood, went to the same school, attended the same church, and played in the same park. Although their income and social standing did not match affluent Whites', Black residents also enjoyed a rich organizational life.[27] With these insights in mind, the next section explores the short- and long-term effects of civic structure on post-Katrina reconstruction.

The Geography of Resilience

Comparing the effect of civic structure on repopulation in the city's high and low areas, we find that there is a tale of two recoveries. Although community civic structure contributes to repopulation in both areas, the positive effect of civic resources is much greater in the

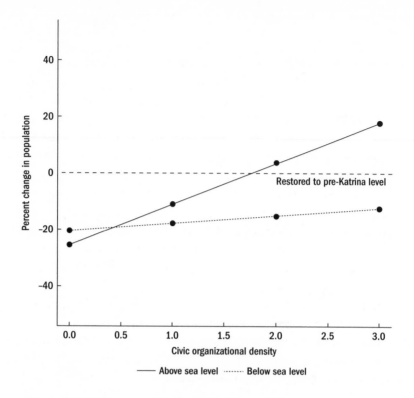

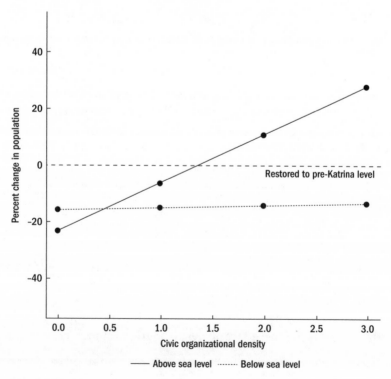

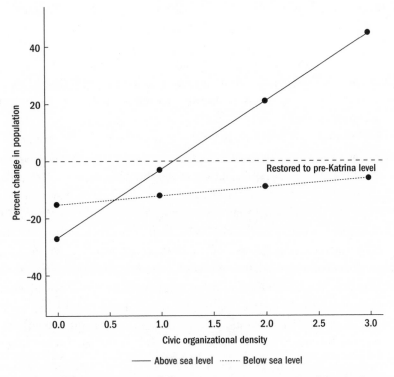

Figure 4.1.a–c. Predicted repopulation rates by civic organizational density, June 2011 (4.1.a), 2013 (4.1.b), and 2015 (4.1.c). For June 2015, one observation (Iberville Development) is deleted because the public housing was demolished in September 2013 and only one address was counted in June 2015.

neighborhoods located on a higher ground, while the neighborhoods below sea level lag far behind. The plots of Figure 4.1 predicted the repopulation ratio as per the increase of civic organizational density in three years—2011 (a), 2013 (b), and 2015 (c).[28] Overall, the slope of the solid black line (high-lying areas) is steeper than that of the dotted line (low-lying areas), which means that for the same unit increase in civic density, population increase is greater in high-lying areas than in the low-lying counterparts. In 2011, with the same level of civic structure, the neighborhoods above sea level had a higher level of repopulation than those below sea level.[29] The gap between the two lines grows larger as recovery goes on. For example, in 2013 and 2015, the slope for areas below sea level remains pretty much the same, while the slope for areas above sea level has become steeper than in the previous time periods. Furthermore, the predicted repopulation ratio for below-sea-level neighborhoods remains under 1 throughout the entire time period, suggesting that neighborhoods below sea level have not reached their pre-Katrina population level, and that repopulation is happening very slowly and incompletely despite help from civic organizations.

Let us look at the repopulation pattern in the low-lying area more carefully. Despite at a lower and stagnant rate, civic structure is still positively associated with repopulation in neighborhoods below sea level, which means that civically enriched communities tend to have a higher rate of population return than less organized communities. While this finding seems to buttress the positive role of civic organizations, a close reading suggests that this is not the case. To answer why, we need to think about what repopulation means for the city's low-lying communities. As explained in chapter 1, urban resilience may be enhanced when *fewer* people resettle in areas exposed to continued hazard risks, and therefore, repopulation in highly vulnerable areas does not foretell resilience. Still, this analysis found that community civic structure facilitates repopulation in low-lying neighborhoods, albeit with limited success. In neighborhoods like Pontchartrain Park, civic organizations are striving to build more houses and invite more homeowners to the neighborhood, despite it continuing to be one of the most vulnerable neighborhoods in the city. Its historic role within the community notwithstanding, Pontchartrain Park's slow but steady recovery raises a question about whether repopulation—the central goal of most neighborhoods—portends a promising future for the city.

To the extent that repopulation is understood as a sign of resilience, we might interpret the findings to mean that community civic structure has enhanced resilience in each neighborhood but at different speeds. If we take the different speeds seriously, however, the widening gap between the two geographies tells a more complicated story. In the low-lying part of the city, the stagnant repopulation process has trapped neighborhoods between full-fledged recovery on the one hand and persistent blight on the other. While some residents celebrate the efforts of their community organizations, others observe the vivid reality of post-Katrina dilapidation: abandoned homes, unelevated houses, and the disintegration of the community. Contrary to those believing in the rebirth of the city, people in the low-lying neighborhoods are skeptical about the promises that things will ever be the same or even better than before. Ten years after the hurricane, residents in Pontchartrain Park commented that the flavor of their neighborhood was quite different from its pre-Katrina atmosphere.[30] Their pessimism is distressing when compared to what is happening in the opposite parts of the city. On the high ground, community civic structure is working just as many had envisioned—attracting more people, building social relationships, and proving that New Orleans is, after all, a resilient city. The repopulation and rebuilding processes have taken preexisting inequality to a new level by geographically separating residents and concentrating vulnerabilities in the city's unsafe areas.

The Geography of Vulnerabilities

Thus far, we have learned that the geography of repopulation is sharply divided by sea level, and strong community civic structure has positive yet disparate effects on repopulating the city's high and low areas. In this section, I delve into the signs of social vulnerabilities in these two areas. Overall, Katrina has widened the spatial gap between areas that had once shared similar levels of social risks. Table 4.2 presents a cross-tabulation of the social vulnerability indicators in the pre- and post-Katrina period (2000 and 2010) by sea level as well as of the difference between the two periods.[31] Greater values in the difference indicators suggest that social vulnerability increased between 2000 and 2010. When pre- and post-Katrina values are compared, vulnerabilities in the neighborhoods on the higher ground have been reduced, while low-lying neighborhoods have become more vulnerable. In high-lying neighborhoods, the average poverty rate has been reduced by about 4 percentage points over a decade, far surpassing the citywide decrease of 0.2 percentage points. In sharp contrast, the average percentage of those living below poverty level has increased by 3.76 percentage points in low-lying neighborhoods after Katrina, falling far below the city average. The gap between the two groups has significantly widened after Katrina, given that their pre-Katrina estimates were similar to each other (28.47 to 28.89).

TABLE 4.2. Social vulnerabilities before and after Katrina by elevation. All values are an average percentage of people falling into one of the four categories. Source: The Data Center.

	Above sea level			Below sea level			Citywide		
	2000	2010	Diff	2000	2010	Diff	2000	2010	Diff
Poverty Rate (%)	28.47	24.59	−3.88	28.89	32.65	3.76	27.9	27.7	−0.2
No Vehicle (%)	28.01	18.38	−9.63	27.57	20.94	−6.63	27.3	18.7	−8.6
Elderly Living (%)	36.95	35.89	−1.06	34.03	31.56	−2.47	35.34	33.51	−1.83
Vacant Housing (%)	13.55	21.54	7.99	11.46	27.32	15.86	12.5	25.1	12.6

The percentage of people with no vehicles has decreased in both locations, meaning that more people now have access to vehicles for evacuation in emergency situations than in 2000. However, there is still a discrepancy, as more people above sea level enjoy access to vehicles than those on the lower ground. In fact, the percentage point change in low-lying neighborhoods is smaller than the citywide average (8.6 percentage points), indicating that, comparatively speaking, low-lying neighborhoods did not gain much in terms of resident mobility. Likewise, in both areas, there has been a substantial decrease in the percentage of the elderly living alone. The decrease is greater in the high-lying neighborhoods, however, and the decrease in the low-lying neighborhoods is still below the city average.

Housing vacancy rates show the starkest difference between communities below and above sea level. Vacant buildings are often associated with blight and underdevelopment, so a high vacancy rate indicates greater depopulation and deinstitutionalization of an area.[32] Before Katrina, neighborhoods in both areas had similar vacancy rates of under 15 percent. After Katrina, the city experienced soaring vacancy rates, and approximately a quarter of the entire city's residential units remained unoccupied (25.1 percent). Among them, communities in vulnerable locations were hit much harder than less-flooded, less-vulnerable areas. On average, more than a quarter of below-sea-level neighborhoods' houses were empty (27.32 percent), while slightly over 20 percent of the units of safely situated neighborhoods remained unoccupied.[33]

By all accounts, social vulnerabilities in the city's lower grounds have been exacerbated to a greater degree than those located in the safer places. Although the city celebrated a strong comeback,[34] the geography of vulnerabilities remains uneven and divided, rendering some groups of people more susceptible to the next disaster than others. Already occupying the city's most precarious locales and having suffered from the catastrophe of Katrina, these neighborhoods have gotten poorer, less mobile, and more sparsely populated than before Katrina made landfall. In other words, these neighborhoods are more susceptible now to future risks from climate change and natural disasters. In contrast, neighborhoods on the higher grounds have been able to enjoy the benefits of the post-Katrina recovery. The gap along the geographic fault line has widened, jeopardizing the life chances of those who have returned to the city's most insecure areas. Does community civic structure help close the gap among the neighborhoods, or does it deepen the spatial vulnerabilities between high and low grounds? To answer these questions, I estimate the effects of community civic structure on post-Katrina vulnerability by examining the interaction between land elevation and the community civic structure variables. Figure 4.2 shows the predicted values of four social vulnerability indicators measured by the increase in the civic organization density.[35] Again, this is measured for neighborhoods below and above sea level. The solid line represents the high-lying neighborhoods (*Above Sea Level*), and the dotted line represents the low-lying counterparts (*Below Sea Level*).

Depending on where your neighborhood is located, then, community civic structure plays a different role in alleviating vulnerabilities. First, civic structure contributes to slowing down poverty rates in neighborhoods above sea level, but not those below sea level. Also, the speed of poverty reduction is much faster in higher neighborhoods than low-lying ones (see Figure 4.2.a). In the high-lying neighborhoods, there is about a ten-percentage-point drop in the poverty rate from 2000 to 2010 per one civic organization increase per household. In low-lying neighborhoods, there is actually a slight increase in poverty rates, by approximately two percentage points. While civic community structure clearly helps improve the poverty situation in higher neighborhoods, it has a negative impact on reducing the number of poor people located in lower neighborhoods.

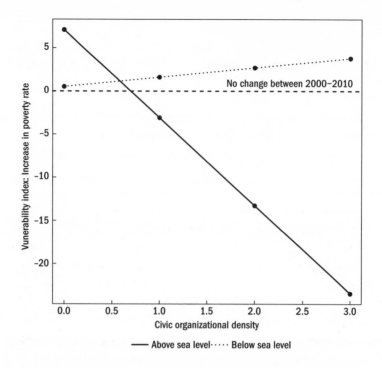

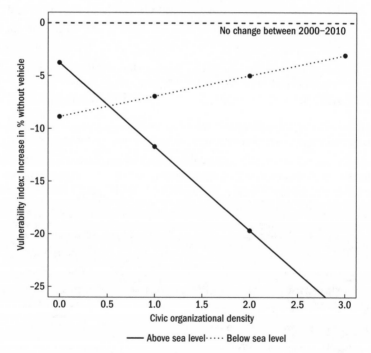

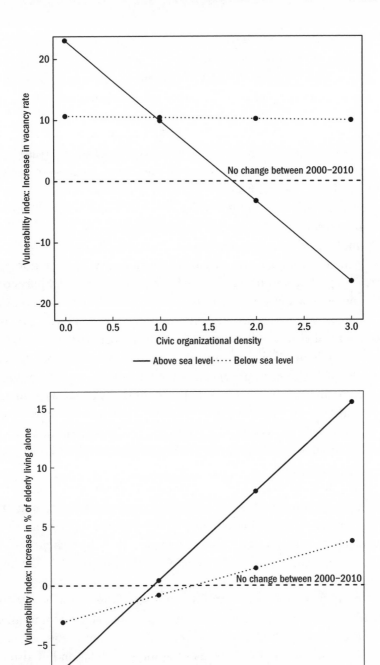

Figure 4.2.a–d. Predicted vulnerability index by civic organizational density by sea level.

Similarly, the differential effect of community civic structure is also clear with respect to automobile access (see Figure 4.2.b). While increased civic density contributes to diminishing the percentage of people without a car in above-sea-level neighborhoods, it does not have the same effect in areas below sea level. As civic density increases, the percentage difference decreases, which means that in areas below sea level, neighborhoods with strong civic structures tend to experience *less* improvement in resident mobility than neighborhoods with fewer organizational resources.

A similar pattern is found in vacancy rate changes (see Figure 4.2.c). On the higher ground, neighborhoods with more civic organizations experienced greater improvement in reducing vacancy, as neighborhoods with higher civic density tend to have reduced vacancy rates over the ten-year period. In contrast, in communities below sea level, civic organizational density rarely contributes to the reduction of vacancy rate. There is no definite relationship between civic organizational density and vulnerability, meaning that higher civic density leads to few changes in already-high vacancy rates. When everything is equal, a neighborhood without any civic organization is likely to have a ten-percentage point increase in the vacancy rate; however, if the number of civic organizations increases to three per person, the vacancy rate change rises twenty percentage points.

Finally, however, civic structure does not seem to help reduce the number of elderly people who are likely to "die alone" in natural disasters (see Figure 4.2.d).[36] In both areas, having more civic organizations is associated with a greater number of single-elderly households, while the rate of increase in this vulnerable population is greater in the high region.

In sum, the effects of community civic structure are unevenly distributed across the city. Despite little media spotlight, the communities located in the city's higher terrain benefit more from the presence of civic organizations, not only by gaining more population but also by attracting a more resilient demographic. Already exposed to the risks from the proximity to water, neighborhoods below sea level do not enjoy the fruits of civic activism as much as their higher counterparts. In addition to perennial exposure to natural hazards, those who returned to the city's low-lying areas bore the burden of growing poverty, reduced mobility, and the hollowing-out of their communities. The growing poverty gap is particularly worrisome given that New Orleans is already a poor city. About one in four people in New Orleans lives in poverty, and the city's poverty rate (27.7 percent) far exceeds the national average (15.6 percent). The concentrated poverty in risky areas suggests that occupants in these areas are already exposed to significant hardship in their daily lives and would only experience further difficulties in the event of a future disaster.

Why is civic structure associated with deteriorating conditions in the low-lying neighborhoods, but improvement in the communities on a higher ground? The reason could be that civic organizations are strong enough to attract people back to the flooded neighborhoods, but not strong enough to lure the kind of people who are willing to invest their resources again in high-risk areas. Brad Pitt's Make It Right Foundation, for example, helped people in the Lower Ninth Ward come back by building them affordable, environmentally sustainable homes there. Despite visible efforts for repopulation by these civic organizations in the early stage of recovery, the occupancy rate in the Lower Ninth Ward has plummeted since Katrina, where almost half (48 percent) of the residential units remained unoccupied in 2010 compared to one-fifth (18.3 percent) in 2000. On the other hand, civic activities on the high land send a strong signal to returnees and new settlers in the city. As people carefully gauge the risk of coming back to resettle, a preexisting civic structure can help reassure their decision to invest in the properties that are safe from natural disasters.

Furthermore, to reduce blight, civic organizations may have unintentionally encouraged the concentration of vacant lots and vulnerable populations in certain neighborhoods. Recall that on average, low-lying neighborhoods had not been any more vacant than their high-lying counterparts; in fact, the median vacancy rate was higher in the area above sea level (12 percent) than below sea level (10.2 percent). After Katrina, the trend reversed. The vacancy rate has more than doubled in low-lying areas (26 percent), while the higher areas sustained a relatively low increase (18 percent). This chapter's analysis suggests that community-based recovery efforts may fall short of generating the type of density that the neighborhood activists had hoped for. After Katrina, local civic organizations in flooded communities cooperated with the

NORA, a state agency administered with federal funding, to revitalize depressed communities including the city's most heavily flooded areas such as the Lower Ninth Ward, Broadmoor, Gentilly, and Pontchartrain Park.[37] NORA won a highly competitive federal grant called the Neighborhood Stabilization Program (NSP) and cooperated with select neighborhood associations to remove blighted and abandoned properties and build affordable housing units for low- to middle-income homebuyers.[38] Nationally renowned neighborhood associations including the Broadmoor Improvement Association (BIA) and MIR in the Lower Ninth Ward partnered with NORA.[39] In the second phase of the NSP, 87 percent of the expenditure (about $27 million) was used for building homeowner (55 percent) and rental (32 percent) units in these neighborhoods.[40] These efforts, targeting storm-damaged communities and low-income residents, might have resulted in increasing both vacancy rates (by demolishing damaged properties) and occupancy rates for people below poverty level (by building affordable housing). Back in Pontchartrain Park, NORA intended to build modular homes to secure qualified homebuyers and turn over 125 lots to developers who would then build additional homes. However, the process has been slow, with only a handful of lots turned over each year. Furthermore, since the program was intended for low- to middle-income residents, those who could actually afford the newly built homes were often overqualified to apply for the housing program because their income was too high. By taking on recovery activities that targeted low-income residents, civic organizations could increase the population count, and yet these activities paradoxically deepened the spatially uneven redevelopment pattern.[41]

The influx of poor residents after the flood brought about a new source of contention and chasm within communities. As old residents moved away and rented out their homes, renters quickly filled in the vacancy. The native homeowners of Pontchartrain Park were worried that these "Section 8" renters were different from themselves, and were loud, fussy, and aggressive. Old residents were concerned that their community identity as a neighborhood of middle-class homeowners might be diluted by renters, who, according to them, had households composed of large numbers and disrupted the existing social order of their stable Black community. Although most of them were also African Americans, they were still "new" residents in the sense that their familial and social circles did not originate in the Park. The civic efforts to protect the community's legacy, combined with the imperative to bring people in, resulted in transforming the very characteristic of the neighborhood that they had hoped to preserve.

In addition to the limited role of civic organizations, an important factor to consider is how government aid, or lack thereof, contributed to concentrating the vulnerable population in the city's low-lying region. After Katrina, the Louisiana state government established the Road Home program to assist in the rebuilding of damaged houses. Funded by the federal government through a Community Development Block Grant (CDBG), the Road Home program disbursed $9 billion to 130,000 in-state homeowners, averaging about $70,000 per applicant.[42] Although some expressed satisfaction,[43] the Road Home grants had disproportionate effects on households in severely flooded, low-income communities. The biggest issues were that the program was designed to encourage rebuilding rather than relocation, and that post-Katrina compensation was tied to pre-Katrina socioeconomic conditions.[44] The compensation was lower for those considering a buyout option than for those who rebuilt their damaged homes. Furthermore, the compensatory formula was based on the pre-Katrina home values rather than the extent of damage incurred, which made it hard for owners of the low-valued properties to complete reconstruction in a timely manner.[45] For example, the average amount of compensation for Louisiana House District 105, which includes part of coastal New Orleans and Gulf Coast parishes, averages at $55,731, an amount that is far below the statewide average of $70,000. Moreover, uninsured properties were subject to an automatic penalty of 30 percent on their grant award, and this policy decreased the grant amount for houses with no insurance, which tend to be low-income households.[46]

The initial delay in implementing the program added financial burden for those who could not afford to pay their mortgage and property tax nor find alternative housing while waiting on disbursement. Although the Road Home program ran the Small Rental Property Program with $429 million, the amount of funding was too small to help rebuild affordable rental units and thus insufficient to help renters return to the city's safer areas. In fact, the fund was able to replace only one of three pre-Katrina rental units, placing an undue burden on the city's poor residents.[47]

In addition to the financial difficulties caused by the delay of and deficiency in government aid, the civic effects of government policy should also be noted. More often than not, urban programs that are supposed to enhance the well-being of local residents—such as neighborhood empowerment programs—tend to dampen civic engagement for those who may benefit from them.[48] In navigating byzantine bureaucratic procedures and dealing with street-level bureaucrats face-to-face, the potential recipients of the government aid, many of whom are from marginalized communities, experience frustration, despair, or humiliation. Although not measured here, the occupants of high-risk areas often reported mental distress and anger toward the government.[49]

The Geography of Race

As a final query, I ask whether civic structure changed the racial makeup of the city. This question is especially important given the current demography of New Orleans. While post-Katrina New Orleans has regained over 70 percent of its pre-Katrina population, the color of the city is different from the past, and has become lighter than before. Although the African American population used to account for two-thirds of the city's population (67 percent), now the proportion has fallen to 60 percent. In contrast, the city's White population has increased from 28 to 33 percent, and the Hispanic population rose from 3.1 percent to 5.3 percent.[50] New Orleans was a divided city before Katrina, with more minority populations residing in the city's lower areas, and Whites occupying the higher ground. To gauge the relationship between civic structure and the racialized geography of the city, I estimate the decennial changes in percent Black and White in each neighborhood and regress these values against civic organizational density (Figure 4.3).[51] By any measure, the impact of civic resources fares differently for the two racial demographics. Figure 4.3 shows the changes in the Black and White populations, respectively, in the areas below and above sea level. In the areas above sea level, civic organizational density is positively associated with increasing the proportion of the White population in a neighborhood. Changes in percent White in this area are already positive, meaning that the neighborhood has a larger White population than in 2000. Civic structure adds to this trend by helping the gain in White population. As a neighborhood adds

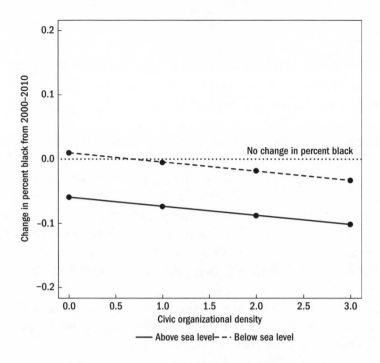

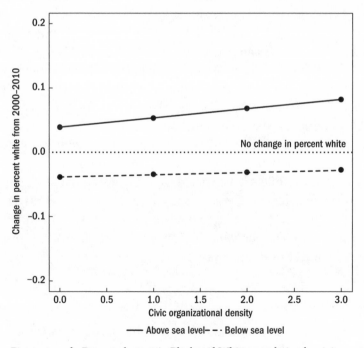

Figure 4.3.a–b. Percent changes in Black and White population by civic organizational density.

one civic organization per 100 households, there is about a 2 to 3 percent increase in the White population compared to its pre-Katrina rate. This presents a sharp contrast with the trend in Black population. As shown in the first graph in Figure 4.3, the percent change for Blacks has negative values in safe areas, which means that the proportion of African Americans in each neighborhood has already decreased regardless of the civic structure. To make matters worse, increasing civic density further propels the decrease of Blacks. The higher the density becomes, the greater the decrease in the percentage of Black population. The proportion of African Americans has significantly decreased in about half of the city above sea level, while the proportion of Whites has increased in the same area. Community civic structure has assisted this diverging trend.

Things look quite different in the neighborhoods below sea level, which are presented with dotted lines in Figure 4.3. For Blacks, increasing civic density is still associated with a greater decrease in their population, although the relationship is not so strong. In areas with a low level of civic density (civic density < 1 per 100 households), the values are still positive, which means that areas with some civic organizations still gained more African Americans than in the past. Overall, the percentage of Whites has decreased in these neighborhoods, noted by the consistent negative values (see Figure 4.3.b). The proportion of Whites has decreased in vulnerable areas regardless of the civic density, contrary to the uplifting role it played in the safe areas.

Comparing the Black and White populations, community civic structure has contributed to increasing the White population in the city's safe areas, while it is associated with driving out the Black population in the same region. The geography of vulnerability fares disparately for the White and Black populations in each area, and the difference widens the gap between what African Americans and Whites would suffer in the case of future disasters.

Post-Katrina New Orleans: A Two-Tiered City

The long-term effects of marked geographic segregation can be detrimental. Not only do fewer African Americans get to enjoy the kind of civic benefits available in the city's safe, high-lying areas, but more communities of color are exposed and susceptible to uncertainties brought about by natural disaster. If another hurricane of Katrina's magnitude were to hit the city, a disproportionate number of African Americans would be affected; far fewer Whites would be affected. In this sense, the civic capacity entrenched within neighborhood boundaries is inseparable from racial and spatial inequalities.

A recent survey reflects the growing geographic divide between Whites and Blacks. When asked about the post-Katrina quality of life and their prospects, Blacks and Whites in the city gave sharply divided responses. While 50 percent of Whites responded that the quality of life has improved or remains the same as before Katrina, only 17 percent of the Black residents said the same thing. The disparity is not because Whites are generally more satisfied than Blacks about how recovery unfolded; rather, the divergent responses may have to do with where they resettled after the storm. Although the surveys do not reveal where the White and Black residents currently live, comparing the neighboring parishes reveals that the White response is not uniformly positive but varies significantly by geography. The White residents in Plaquemines and Saint Bernard Parishes, who experienced severe flooding and destruction of their communities during Katrina, responded in a similarly skeptical way as New Orleans's Black residents, unlike other Whites. For instance, 48 percent of the residents in Plaquemines Parish said the quality of life in their community has gotten worse, similar to 45 percent of Black residents—this is far higher than the mere 13 percent of Whites in Orleans Parish who responded in the same way.[52] The racial difference, therefore, represents the divergent conditions in their communities after the storm.

This chapter shows that community civic structure has an enduring effect on how neighborhoods are reshaped after a disaster. Not only were civic organizations important in facilitating repopulation, they also continued to affect neighborhood demographic makeup after the initial rebuilding effort ran its course. The preexisting civic structure has amplified the divide between the areas that are safe from climate hazards on the one hand, and those that are exposed to risks on the other. While neighborhoods above sea level have gained more people and reduced social vulnerabilities thanks to their civic organizations, those below sea level did not enjoy equal civic benefits and have accumulated greater demographic and social risks than before the flood.

In this sense, what we observed as apparently remarkable recovery in the flooded neighborhoods of Broadmoor and Village de l'Est may in fact be only successful by one narrow definition. Compared only among themselves, these exemplary neighborhoods regained significant numbers of residents thanks to their community civic structure, even after accounting for the level of flooding. However, these neighborhoods do not represent the fate of all flooded neighborhoods, let alone the future of the city. From the perspective of the entire city, the benevolent civic effects are quickly overwhelmed by the more expedient repopulation in the neighborhoods on the higher ground. Uptown, for example, is enjoying an influx of young professionals and the new cultural institutions they bring, while the Seventh Ward and Pontchartrain Park are home to significantly more people below poverty level than before Katrina. In a subtle way, the civic capacity of vulnerable neighborhoods deepens, rather than disintegrates, the existing racial order and solidifies the systematic disadvantages for those located in the city's less desirable areas.

To be sure, having a strong, resilient civic structure would be better than having no social infrastructure at all. It is also possible that racial inequality might have become even worse had it not been for the strong civic leadership in some communities. However, the objectives of these civic organizations—mostly aiming at population gain and community revitalization—do not help close the gap across communities nor reduce relative vulnerabilities, both of which are crucial parts of building urban resilience. The long-term cost of haphazard or uneven redevelopment in the city's risky areas falls exclusively on the residents in the low-lying areas, who have now become poorer and more vulnerable than before. Stagnant property values, fewer amenities, and higher insurance rates are some of the unseen costs of inhabiting the low-lying parts of the city. If we recall that one of the major reasons for the public outcry against rightsizing was the relative depravation felt by the residents in the devastated communities, it's clear that these feelings of loss are likely to persist, or even worsen, long after Katrina's physical wounds are gone.

Conclusion

Like many American cities, New Orleans's racialized urban history during the twentieth century is reflected in its geography. Economically empowered yet socially discriminated against, the growing Black middle class settled in the city's low-lying areas and formed intimate communities. Civic structure, therefore, was firmly embedded in neighborhoods, as people invested not only in their homes but also in their schools, churches, and neighborhood associations. Our common understanding of inner cities does not apply here, as residents developed informal social ties by participating in organizational activities.[53] When community identity is strongly attached to place, it is difficult to suddenly sever the ties and move out. Although Katrina decimated both their houses and their community, people felt that taking buyouts for their properties would have been akin to betraying and denying their collective memory and history.

At the same time, however, the attachment to place, and the resultant community actions, did not solve the fundamental underlying problems of inequality and vulnerability. The boundaries of community civic structure tend to draw the boundaries of recovery, and the bordered recovery process persists throughout the various phases of post-Katrina redevelopment. The social and civic structure of communities gradually (if unintentionally) transformed the city into a two-tiered place, divided by different life opportunities for Blacks and Whites and by the location of their residences, whether above or below sea level. Without a centralized authority to oversee and regulate the pace of reconstruction, some communities were left on their own to survive, and indeed some thrived beyond expected capacity. Civic structure seldom integrated old and new residents of different races, however, who are increasingly sorting themselves along racial and geographic lines after Katrina. Although sustaining the life of these communities is certainly a meaningful undertaking, the gradual deterioration of these communities that has resulted from taking a haphazard approach to revitalization may ultimately deprive these places of sense of community that residents have been hoping to restore.

The dual role of community civic structure, explored in this chapter, raises a question about why civic organizations, purported to help residents recover and rebuild, end up increasing vulnerabilities rather than reducing them. To probe this question more closely, we need to look at the goals, motives, and outcomes that these organizations pursue. The next chapter takes a close look at two neighborhoods—Broadmoor and

Freret—to examine the mechanisms through which civic capacity works, but in a limited way. Focusing on economic self-reliance tends to direct resources toward visible changes in a neighborhood, which requires attracting homeowners and new businesses rather than disadvantaged residents such as renters and those living in poverty. The "business-as-usual" approach of these civic organizations, which focuses on revitalization and rebuilding, tends to justify the notion that rebuilding civic infrastructure, businesses, and damaged homes is the right approach, without considering the larger impact of reviving their neighborhoods.

5

The Making of Resilient Communities

Many residential, community-based groups formed either
just before or just after the storm to protect physical and social space. In most cases, they pursued parochial projects.
I was impressed by the spirit and dedicated leadership of
many of the groups. Nonetheless, most saw their opportunities in reference to others as a zero-sum game.
—Edward Blakely, *My Storm*[1]

In his recollection of neighborhood-based civic organizations in New
Orleans, Edward Blakely lamented the parochial nature of community
groups and their activities. According to him, the city's civic organizations were fragmented by politics, religion, race, and ethnicity, and there
was no central coalition that could carry a "civic vision" beyond the
interests of each group.[2] Although he gave credit to community organizers for their commitment in resurrecting their own communities,
Blakely observed that their commitment was often narrowly defined,
and that their interests would often clash, making post-Katrina recovery
a zero-sum game. On the one hand, the city's affluent and less-damaged
communities did not support spending resources on the city's disadvantaged and heavily flooded communities. On the other hand, knowing
this lack of sympathy existed, residents in damaged neighborhoods
worked to secure any resources before they were made available to others and viewed a citywide solution as an attempt to shrink their presence
in favor of less-affected communities.[3]

A nationally renowned urban planner and the recovery "czar" of
post-Katrina New Orleans, Blakely was appointed by then-mayor Ray
Nagin as the executive director of the Office of Recovery and Development Administration. Despite receiving much fanfare among urban
planning experts nationwide, Blakely's plan to revitalize the city did
not gain support but backlash from citizens, which made him even-

tually step down in July 2009. Shortly after his resignation, Blakely published a memoir in which he described what went wrong during the early phase of recovery and how political, social, economic, and personal hurdles delayed and derailed post-disaster planning and compromised his role as the chief of recovery planning. According to Blakely, one of the fundamental hurdles was helping overcome the deeply held distrust of government and integrating citizen opinions across racial and economic divisions. He further reported how low-income communities sought to secure resources whenever they were available, before any citywide plans could be discussed.[4] For him, the speedy recovery process was not so much a sign of undying resilience as the manifestation of the competition among neighborhoods, which portended uneven and unhealthy redevelopment for the declining city.

Unpopular as he was during his two-year term, his scathingly frank comment deserves a deeper discussion. While the tone may differ, the challenges of making a citywide plan have been well documented elsewhere, especially with regard to the conflicts among citizens and between citizens and government.[5] Not only did problems derive from the ineffective vertical communication between local community groups and government agencies, but there had been subtle yet salient conflict *among* communities even prior to Katrina. Kristina Ford, who was New Orleans's director of city planning from 1992 to 2000 and served as the chief of staff to the deputy mayor in 2010 and 2011, observed similar kinds of civic competition for the city's resources during the public meetings for the city's 1999 Land Use Plan.[6] In drafting the Land Use Plan, Ford's department sought answers from citizens as to what they wanted their city "to look like, feel like, and be like in twenty years?" In answering the question,

> [C]itizens respond . . . by declaring that they want the civic amenities that other, more-favored neighborhoods already have. These civic jealousies are often quite specific. . . . Other civic jealousies are more general, as when citizens tell planners they want community centers, playgrounds, and elementary schools "nearby," or that they want safe places to walk—all of which they believe (whether or not it's true) other neighborhoods enjoy.[7]

As described above, citizens negotiated their desire to better their neighborhoods *relative to* other neighborhoods, and what Ford termed as "civic jealousy" had been deeply ingrained before the storm. The post-Katrina rebuilding process only intensified the conflict. When I asked whether neighborhoods were cooperative or competitive during the reconstruction process, a city official's response echoed what Ford described. There were many neighborhoods whose residents "felt they were being beyond neglected and targeted for abandonment." In these neighborhoods, people often thought, "maybe there were officials who were trying to wipe out their neighborhoods."[8]

The sentiments of relative deprivation lingered long after Katrina. Indeed, residents expressed anger and frustration when the city tried to collect their opinions on the citywide master plan in public meetings. Those who lived in the neglected sections of the city were angry about the city government's action to establish a long-term plan without paying adequate attention to their immediate concerns. In a public meeting for the city's Comprehensive Zoning Ordinance, a resident from the Lower Ninth Ward expressed frustration about the seemingly inadequate gestures suggested for infrastructural improvement to the representatives of the City Planning Commission:

> As far as the sewage and water board is concerned, I think it is a very silly idea to build all of this, implement all of this [zoning change], without getting infrastructure . . . without having streetlights, or [a] fire station. From what I am told, it's against the law to not even have a fire station, because there is lots of water we are separated by. There is no way we are able to live in this area without having fire station, police station, streetlights, and streets properly fixed. I just don't agree with that. It's silly. . . . Around Lakeview, Canal Street . . . everything is done in that community. And I wanna know, Holy Cross area, they always get everything. Holy Cross area they have their own association. They will always get what they wanna get because of people that run the committee. We don't have a voice here. . . . We need help here. And we are paying taxes! What are we paying taxes for?[9]

For those in the Lower Ninth Ward, the paucity of basic infrastructure was in stark contrast to other flooded communities'. The Holy Cross neighborhood revived much more quickly. Located south of the Lower Ninth Ward, Holy Cross made significant progress under the leadership of its neighborhood association. Likewise, the Lakeview neighborhood, an affluent lakefront community, restored more quickly than the Lower Ninth Ward despite a comparable level of damage from the storm.[10]

While people from the Lower Ninth Ward were struggling with inefficient government services, residents in other neighborhoods rolled up their sleeves to recuperate their own neighborhoods without the government's help by hiring contractors, recruiting planning professionals, and staffing full-time workers in their respective neighborhood organizations. In so doing, they formed what public administration scholars call "private governments"[11]—a set of voluntary, exclusive organizations formed within the existing local governmental jurisdiction. Galvanized by civic motives, these private governments, in the form of neighborhood associations, housing services, and community development corporations, occupy primary positions in New Orleans's recovery. Indeed, the rise of resilient communities blurred the boundary between civic and private governance, foretelling the tendency toward market-based, privatized post-disaster efforts.[12]

To bear out this point, this chapter scales down its analytic focus to the community level and explores how the idea of community self-reliance developed—and how it continues to serve as a dominant force in the post-Katrina period. I bring attention to the ways in which the norms of community *self-reliance*, cultivated by the city government to substitute for insufficient government resources, transformed into the idea of community *resilience* before, during, and after the storm. Five years after Katrina, neighborhoods had returned to their normal business of community development, striving to bounce back and expand. I found little evidence, however, to suggest that such mode of community resilience strengthens the bond between neighborhoods. To the contrary, the efforts for neighborhood revitalization helped each community effectively become a self-sufficient governing unit and fortified existing neighborhood boundaries. Community resilience was differently understood and accomplished across neighborhoods, depending on the kind of preexisting resources available in each community.

The conflation of civic and private governance in the wake of Katrina resonates with what Cedric Johnson called "grassroots privatization," whereby the dynamics of neighborhood recovery are governed by the neoliberal logic of privatization, competition, and marketability.[13] This begins with a broad shift. As he mentions, "the pressures of competition between locales to attract investment has created a highly variegated order within the international economy . . . and cities like New Orleans occupy a diminished, peripheral, and precarious place under these emergent arrangements."[14] Following the national and international push for pro-market reforms, neighborhoods have also been enlisted as part of this neoliberal wave and sought to stay buoyant by attracting more people, businesses, and infrastructure. The intra-city competition was detrimental to individual neighborhoods in the context of the city's overall declining economic and demographic outlook, and the competition continued to influence how these neighborhoods fared after Katrina. Thus, it would be insufficient to attribute the rise of resilient communities after Katrina to a surprising, unexpected outpouring of civic reaction that is different from the community development trajectories in ordinary times; rather, this chapter reminds us that Katrina reinforced, rather than changed, the existing course of privatized local governance by providing a moral impetus for self-sufficiency.

The story I tell in this chapter defies sociologists' conceptualization of urban neighborhoods as spatially connected units within a city. Urban sociologists use the term "spatial diffusion" to describe the process of neighborhood interaction. In his examination of Chicago neighborhoods, sociologist Robert Sampson argued that urban neighborhoods and their community outcomes are spatially concentrated, and neighborhood outcomes are not only a function of each community's internal characteristics but are also influenced by the conditions of adjacent entities.[15] Simply put, spatial diffusion means that what happens in neighborhood A is not only a function of A's internal characteristics, but also partially a result of what happens in adjacent neighborhoods. The idea of spatial diffusion is also used methodologically, wherein a researcher should take into account the interdependence among spatially adjacent units in statistical analysis.[16] The conceptual and methodological advances on spatial interaction reflect the flexibility and arbitrariness of the sociopolitical jurisdictions within a city. In fact, the delineation of neighborhood boundaries has been historically malleable, and people have flexible ideas about what to call their neighborhoods or where their residence belongs. Although New Orleans's neighborhoods seem to have acquired their characters and rough outlines long ago, the city's designation of seventy-three distinct neighborhoods is a recent invention. It appeared in the 1970s, when the mayor's office of policy planning drew neighborhood boundaries to distribute the CDBG allowed by President Lyndon Johnson, which evolved in the 1980s to the current boundaries that also conform to the federal census tract boundaries.[17]

As neighborhoods are understood to be spatially interdependent, permeable social boundaries, post-Katrina recovery is also expected to be a bit "messy," with lots of spatial interaction crossing local divisions. However, as shown in the quantitative analysis in chapter 4, there is little evidence to support this idea. Neighborhoods—or more specifically, neighborhood-based resilience outcomes—were not necessarily spatially correlated, and yet they affect one another for an extended period of time. Admittedly, spatial diffusion did occur in the early period of recovery, when the increasing number of returnees in one neighborhood could be positively associated with repopulation in adjacent neighborhoods. Although repopulation did diffuse across the city in the beginning, the spatial diffusion pattern dissipated over time and eventually disappeared, suggesting that, in the long run, neighborhoods may not reciprocate as much as we would expect.

This stands in contrast with the fact that the exposure to risk, such as the depth of flooding and land elevation, does not vary by neighborhood boundaries but is spread continuously across space. Land does not abruptly go up or down at the edges of socially defined neighborhoods; likewise, water does not stop flowing along the lines of community borders. In other words, the city's ecological landscape cannot be as clearly demarcated as socially constructed neighborhood boundaries—and yet, neighborhoods are such powerful units that drive independent recovery patterns. To the extent that neighborhood institutions actively pursue redevelopment, they operate within those socially defined borders, and geographic proximity may not automatically connect neighborhoods together. The discrete patterns of recovery laid out in this chapter demonstrate why community resilience may not always correspond with long-term sustainability goals at the city level. When communities pursue spatially targeted, locally beneficial strategies, the scope of development tends to be confined within neighborhood lines. Also, specific modes of development vary from community to community, based on the availability of human resources and the preexisting outlook of the given community. This spatial variation, however, does not adequately reflect the distribution of risk and hazard at the city level, separating community revitalization efforts from building citywide adaptive capacity.

To describe this process more closely, I explore a story of two neighborhoods, Broadmoor and Freret, to show the ways in which local neighborhoods pursued resilience once the exigencies of Katrina subsided. The objective of presenting the story of two neighborhoods is not to contrast the success or failure of citizen-activated recovery. By any means, both neighborhoods achieved a good level of success, as many studies and journalist accounts have documented their triumphant civic activities. Rather, I explore these two cases under a different light. The stories of Broadmoor and Freret represent the ways in which neighborhoods' resiliency strategies deepen the dilemma of urban crisis.

On one hand, the Broadmoor case shows the paradox of community resilience in the context of a sinking city. The heavier the land usage and water drainage that occur in Broadmoor, dictated by various civic projects, the greater the level of land subsidence, naturally shrinking the city proper.[18] Broadmoor achieved a marketable status by turning its geographic disadvantage upside down and displaying how civic forces can fight and overcome natural constraints. Based on their strong civic structure, Broadmoorians focused on promoting *social* resilience, whereby residents build educational and cultural infrastructure that can anchor community activities and make a neighborhood more livable. Community organizers focused on restoring the "civicness" of their community by fortifying the civic infrastructure, such as constructing a new community center, library, and a charter school.

On the other hand, the Freret case demonstrates the ambivalent meaning of community resilience in a shrinking city—one with a declining population and increasing blight. Trying to revitalize its commercial corridor, Freret residents sought to achieve *economic* resilience and organized their efforts to find a competitive niche as a convenient consumer district for Uptown and Tulane University clients. Freret Street, located below sea level, is being transformed into a new space for hip bars, restaurants, and coffee shops that invite new residents but do so at the expense of driving out old residents. At the same time, it is also going through a racial transition, where the neighborhood's Black population is being replaced with White and Hispanic residents.

In contrast to the data analyses in the previous two chapters, I employ a qualitative method to reconstruct the narratives of the community members and probe into the nuanced differences between the two neighborhoods. In so doing, I first situate post-Katrina community development in the broad context of New Orleans's changing political economy, to substantiate the claim that the current rise and success of community development initiatives has historical continuity with the self-governing urban development trends in pre-Katrina New Orleans. The narrative of this chapter is thus based on three components: (i) literature review and archival research on the history of community development in New Orleans; (ii) semistructured interviews and conversations with residents, community organizers, owners of commercial facilities, and city officials; and (iii) participant observation of neighborhood meetings, city council meetings, and public hearings on zoning across the city. The data were collected at various times from 2008 to 2013. The interview data were acquired during fieldwork conducted between February and April of 2010. During my stay, I approached and interviewed various groups of people in both neighborhoods as well as throughout the city, and each group of interviewees provided me with diverse perspectives on what was going on in their neighborhood and the city after Katrina. Each conversation lasted a minimum of thirty minutes and up to more than two hours, and I conducted about twenty interviews in total. The two neighborhoods I selected—Broadmoor and Freret—are racially mixed communities with low-to-middle income levels. While they are by no means representative of all New Orleans communities,[19] I selected them because they did not have either obvious obstacles or advantages for recovery (such as extreme poverty or the predominance of a certain racial group), which allowed me to focus on the experiences of the community organizations.

Admittedly, two months of field research is quite limited compared to that of ethnographers who spend much more time, meet a wider range of people, and immerse themselves completely in the field. However limited the field study may be in its duration and immersion, the qualitative data I gathered in the field research still serve as well-qualified sources for triangulating with the quantitative findings of the previous chapters. When interviewing people and observing meetings at various levels of local jurisdictions, I found that my interviews and observations converged with quite similar conclusions to what existing literature has discussed,[20]—namely, that neighborhoods strove to achieve autonomy and self-governance, and some were effective while others struggled. However, this chapter's contribution lies in attending to the spatial boundaries in which the specific mechanisms of resilience building occur in neighborhoods. Throughout my field research, I found that neighborhood designations were not just historical and cultural constructs but socially embedded units; development strategies and serviced clients were identified and sorted out by each neighborhood's residents. Civic capacity, expressed through voluntary, collective participation for advancing the public good, was cultivated within these neighborhood boundaries.

Another important theme of this chapter is to recognize the historical continuity of the idea of community resilience. Although the term "community resilience" has mostly been discussed in the context of natural disasters since Katrina, the ideas undergirding what constitutes a resilient community were already entrenched in the political economic context of American cities. Urban development policies, most of which had been designed without factoring in the variables urban crises could contribute, emphasized neighborhood self-reliance as the core ideology for urban revitalization.[21] Focusing on specific needs facing their own neighborhoods, residents engaged in various local initiatives—fair housing, historic preservation, and crime control, to name a few—with varying degrees of success. These self-governing communities, however, were not entirely a civic product. They emerged out of a necessity to complement the decimation of public resources for adequate service delivery. In this sense, self-reliant communities tend to blur the boundary between civic-spiritedness and private interests. On the one hand, neighborhood self-governance is a civic matter in that it requires voluntary engagement from its members to achieve an equitable and fair outcome; on the other hand, neighborhood-led initiatives ultimately pursued semiprivate interests, as the type of desired public goods tended to be narrowly defined and the scope of the public goods provision confined within neighborhood boundaries. The gradual shift of focus from political empowerment to economic development thus suggests that civic engagement does not just mean nurturing a sense of belonging and civic-mindedness but also realizing the concrete interests of the most engaged community members. Tracing the slow but consistent patterns of privatized neighborhood development in New Orleans illustrates this process.

The Rise of Self-Reliant Communities in New Orleans

Post-Katrina reconstruction was a process that solidified the changing notion of neighborhoods from socially defined regions to economically viable units in the city. A series of political economic changes from the 1970s through the 1990s laid a foundation for local communities to undertake an active role in urban development, which included providing core services such as security and beautification as well as attracting nongovernmental investment into their communities. This process was victorious for some but contentious for others, depending on the degree to which a neighborhood could sustain itself by securing a stream of resources both internally and externally. The implicit boundaries around local neighborhoods not only enhanced residents' sense of belonging and civic-spiritedness, they also came to serve as basic units of informal governance recognized by residents and governmental authorities.

The 1970s and 1980s: The Emergence of Neighborhood Groups

Amid instability in the city's formal political power channels in the 1970s, neighborhood groups became active to influence a variety of citywide policies including historic preservation, public housing, housing subsidies, neighborhood revitalization, and schools. Two national trends spurred the growth of neighborhood movements.[22] First, HUD stopped subsidizing new development in Eastern New Orleans that was supposed to have housed middle- to low-income residents. Middle-class support for public housing had also waned because of the new view that the massive housing projects of the past were unmanageable, and the fervor over public housing had disappeared along with discontinued public funds. The concept of public housing as a public good no longer existed within the public imagination, and thus development projects fell mostly into private hands.[23] With weakened public assistance for housing, residents and private developers could exert free rein on the eastern part of the city—a low-lying area that held the possibility of land subsidence.[24] As middle-class Black families moved to New Orleans East and formed more socioeconomically homogeneous neighborhoods, it took less effort for neighborhood groups to undergird the interests of private developers and homeowners than to negotiate with the federal agencies that had specific demands for funding public housing projects.

Second, the Nixon administration halted housing subsidy programs for low- to moderate-income families. The demise of housing subsidy programs and a revived interest in urban neighborhoods galvanized neighborhood groups to engage in charting housing policy themselves. The moratorium on housing subsidies, coupled with the sharp recession of 1974–1975, directly affected the local housing market and further delegitimized the authority of city housing policy makers.[25] The Housing and Community Development Act of 1974 (CDA) further eased the entrance of neighborhood groups into the policy-making arena as the local government began to recognize neighborhoods as viable units of governance and the receivers of federal funding. Consolidating the preexisting seven grants-in-aid, the CDA funneled block grants directly to local governments with a population of fifty thousand or more. Not only did the CDA allow greater flexibility for dispensing CDBGs, it also embedded citizen participation within the grant application procedure. Preparing for CDBG application required local knowledge of community problems, and neighborhood groups played a central role in identifying local issues and enhancing the feasibility of proposed programs.[26] In proportion to the devolution through block grants and the rise of newly formed neighborhood associations, the formal policymaking arena in New Orleans shrunk and no single power center could mobilize sufficient resources for housing matters. Whereas a group of powerful cliques had set and implemented the agenda for housing policy prior to the 1970s, a plethora of housing advocates emerged in the housing policy arena thereafter. Private businesses were cautiously gauging pros and cons of establishing themselves New Orleans and its vicinities, government agencies were caught in the quagmire of the resulting impasse in adequate housing policy implementation, and neighborhood groups were engaged in issues that served the interests of respective communities.

In addition to political trends, local demographic change also rekindled interest in urban neighborhoods. Despite the general movement of Whites into suburban vicinities, young generations chose to dwell in the old neighborhoods of the city, rehabilitating old houses and ultimately gentrifying their neighborhoods. The increased activities of young homeowners resulted in the ascendance of neighborhood-led organizations, and yet the generational replacement served to accelerate the displacement of poor and elderly people who had previously occupied the old buildings.[27]

With these external factors present, the city government continued its explicit efforts to facilitate neighborhood self-governance. The macroeconomic downturn and substantial loss in tax revenue—for example, about $52 million in revenue losses from residential properties in 2003—caused delays in improving city services and left taxpayers less trustful of the city government's ability to deliver appropriate services to residents. To compensate for the service underprovisions caused by cutbacks on manpower, budget shortfalls, and program reductions, locally elected government officials considered various ways to capitalize on the energy of individual citizens and neighborhood organizations and to share the responsibility for providing and funding essential city services.

One of the government programs that materialized with this strategy was the neighborhood-based security and improvement district, whereby property owners in a neighborhood paid a special tax in addition to what they would normally pay to the city or state. Extra fees were imposed on residential and commercial lots for additional public and private security patrols. As of October 2010, twenty-six neighborhoods were participating in private securitization.[28] These types of neighborhood-based services were not solely based on the community's economic capacity but rather they reflected the increased civic power of neighborhoods and their interest in self-reliance. Joining a special tax district is determined by voter referendum, and the process often involves heated discussions on whether the benefits will outweigh the costs, as was the case in the affluent French Quarter and Lakeview neighborhoods.[29]

Another attempt to decentralize public service provisions was the Impact Neighborhood Strategy, where the city promoted rehabilitation projects in old, blighted parts of the city and engaged community and faith-based organizations, banking and lending institutions, and public officials in the rebuilding process. The Strategy chose several neighborhoods for redevelopment, and active neighborhood leadership and community engagement constituted the core criteria for which were selected. Tremé was chosen, and the city government formed a partnership with financial institutions, neighborhood churches, and community-based organizations to rehabilitate blighted owner-occupied housings. With $1.2 million from the CDBG and funding from local banks, the Impact Neighborhood Strategy established an institutional structure to encourage homeowners to repair, renovate, and beautify their properties. Again here, neighborhoods were encouraged to be independent, self-reliant entities that competed against one another to secure government resources and prove their viability.[30]

Not only did neighborhoods assume the necessary housekeeping duties inherent in establishing these government-assisted programs, they also voluntarily addressed community-specific issues. A newspaper article featuring a neighborhood association in Village de l'Est represented such a case (Figure 5.1). Described as an active organization since the late 1960s, the neighborhood association took care of the neighborhood's most dire problems, which included imposing strict rules and issuing fines to the dog owners who would otherwise abandon their dogs on Michoud Boulevard in their community. But more important, the active neighborhood association mobilized its community members to maintain, repair, and upgrade the community through such activities as pressuring a state division cement company to spend money on removing cement dust and cutting grass on neutral grounds along Dwyer Boulevard. Furthermore, residents of Village de l'Est successfully lowered their own flood insurance rates by fielding a slab elevation survey for the homes and countering bad publicity about the flood risks in their community. In organizing these collective endeavors, the residents acknowledged that what they were doing was in fact normally the function of the city government. "With the city having budget problems, they are not able to cut the grass as often as we would like," noted a resident. "But if more of us would do this, we would have a better-looking city and less of a budget-balancing problem in city government."[31]

Page 24   Saturday, September 20, 1980   The Times-Picayune/The States-Item

United:

Residents Of Eastern N.O. Development Have Conquered Their Growing Pains

By ANGELA M. CARLL

The small community of Village de l'Est is one of the most cohesive and well-organized neighborhoods in the city.

Developed in response to the increased demand for housing brought about by the introduction of the National Aeronautics and Space Assembly facility, this eastern New Orleans community has met and conquered more problems than have many older and more established neighborhoods.

A pie-shaped area bounded by Paris Road, Chef Menteur Highway and a bayou flowing into Lake Michoud, many of its residents are families who follow the properties and recessions of the space center, creating a necessarily transient community.

Yet, Village de l'Est has had an active neighborhood association since the late '60s which has enabled it to preserve the atmosphere of a community that cares about itself.

The first problem this Michoud community addressed was the proliferation of stray dogs in the neighborhood.

"Not only do people let their dogs out to run in the morning and evening," explains resident Dee Jenson, "but people also bring dogs and cats and drop them at the end of Michoud Boulevard and abandon them."

Residents worked with the Society for the Prevention of Cruelty to Animals and staged a "dog round-up". The SPCA also agreed to issue fines to dog owners who failed to comply with the parish leash law, did not have their dogs vaccinated, or failed to confine their pets securely.

Association president James Person reports the community now is virtually free of stray and loose dogs.

The neighborhood's next problem involved a fine film of cement dust residents would find on their cars and in their houses.

The residue was coming from the Louisiana Cement Division plant of OKC Corp. on Intra-coastal Drive about a mile and a half from Village de l'Est.

"Our pets were dying, our shrubs were dying, and it was a definite health hazard," recalls resident Allen Nagele. "Not only that, but once the dust was mixed with water, it was virtually impossible to get off your cars or out of your house."

Residents finally persuaded the cement company to spend about $2.5 million to have the problem corrected, and at latest report have not had to contend with any more dust.

Residents also have countered bad publicity about the flooding in their neighborhood by scheduling slab elevation surveys before applying for flood insurance.

"We've been able to qualify for very low flood insurance rates as a result of our surveys," says resident Dolores Dalon. "And we're proud to be able to even offer a group rate on the surveys through our neighborhood association."

The latest example of neighbors working together to improve their community can be seen as a group of residents on Dwyer Boulevard have begun cutting the grass on the neutral grounds in front of their houses.

"With the city having budget problems, they are not able to cut the grass as often as we would like," notes Person, "but if more of us would do this we would have a better looking city and less of a budget-balancing problem in city government."

Although residents readily admit much of their community is of a transient nature, they still feel they have the spirit of the older, established neighborhoods.

"We're beginning a neighborhood anti-crime program," says Persons, "which will make our neighborhood safer and more inviting than ever."

—Staff Photo By Bryan S. Berteaux

Michoud Boulevard Corner: A Sign Of The Times

Figure 5.1. Newspaper coverage for Village de l'Est neighborhood association on September 20, 1980. Source: *Times-Picayune/The States-Item* from the New Orleans Public Library Digital Archive.

The delegation of city services to individual neighborhoods inevitably resulted in widening the livability gap between resourceful neighborhoods and their disadvantaged counterparts. Naturally, the special tax district scheme appealed to those neighborhoods that have strongly organized associations, tight community identity, a high percentage of homeownership, and a substantial tax base. In other words, the predominantly White, middle class, homogeneous areas would most likely establish private tax districts and receive benefits. The disparity in neighborhood tax bases bred a system of elitist neighborhood districts where the more affluent communities, such as the Garden District, were willing and able to pay for extra services at their own cost, while poorer neighborhoods with a thin tax base deteriorated more rapidly as necessary services were diverted to those areas that paid the special tax.[32] In sum, poor Black communities had to bear the brunt of an incompetent public sector and privatized services.

*The 1990s and 2000s: The Era of Community
Development Corporations*

The codependent relationship between neighborhood groups and city government continued in the 1990s. With the waning city economy and decreased federal support, the administration of Mayor Marc Morial (1994–2002) sought to integrate private sector actors into the housing policymaking process to rehabilitate the real estate market.[33] In addition to the direct citywide program on neighborhood revitalization mentioned above, CDCs also proliferated in high-poverty areas. Aimed at transforming vacant and abandoned properties into affordable housing, CDCs in the 1990s garnered support for various national and local organizations. The Local Initiatives Support Corporation, a national organization created to mobilize resources for local community organizations, established a New Orleans affiliate and propelled the development of CDCs. The Division of Housing and Neighborhood Development used federal CDBG and Home Ownership Made Easy (HOME) funding to provide operating support. Preexisting faith-based organizations and advocacy groups, such as All Congregations Together, the Jeremiah Group, and the Association of Community Organizations for Reform Now (ACORN), also participated in channeling community organization with community development.[34]

Despite the rise of CDCs during the 1990s, little consensus existed as to what role CDCs should play in community development. As Lowe and Bates explain, "Some, particularly nonprofits, supported CDC efforts at individual and community empowerment. Others, especially those with private sector connections, placed greater emphasis on efficient housing rehabilitation."[35] This "clash of values" represents the gradual role change of community-based organizations from advocating political empowerment to spearheading economic development. Although a seemingly equal emphasis was placed on both goals, it became clear over time that CDCs would invest their resources in property development and neighborhood revitalization. This also meant that the viability of CDCs depended on the availability of financial and institutional resources to fight abandonment. In the late 1990s, the ebbs and flows of external resources determined the scope of action by CDCs. In prosperous times, CDCs enjoyed a wealth of funding from national, regional, and local philanthropies and businesses and could expand their organizational and production capacity. In contrast, in the 2000s, the diminished national and regional support contracted the CDCs' capacity to address vacancy and abandonment.[36] Regardless of these fluctuations, however, the idea of economic self-reliance remained a crucial element of community-based movements and defined the nature of civic capacity that culminated in the wake of Katrina's devastation.

After Katrina, CDCs continued to maintain a presence in community development, channeling external resources into local neighborhoods. Preexisting CDCs revamped their organizational structure to coordinate recovery efforts, while many neighborhoods established new CDCs to accommodate growing needs for community-driven reconstruction. CDCs in highly flooded areas, including Gentilly, Broadmoor, Central City, and the Lower Ninth Ward, participated in the consortium of the NSP. Administered by HUD, the NSP selected which NORA and community development organizations would receive federal funding to construct and renovate affordable houses. In the process of rebuilding damaged properties, some of these organizations declared a shift in focus from advocacy to community development. For example, the Lower Ninth Ward Neighborhood Empowerment Network Association (NENA) began as a grassroots community organization for equitable recovery and pivoted to become a fully developed "private entity"[37] that engaged in redevelopment projects such as building new, affordable houses in the neighborhood.

Once considered to be complementary entities for the city government, CDCs now gained moral support as an alternative to the local government body that serves community interests. In a volume on post-Katrina civic engagement, Pat Evans and Sarah Lewis claimed that "neighborhoods themselves serve as the building blocks for recovery and should guide post-Katrina community engagement."[38] Post-Katrina community building, they further argue, is "based on the fundamental goal of obliterating feelings of dependency and replacing them with attitudes of self-reliance, self-confidence, and responsibility."[39] The prominence of neighborhood self-reliance was contrasted against the inefficiency of local government, with the end result that the swift, effective neighborhood responses to disaster recovery were done "in spite of, rather than in collaboration with, the city's disaster response."[40]

Broadmoor and Freret's stories demonstrate what these neighborhoods pursue as self-reliant strategies. Far from being exceptional, the ecology of community organizing in post-Katrina New Orleans has followed a pattern whereby community "organizing," which aims to embrace broad political issues and thus requires citywide coordinated action beyond neighborhood boundaries, has given way to a community "development" perspective that is predicated upon the ideas of well-being, safety, and economic development.[41]

The Rise of a Socially Resilient Community: Broadmoor

On a humid September evening in 1929, about a thousand residents gathered at Saint Matthias Catholic Church in the Broadmoor neighborhood, outraged and frustrated by constant flooding and the suffering it brought. The meeting was organized by the BIA, and the residents had come to hear from city officials on the Sewerage and Water Board about the city's plan for solving the neighborhood's chronic drainage problems. Joseph Rault, vice president of the BIA, commenced the meeting, and residents called for a gubernatorial action to propose a flood relief bill in the legislature as soon as possible. "I have never ceased to call the attention of the public to the danger from heavy rainfall," said George G. Earl, superintendent of the Sewerage and Water Board. His solution to the polemical flooding problems in Broadmoor was to spend more on drainage improvements. He said, "I have included in my report and recommendations between now and 1942, to keep up with the growth and expansion of the city, $65,000,000 would have to be spent to provide adequate sewerage and drainage development."[42] Not only did he emphasize the Board's financial commitment in the drainage system, Earl also assured that the allocated money—which is worth $976 million in 2020 dollars—would be spent for the "benefit of the Broadmoor section."[43] The superintendent assured residents that this large sum of money, collected from public finances, would be used to protect a tiny neighborhood of 0.56 square miles, which is far less than one percent of the city's total area of about 350 square miles. "Other sections are making similar requests for relief and ask for improvement of present conditions even as you do," he continued. "Most of the four million dollars which have been obtained for drainage development through the bond issue and taxation will be used to better drainage conditions in the Broadmoor area. Everything, financially and physically that can be done is being done for the section," he concluded.[44]

The anger, frustration, and little bit of hope that surfaced during the meeting present a striking similarity to one of more than a hundred meetings held after Katrina in 2005. About eighty years later, residents gathered once again—this time to protest the city's plan to flood the neighborhood forever. Although there was no official announcement to declare the neighborhood a green space, the public quickly interpreted the proposal to mean that some neighborhoods, including Broadmoor, would disappear. Feeling the threat of their homes being completely bulldozed, residents organized rallies and protests against the city's announcement. More important, they drafted a four-hundred-page proposal for neighborhood redevelopment and submitted it to the BNOBC in order to prove their vitality and argue against the commission's abandonment plan.

This experience remained a proud memory for Hal Roark, a native of New Orleans and a Yale graduate, when I interviewed him in a meeting room at the BIA about five years post-Katrina, in 2010. Renovated and repurposed from a single-family house, the BIA office was located on a quiet street and exuded a "neighborhood" feel by looking cozy, comfortable, and approachable. Despite its quite informal and casual setting, however, BIA was far from a social club, as Roark's unassuming yet confident remarks demonstrated. He had been a real estate developer before becoming the executive director of the Broadmoor Development Corporation (BDC) in 2006, the neighborhood's first CDC. Established quickly as a sister organization of the BIA, the BDC played a crucial role in rebuilding abandoned, vacant, or damaged housing and then putting those houses back on the market.

Roark's philosophy on community activism was clear: be strategic and professional. The BDC was created to propel housing reconstruction and the revitalization of the real estate market in the area. Instead of taking a grievance-based approach, he emphasized that business-oriented, professional community organizing would yield a more constructive and tangible outcome:[45]

I think, the big concern that I have for a lot of community organizing groups nationally, now this may not be the case in practice, but it's sort of the chain that people think in [a] loose general way about community organizing, is too much community organizing is like, you organize people, and you just protest. . . . You have get [the] public [to] buy in around the legitimate issue, and show legitimacy through protest, so I am not against that phrase. But the problem is, when we think about this, and the media covers it, you have to eventually take that political power that you gather through the protest phase, and have to become directed and cemented in some kind of focus. That then achieves the outcome of the political vision that you're protesting for. And the problem that I see with too much community organizing is that it never gets out of the protest, it doesn't get out of the protest phase effectively and fast enough into the operational phase. So for us, the BDC is the manifestation of all the Broadmoor protest, it's just that we're the operational [and] institutional manifestation of the protest.[46]

For Roark, community development strategies were the "operational [and] institutional manifestation" of the political protest; he recognized that as protesting alone had not been able to bring about visible changes to the neighborhood. Throughout the interview, he constantly emphasized how the BDC took a pragmatic approach for the benefit of the Broadmoor neighborhood, and it was clear that he adopted the language of business management in his dealings. For example, "organizational diversification" within the neighborhood is one of their strategies. Three other nonprofit organizations spun out of the BIA, including the BDC, Broadmoor Charter School Board, and Broadmoor Community Care Services. Instead of being subsumed as new departments under the BIA, these organizations were separately created and assumed very specific tasks, such as home building assistance and the creation of a charter school. This was a conscious strategy, designed to avoid overwhelming the BIA and to ensure that even if one organization failed, it would not affect others.

Another term that was frequently mentioned was "public–private partnership." The BDC collaborated with many external organizations such as Harvard, MIT, and the Carnegie Corporation of New York. The BIA and BDC each collaborated with the Harvard Kennedy School and received a $2 million grant to rebuild the Rosa F. Keller Library.[47] As a neighborhood that most closely reflects the city's overall demographics and symbolizes resilient local activism, Broadmoor quickly attracted attention from various high-profile corporate and philanthropic organizations including the Clinton Global Initiative, the Shorenstein Company, the Shell Oil Company, and Mercy Corps.[48]

LaToya Cantrell, then-president of the BIA and the current mayor of New Orleans, also confirmed this vision. Before Katrina, Cantrell had already been working to resolve neighborhood problems around her own property regarding slumlords, drug trafficking, and blight. Then, after Katrina, the BIA asked her to join and lead the organization, where she became the president. As a neighborhood association, the BIA aims at expending resources to areas "where the needs are the greatest" to continue to receive help from external organizations. In the interview, she emphasized that the BIA works to identify issues such as blight, slumlords, crime, and drug trafficking that tended to be concentrated in a poor section of the neighborhood. However, she also emphasized that these issues are not related to a single racial group or assumed to be associated with the poor. Bringing race to the forefront of neighborhood recovery almost seemed to undermine, rather than highlight, the broader goal of the BIA, which is to promote the welfare of its residents. Although these social ills clearly had a racial undertone and the African American section of the neighborhood clearly lagged in repopulation, Cantrell made it clear that she and her association would focus on serving the most immediate needs of the residents.

Both leaders had a clear idea about what resilience means for their neighborhood. For them, resilience meant engaging in resistance: residents made concerted efforts to protect their community against the city's rightsizing plans. Also, as Roark mentioned, resilience meant "getting things done" by producing concrete, tangible results rather than delivering complaints via political protests with no tangible outcomes. Showing community resilience in Broadmoor involved proving an ability to sustain itself without government help by drafting a neighborhood master plan without government assistance, rebuilding damaged properties with speed, and eradicating signs of blight and degradation—including those that had plagued the neighborhood even prior to Katrina.

This language of self-sufficiency and sustainability was clearly articulated in the neighborhood meeting that I attended on March 15, 2010.

Held at the newly built gym of the Andrew H. Wilson Charter School, the meeting had a great turnout of about sixty to seventy people. The meeting began with a welcoming speech by LaToya Cantrell:

> Thank you so much for coming out tonight. I see a lot of new faces or fresh faces and just thank you for being here. It's always encouraging when you have meetings and you see new residents coming out, even if it's for the first time, or just returning. We know you can't make every meeting, but just knowing you have it on your agenda, that it's in your plans to participate in the recovery and sustainability of this community. We appreciate that.[49]

The meeting went smoothly and as scheduled, and the BIA and BDC staff members announced new programs and took questions from residents. Maggie Carroll, then the secretary of the BIA, reported on the minutes from the previous meeting. First, she mentioned the progress on the Rosa F. Keller Library, a newly constructed public library in the neighborhood funded by the Carnegie Corporation. Next, she reported on the arrival of the new interns from Tulane, Harvard and Bard College, who would mainly work with the BDC to promote housing redevelopment in the neighborhood. Third, she thoroughly explained the progress on the Andrew H. Wilson Charter School in which they were sitting, which was one of the first schools that reopened in New Orleans after Katrina:

> There is also a call for residents to get more involved with the BIA. Charles Montgomery, architect of HMS Architects, spoke about green design that went into the Wilson School design, which is being recognized as having the gold status. Architects were able to maximize the amount of play space for the block, introduce rain collection systems with a cistern that can hold 25,000 gallons that will be used to irrigate the lawns. Rainwater is collected through the permeable paving material in the courtyard and rain guards on the west and north side.

Finally, Carroll briefed the attendants on the BIA's partnership with the YMCA, which provided an afterschool program to complement the athletic activities at Wilson School:

LaToya spoke about our YMCA partnership and how the YMCA facility was part of the original proposal to the state, but the square footage was insufficient. Initially, the state did not believe that the site could accommodate a gym. The BIA fought long and hard to make sure that the Wilson students had a gym on campus even when the state told us to forget about having a gym. The YMCA has begun hosting an afterschool program out of the gym. The BIA is currently working to raise money to purchase a core divider, so that different activities can take place at the same time in the gymnasium. Meeting adjourned.[50]

Carroll's detailed review of the previous meeting demonstrated the progress of the neighborhood as a socially viable unit with plenty of human and material resources. Indeed, the general atmosphere of the meeting was upbeat, and residents were hopeful about where the neighborhood was headed. In addition to the construction progress on the Wilson School, the meeting also introduced volunteering opportunities for summer camps and community programs for Broadmoor residents. There was an introduction for the Apex Youth Center, which was run by a couple to address youth development in Broadmoor. Also, one of the volunteer students from Bard College introduced the Wilson summer camp for civic empowerment. In addition to the educational programs run by community members, the BIA hosted social and emotional wellness services. Kyle, one of the interns for the program, came up to "invite you guys, residents, anyone affiliated [with] Broadmoor, those who live, work, and worship in Broadmoor and anyone affiliated with the school to come on board with us and help inform the development of this program because it's for Broadmoor, so we'd like to have Broadmoor as a part of the organization."[51]

Pursuing social resilience was an important part of neighborhood-based recovery. After Kyle's introduction, Cantrell mentioned how these social wellness programs were prepared to meet "the needs of the community" by "providing social services and human services." Furthermore, it was when the president of the BIA delivered the closing speech that the idea of self-reliance clearly sounded synonymous with resilience and self-sustainability:

There is no way that the BIA would go back to where we were pre-Katrina. We just can't. We have started a development corporation, the

Broadmoor Charter School Board, and of course we have the BIA. And so in looking to long-term sustainability, we will be coming before the community and together drafting a plan and a vision for how we are going to be self-sustainable.[52]

Cantrell's remark demonstrated the dedication community leaders had to making the community sustain itself. Not surprisingly, residents' responses to the activities of the BIA were generally positive. While they were invariably critical about the slow and unresponsive government, they found that the BIA effectively filled the gap for services by working closely with residents and solving their issues. Five years after the storm, many blocks in the neighborhood seemed to have returned to pre-Katrina normalcy, and there remained no signs of fierce resistance against the "green dot" plan to turn the community into parkland, except for the occasional banners and pickets that read "Broadmoor Lives"—a phrase coined at the height of the neighborhood reconstruction period to represent the shared community spirit.

The residents I met in casual environments—whether in a backyard, at a cafeteria in their workplace, or inside a home—praised the BIA for getting things done and reaching out to people who did not have the resources to rebuild. Aida Gray, an elderly Black lady who has lived in Broadmoor throughout her life and who runs a nursery at her home, was quite pleased with what the BIA had done for the community:

If you have [a] problem, you call the office and you state your problem, and they handled it. I'm not going to have a bulb in my corner and I didn't like when the guys would get out there and my children or my grandchild would be in the yard, and they'd be cursing and all that, I didn't want it, I didn't buy a house for that. So I called them and they handled it.[53]

For Aida, one of the neighborhood association's most important tasks was to maintain safety and order in her block, and the BIA paid attention to her needs. Although it was not clear exactly how the neighborhood association might have handled the disorderly behaviors, Aida seemed quite happy about the fact that the BIA was responsive to her demands with regards to quieting down the commotion. As I was talking to Aida, her next-door neighbor Larry, a middle-aged White man who runs a construction business, spotted us and made his own interjection. He concurred with Aida and stated, "I think they have been probably the best association in the city. Out of all the city, out of all the associations that I am familiar with, I think the Broadmoor Association is probably the best in getting things done."[54]

The social resilience exhibited by the Broadmoor community stands in sharp contrast to the perceived lack of accountability on the part of the city government. Quite opposite from the positive attitudes toward their neighborhood association, residents showed a high degree of distrust and frustration toward government in general. Even when I did not directly ask about their opinions on government, residents would often jump in to criticize it. Larry, for example, explained how he was at first deemed overqualified for the Road Home grant because of his income but then became eligible for the grant again as the rules changed. While lamenting the inconsistency he experienced with the Road Home grant application process, he stated that he thought government officials were profiteering by delaying the process:

> In the course [of disaster relief], the bureaucrats that managed everything got paid. The longer it took, the harder it was to get things done, they stayed in and got paid. Whereas all of us at the bottom of the—bottom of the food chain, so to speak—didn't get anything.[55]

Because I was not sure about what he meant by "the bureaucrats," I asked for clarification:

AUTHOR: So, by bureaucrats, you mean the federal agents? Or city officials?

LARRY: Yes. All of them, all of them. It makes me worried about [the federal] health care, because what they did to us after Katrina, there's no way you can depend on any of these guys . . . [T]he only way we got along here, the only way most people survived in the city was friends, faith-based organizations, and other volunteers. . . . We had Mormons from Utah. We had, you know, any kind of organizations, we had tourist groups coming down here. We had Christian groups coming here. Lots of Catholic groups. I don't remember any Muslim groups, nah, there's no Muslim groups.[56]

It is interesting to note that Larry drew a comparison between different religious groups, i.e., Christians versus Muslims. Although religion was not part of our initial conversation, Larry frequently mentioned that many of the volunteer organizations were faith-based groups, especially those tied to the Christian tradition. Throughout the interview, he drew an "us versus them" distinction: "us" included the neighbors, BIA, and Christian volunteers, while "them" included government at all levels, Muslims, and (later) the insurance companies.

Broadmoor's Invisible Boundaries

Larry's opinion about "outsiders" resonated with a male participant's comment in the BIA meeting. He similarly expressed concerns about the increasing number of newcomers in the neighborhood. During the meeting, a White, middle-aged resident raised his hand and commented on the changing makeup of the neighborhood:

> So all the people who have been displaced by all the property taken out of public housing with vouchers and moving into different parts of the neighborhood and there's a migration also of people of different backgrounds and cultural backgrounds moving into the neighborhood, there's change in the neighborhood. . . . So you see different people in the neighborhood who once weren't in your block and you don't have no relationship with them because sometimes they are renters, sometimes they are foreigners, and you have some kind of way to interact with those kinds of situations—I'm just putting that on the table.[57]

Indeed, although there was no explicit discussion of race and class within the neighborhood, the repopulation patterns within the neighborhood show that race is indeed a significant factor of the demographic change in the neighborhood (Table 5.1). Overall, Broadmoor lost a third of its Black population (33 percent) between 2000 and 2010, while Whites decreased by 16.9 percent and Hispanics increased by 34.5 percent. Subgroup divisions within the neighborhood further show that the recovery happens more slowly for Black residents than other racial groups. The neighborhood is composed of three subgroups (A, B, and C), which are divided by three major thoroughfares: Fontainebleau, Broad,

TABLE 5.1. Repopulation rates in subgroup areas in Broadmoor.
Source: The Data Center.

	Subgroup A	Subgroup B	Subgroup C	Broadmoor
Population (2010)	1900	2198	1283	5381
% change from 2000	−16.50%	−35.80%	−16.40%	−25.60%
White (% change from 2000)	36% (−18%)	7% (−1%)	55% (−19%)	28.8% (−16.9%)
Black (% change from 2000)	51% (−21%)	86% (−40%)	32% (−22%)	61.1% (−33.0%)
Hispanic (% change from 2000)	8% (+21%)	5% (+64%)	7% (+32%)	6.7% (+34.5%)

and Napoleon Avenues (see Figure 5.2). The uppermost section is subgroup A, the lower right is subgroup B, and the lower left is subgroup C.
Subgroups A and C are racially integrated, and subgroup B is the majority African American area. In terms of population change, subgroup B,
the most populous and heavily African American section, underwent
the most significant population changes. The entire subgroup B shrunk
in its size by 35.8 percent—over twice as much as the other subgroups,
which show—about 16 percent population decrease within the past ten
years. Furthermore, a significant part of the population loss occurred
among Blacks, which diminished by 40 percent from 2000 to 2010. In
the other subgroups, White and Black residents left the neighborhood
at similar rates—around 20 percent—and yet the loss was still more
significant among Black residents, by 2 to 3 percentage point margins.
The Hispanic population has made up for the loss of population in the
neighborhood. They increased in number in each subgroup, especially
in subgroup B.

In addition to seemingly innocuous census tracts, neighborhood
boundaries also resulted in tangible differences when an active neighborhood organization could not extend its assistance to properties outside the
boundaries of the neighborhood. Neighborhood associations work within
clearly demarcated borders, and these borders determine who gets to
enjoy the benefits of successful civic activism and who does not. This distinction was revealed somewhat unexpectedly in the neighborhood meeting I attended on March 15, 2010. Staff at the BDC and the BIA announced
that there would be private funding available to open a coffee shop in their
newly renovated Keller Library; a student volunteer from Bard College
showed a fifteen-minute documentary on what people like about their

BROADMOOR SUBGROUPS

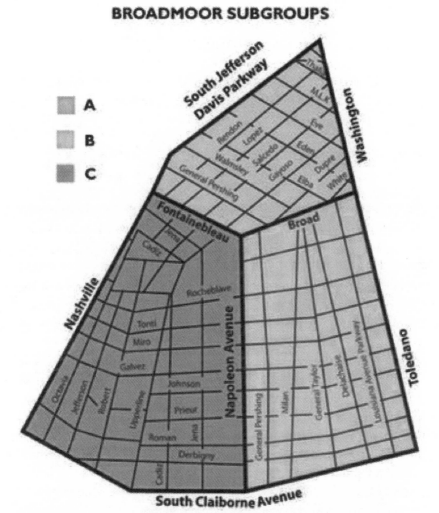

Figure 5.2. Map of Broadmoor. Source: Broadmoor Improvement Association.

neighborhood; and there were also housing swap opportunities between Broadmoor and Gentilly.[58] Then, in the Q and A session, one participant asked a question about whether the BDC could help fix her house:

> PARTICIPANT: What if you, you say ya'll fix our homes? If you have a house and you are not able to come back in the house because it got messed over, how could I get you over and fix the house?

BDC STAFF: Fix your house in Broadmoor?

PARTICIPANT: No, it's ... not IN Broadmoor. It's over down on Jackson [Avenue, in Central City].

STAFF: Okay ... [Audience laughs] The Broadmoor Development Corporation, as much as we wish we could help the entire city, we are bound to the Broadmoor boundaries ... Broadmoor is Claiborne Avenue, Nashville, Toledano [Street], Washington [Street] up to Jeff Davis [Parkway].

PARTICIPANT: Okay, but it don't go to Jackson? Or Claiborne?

AUDIENCE: No ... no ...

The simple question seemed to baffle the staff as well as the attendees in the meeting, one of whom suggested consulting with the property holder's own neighborhood association. The property was located just outside the neighborhood boundaries—Jackson Avenue is about six blocks east of Toledano Street, which is the eastern boundary of the Broadmoor neighborhood. The question caught people's attention because it was asked in a context of staff members reporting significant progress achieved within the community.

The idea of self-governance reached its apex when Broadmoor was designated as the first neighborhood improvement district in Louisiana, in 2010. With a parcel fee of $100 assigned to each property, the BIA could collect those fees from the city government and could spend the money to improve the quality of neighborhood life. In 2015, residents once again renewed its status and voted for renewing the fee, which would amount to $17,000 a year and be used to hire more full-time BIA staff members.[59] Through NID, Broadmoor seeks to become more self-sufficient than before, as the BIA's message shows:

Broadmoor doesn't depend on the kindness of strangers, we depend on our friends, neighbors and families to make "Broadmoor: Better Than Before."[60]

Also called a "business improvement district," the neighborhood improvement district is a quintessential example of neoliberal urban governance, whereby private resources are pooled together to provide services within the designated neighborhood boundaries. To date, more than two dozen such districts are spread out in New Orleans to provide various services from security to streetlights.[61] Providing "club goods" to an exclusive group of residents, these institutions have been known to pose challenges for broader urban integration.[62] Broadmoor's experience shows how the civic victory for achieving community resilience is intertwined with the idea of self-governance as the guiding principle for community development.

The Pursuit of Economic Resilience: Freret

Located south of Broadmoor and close to Tulane and Loyola Universities, Freret was a small neighborhood with a population of 2446 as of 2000.[63] African Americans composed the majority of the population (83 percent), and the neighborhood has historically been a mix of residential and commercial establishments with working- and middle-class families. Since its inception, Freret has embodied a "walking city" model,[64] where homes were built close to each other, sidewalks and streets were often used for social gatherings, and residents were just a short walk away from shops and churches.[65] Thus, residents encountered each other on the streets, in the shops, and on their way to churches and schools. Although Whites and Blacks remained segregated, they still formed a close-knit community—until automobiles and expressways allowed for sprawl and suburban development. Concerned with integrated education and increasing crime, White residents in the neighborhood chose to relocate to the suburbs and turned the area into a majority Black neighborhood.[66]

Compared with the social cohesion in Broadmoor, Freret pursued economic solutions to revitalize the community, and their neighborhood association, the Neighbors United (NU), played a central role. It is a small organization maintained by the residents who work full time as school teachers, architects, and barbers.[67] Compared to the BIA, the NU failed to secure strong leadership to help transform the pre-Katrina informal organizational structure into an institutionalized form of civic power. It took on some of the issues pertaining to neighborhood recovery by participating in the neighborhood redevelopment plan led by the city council (commonly known as the Lambert Plan) after the mayor's rightsizing plan was annulled. However, without the kind of imminent threat of removal that Broadmoor residents had faced, community leaders at the NU did not actively seek external assistance, nor did they create a sophisticated organizational structure to tackle the major issues in redevelopment. I spoke with Andrew Amacker, a young Black man, former vice president of the NU, and a resident of the neighborhood. We met at Village Coffee, one of the new businesses that opened on Freret Street after Katrina. During our conversation, he explained why his organization had not been as successful as the neighboring BIA:[68]

> And I would say, after the storm, even though we didn't have any paid staff, were doing a little bit better than average. You know, we weren't nearly as involved and active as like Broadmoor, and the Phoenix of New Orleans [in Lower Mid-City], or Lakeview Civic [Improvement Association], but you know, we were more like, say, Mid-City Neighborhood [Organization], or Gentilly. But over time, as the planning thing got less and less hot, and people start to drop off, because we were spending a lot of energy doing things instead of recruiting folks, it became harder and harder and harder to do things and keep up.[69]

Andrew deplored the fact that the NU does not have the same amount of financial help as the BIA and saw that as one of the main reasons his organization was unable to keep full-time staff and pursue an agenda like the BIA. As our conversation continued, Andrew, representing Freret, frequently drew a comparison to what was going on in Broadmoor— for him, the financial stability of the BIA meant the ability to sustain the organization and make it more professional than his neighborhood's NU:

> I wish we had some staff, so that way we could help push things a lot further, a lot faster . . . because I know after the storm volunteer groups would say, "Hey, can we do stuff?" And, you know, even though we have things for them to do, we just hadn't sat down to really plan it and think about it because we just didn't have the time. At the same time, I was fixing my house, Jane [a member of the NU] was renovating a rental property, and Dean [president of the NU] teaches, so he's out except for the summers. You know, we all got our day jobs, or daily lives. So it makes it really hard to push more than one or two big things. And, after the storm,

you need to have an organization that could push ten things. You know like Broadmoor, really, if you had the staff, we would have done almost exactly what they did [in Broadmoor], only with more of a commercial emphasis because we have [Freret and Dryades Streets].[70]

In contrast to the BIA's focus on social resilience, economic revitalization was the central topic in this neighborhood meeting. The audience was much smaller than in Broadmoor—fewer than twenty people, all middle-aged adults. The much larger crowd in the Broadmoor neighborhood had a mix of some kids, their parents, and older residents including the former mayor Moon Landrieu and his wife, Verna. Held in a classroom at Samuel J. Green Charter School and presided over by a city council member, the NU meeting simply exhibited a different atmosphere. While the BIA meeting had a very formal structure for a community meeting—reporting on the last meeting followed by the president's welcome address, a treasurer's report, and the Q and A session—the Freret meeting was more informal. It started with a business investor's proposal to open a daiquiri shop on Freret Street. Introducing himself as a father of two girls and living in Metairie, the investor proposed that he and his partner wanted to open it "to revitalize this area. It's really important to attract customers from Tulane and Loyola [Universities] and have businesses that 'make it.'"[71] He tried to convince the participants at the meeting that his daiquiri place would not make the streets dirty and loud, which residents worried most about. Participants at the meeting spent a long time discussing this new business proposal, weighing on its potential benefits against negative impacts. The discussion ended in favor of the proposal, with the condition that the business establishment would abide by the rules that the owner had initially promised, such as keeping noise to a minimum and cleaning to-go cups on the street.

Gentrified Resilience

While new developments and investments were being discussed in Freret, some of the old business owners felt that the neighborhood was undergoing a transition, and that they were not being invited to be a part of the redevelopment. Although Andrew believed that the NU did not do a satisfactory job due to its few staff members and inadequate professionalization, some residents felt that what the NU was doing was too aggressive. Stan Norwood, a barber at Dennis' Barber Shop and longtime resident of the neighborhood, expressed his regrets when I talked to him. While trimming a customer's hair and beard, he told me at length about what he and his friends felt about the neighborhood's landscape after Katrina—as if he had been waiting for this interview for a long time. Contrary to Andrew's observation, Stan felt that the neighborhood was rapidly changing and pointed out that the lack of "personal approach" by the neighborhood association and city government was driving residents out of the neighborhood for redevelopment, blight reduction, and code enforcement:

> We do have it [the Neighbors United] we do know it, but you know, I go to meetings from time to time, and I find information that I can help people who expressed interests in knowing that they have had problems. Because we are here in the barbershop, we find out more information from dealing with people on a personal level that they do. So to a certain extent, the campaign that goes on for blighted properties. My approach, the last meeting I went to, I introduced to them saying, instead of introducing yourself as a neighborhood association to people and saying, "You have to do something with your house. If you don't do something with your house, there is going to be code enforcement. Since the code enforcement is on you, they are going to do adjudicate your property."[72]

In fact, the strong code enforcement and blight reduction was in the neighborhood recovery plan, in which the NU had participated. In this plan, residents wanted to address blighted housing and restrict multifamily residences through zoning enforcement to "protect the neighborhood." According to the neighborhood recovery plan, "the lack of enforcement has resulted in properties that are not well maintained and [have] higher densities than allowed." Addressing blighted housing was the first "critical" project from the survey, followed by street and drainage repairs, policing, and zoning enforcement.[73]

Stan and his patrons were particularly resentful about the insensitivity of the city government in the code enforcement process and the lack of assistance from the neighborhood association with helping people facing penalties for not following the city code. The housing situation was complex for legacy residents whose families had lived in the neighborhood for generations and who might have inherited a house without proper documentation or a title. According to Stan, the NU did not do a good job reaching out and offering help to these people, but rather let the city government enforce codes with brute force:

> But why not approach those people and say, "Here's how we can help you" *first*, "But if you don't do these things, this is what is going to take place"? So my approach is different. We don't know what everybody's personal situation is. You may have lost your siblings, you may have lost your parents, you don't know what the situation is. . . . [But city officials] don't go through the warning process. If I mailed you a letter, the letter says, "Deal with the property." You don't live there—that's your mom's house. So before you start talking to your sister or brother, what are you going to do about this? So instead of them talking to your sister or brother, what are you going to do about this? So instead of them making contact to help get these people [to] gather, get them through succession, or get them to appoint a person [as the owner] and get the information they need to actually fix the house. [However,] they let code enforcement come out first and let the fines build up first. Now you are pushed to do something, or you sign it over. But I can't pay four thousand dollars' worth of fines, and now your house is done. From that point, it's kind of a difficult situation. It's supposed to be a revitalization project to get people to come out and do what they are supposed to do to their property. But the ways they are taking, I don't totally agree.[74]

Given the significance of the barbershop as a place where African Americans go to discuss and share common experiences,[75] these accounts can be said to reliably capture the feelings of those who were excluded from the redevelopment process. They felt that part of the neighborhood became a target rather than a beneficiary of the community development efforts; instead of receiving assistance for comeback and rebuilding, some of the residents were involuntarily driven out of the neighborhood due to strict code enforcement by the city and neighborhood associations after the hurricane. For Stan and his clients at the barbershop, the neighborhood felt different than before, and the whole process of code enforcement and blight reduction did not consider or sympathize with the difficulties that the residents had with returning to and rebuilding their houses. Although Stan is a homeowner, has a stable job, and thus had no difficulty in coming back to New Orleans after the storm, he shared the stories of his neighbors who could not make it back to their homes and who received little help from the government or the community. While I was talking with Stan, some of the customers at the barbershop who were waiting to get a haircut told him to talk about their experiences with relocation, contractor fraud, and police brutality. For many of them, post-Katrina recovery did not mean returning to the old and familiar neighborhood. Rather, it ushered in a new yet different community:

> RESIDENT A: [The] neighborhood now feels different. To a certain extent it is better, but it is not better for the people who [used to] live here. Because the information, the help, is more readily available to the people that are not from the neighborhood than is to the people who have already been there. . . . We had to read the newspaper to find out that the Freret Street Business[men's] Association [was] given a five-hundred-thousand-dollar grant. We [the barbershop] have been here forty-eight years . . . but we didn't really know who the business association was because there was only three people. Post-Katrina people. You know what I mean? We did not know them at first, we didn't know them at all. We know them now, but they have their own set of agenda. . . . There are now more new people and things are not what it used to be. . . . We [old residents] all have the connection. We all have the same issues. To some, there is so much progression going on, and there is. There is a lot of progression going on. But at the same time, there was a transition that brings people from elsewhere, [and] for those people the progression is ten times better than those who were already here. But that information you find out after it is done. You know what I mean? So that is just how it is, unless some things are done purposely that way.[76]

To old residents, the revamped civic association seemed to serve the interests of "post-Katrina people" who were believed to bring capital and business and thus revitalize the neighborhood. Indeed, after Katrina, the neighborhood experienced an economic boost along its commercial corridor. New retail businesses—a juice shop, coffee shop, and po'boy place, to name a few—opened and occupied almost every block on Freret Street, and the property values and rents also increased.[77] During the "Freret renaissance," old residents felt that Katrina had accelerated gentrification by driving out old tenants and businesses. Thus, long-time residents of Freret had to witness the dislocation of some of their favorite places. Dunbar's Famous Creole Cuisine, for example, a beloved soul food restaurant that had operated on Freret Street since the early 1990s, was heavily flooded by Katrina. Celestine Dunbar, the owner of the restaurant, tried to resume business on Freret Street, but between the increased rent and the cost of repairs she could not afford to return to her original location.[78] Instead, after a brief reopening in the cafeteria of Loyola University Law School in Uptown, the restaurant finally got back to full business in Gert Town, a neighborhood north of Broadmoor.[79] Stan sounded angry when he talked about this:

> She [the councilwoman] is more interested in bringing other people than introducing those opportunities to people who are already here. Okay? Ms. Dunbar, who's been around the corner for years, she's in Loyola now. Like I said, the same way brought in from somewhere else, help Ms. Dunbar who's been here twenty years. She's not going to come back? No, she gave up on us. That's what we are talking about. That's the prime example. Ms. Dunbar, she attended a couple of meetings, and again, nobody stopped and gave her assistance, she got taken by a contractor at one point, and nobody did anything to help her. So before getting completely frustrated now they are actually trying to find Dunbar's code enforcement.[80]

Rick Torres, a middle-aged White man who inherited his father's hardware shop on Freret Street and has been running it for almost thirty years, was skeptical about the future of his business because he believed that the street would not be able to resist the natural degradation it had been experiencing prior to Katrina:

> I kind of have a pessimistic attitude about it to a certain extent. . . . About the street and the city. . . . [C]ertain parts of the city, like the French Quarter, [have] tourism. But there is no tourism here so it's hard here. [College students] used to come here years ago. We don't get any

more students. They are mobile. They are going anywhere. They go to Walmart, Home Depot, et cetera. Evolution of this type of business is changing. In large metropolitan cities, the small, independent, mom-and-pop type hardware store is endangered. It's changed because of the big boxes. They can do things I can't do. . . . They just dominate with advertising. . . . So this type of business is a dying breed. People are changing. They are not as friendly as they used to be. The future is very, very [uncertain].[81]

Much like Stan, Rick also realized that the neighborhood had changed as new types of clients and businesses flowed in. However, contrary to Stan—who drew a distinction between pre- and post-Katrina people—Rick viewed the change as part of a larger, macroeconomic transition and therefore was more accepting of the fact that his hardware store might be phased out. While Broadmoor residents seek self-sustainability through a highly formalized structure and various community development programs, people in Freret lack sufficient resources to pursue many of the community programs in a way that Broadmoorians do. Instead, the neighborhood focused on economic revitalization and invited new people into the area. Freret's boundary, in this sense, was more porous than that of Broadmoor's, but not enough to benefit the group of people who were most affected by the storm.[82]

Conclusion

This chapter connects post-Katrina civic resilience with the norm of self-governance that had permeated the city prior to the disaster. The norm of self-governance did not emerge abruptly as a response to the hurricane; rather, it runs parallel to the changing landscape of community-based movements in American cities, which have shifted from political advocacy to economic development, from inclusive politics to exclusive.[83] Through various means of private governance, such as designating themselves as improvement districts or financing their own security, neighborhoods gradually established their own exclusive identities with varying degrees of success. Katrina accelerated this process because it added a civic dimension and moral imperative to the privatized mode of redevelopment. Without being criticized as business-oriented or of gentrifying old communities, post-Katrina neighborhoods could pursue private governance because the need for protecting properties and territory was politically meaningful and desirable to many.

The gradual shift from community organizing to community development in local neighborhood movements continues to define the tone of post-disaster recovery in two main ways. First, the lauded emphasis on community-based redevelopment in fact separates, rather than unites, the city. The "civic jealousy" that Ford mentioned in the beginning of the chapter is relevant in this context. While communities with rich civic resources could focus on internal improvement and solicited satisfaction from residents, neighborhoods with weaker civic bases neither enjoyed the benefits of self-governance nor of government assistance. Second, the drive toward community development makes intra-community vulnerabilities less visible. The focus on neighborhood improvement, via civic and economic projects, ended up disadvantaging many of the neighborhoods' oldest and poorest residents, who did not have the independent means to maintain their damaged properties and thus faced an imminent threat of eviction and demolition. Although housing abandonment was a chronic problem in New Orleans even before Katrina, much of the community rebuilding and recovery focused on blight reduction and code enforcement. As a result, the most vulnerable segment of the population—which the community is supposed to include and represent well—became the target, rather than the beneficiary, of redevelopment efforts. Interpreting resilience as self-reliance validated the pursuit of neighborhood-based recovery as a desirable post-storm recovery strategy because neighborhoods, after all, had to organize themselves as they knew they could not seek support from a decimated city government.

These observations take us back to the central question of this book: whether resilient communities make for a resilient city. The answer is: not always. Without strong government capacity, active local communities only play a limited role in promoting the city's well-being. The various dimensions of civic activism and resilience examined in this chapter show that the hardest problems for the city to solve are still untouched, and that individual actions by local communities may deepen, rather than heal, preexisting chasms that threaten to undercut the city's sustainable future.

Conclusion

Rethinking Civic Capacity and Urban Resilience

This book has discussed how New Orleans has tried to recover from a natural disaster, but it is not primarily dedicated to the understanding of natural catastrophe. Rather, this book uses the example of Hurricane Katrina, as an unprepared-for disruption, to reveal the underlying dilemmas surrounding attempts at urban regeneration. For one, cities have a great potential for recovery because they attract talent, promote innovation, and produce cultural capital.[1] However, the socioeconomic conditions in cities generate various issues that are different from those in nonurban areas and may prohibit cohesive reconstruction. Urban social ills, such as fragmented and underfunded governmental offices, poverty, and high crime rates, can make it difficult to establish a comprehensive plan that can satisfy residents, politicians, and investors simultaneously. Furthermore, unlike suburban neighborhoods—which have more or less homogenous social fabrics—cities boast racial and economic diversity as a source of urban innovation and cultural richness, and yet such varied demographics may also undermine trust among people from different groups and dampen participation in public matters in times of crisis.[2] As much as cities have a wide range of human and physical resources, the deleterious impact of disasters, should they occur, can be much more far-reaching than what would be expected in less-populous areas.

In addition to diversity, a city's concentrated resources make disaster recovery a costly enterprise. Destruction of dense buildings and infrastructure directly aggravates the life chances of city dwellers and seriously weakens the liveliness of a city, and it takes a long time to repair the physical damages and regain the vibrancy it once enjoyed. After Katrina, it was suggested that an estimated $200 billion would be needed to rebuild New Orleans, which amounts to more than $400,000 per person at pre-hurricane population levels.[3] Furthermore, the uncertainty and unpredictability associated with disasters contribute to public health issues that can be difficult to treat, such as mental distress, depression, and anxiety. In addition to the psychological impacts, preexisting social ills—urban poverty, inequality, political corruption, and so forth—are laid bare and further compromise the recovery process. The economic and psychological consequences of natural disasters are interlaced with the city's structural constraints, and these structural deficiencies, fatally exposed in the wake of a disaster, impede the city's recovery efforts.

Given the many obstacles that municipalities must overcome after a disaster, local communities that are active in social and political arenas have a greater potential for adding population and gaining access to better services, even after accounting for their racial or economic differences. In other words, civic capacity boosts loyalty among community members and therefore encourages "voice" rather than "exit." As Albert Hirschman famously argued, people either choose to remain in their original community or leave it, and those with limited options—lower income and less mobility, for example—tend to stay and make their demands known.[4] This explains why, rather than moving elsewhere, many residents chose to mobilize preexisting organizations to reinvest in their original communities, and this process was often more efficient and effective than trying to recover as individuals. The corollary is that in a city with limited political and economic resources, communities can be a good alternative to government agencies for promoting redevelopment.

However, instead of extolling the universal merits of civic engagement, this book takes a cautionary approach and delves into various contexts in which positive and negative attributes of civic capacity can take place simultaneously. Drawing upon the distinction between community resilience and urban resilience laid out in chapter 1, this book demonstrates how civic capacity at the community level, and the success thereof, compromises the pursuit of resilience at a greater spatial scale. Compared to the similar preferences of community members to physically rebuild their own neighborhoods as quickly as possible, a city government must confront a variety of factors that may ultimately force it to prioritize some neighborhoods over others. Facing the long-term challenges of climate change, coastal cities must deal with improving their ecological conditions. Theoretically, the plan to adjust the size of the city involves *Rethinking Community Resilience*, and must account for the instability of community-based reconstruction. With widening inequality and compartmentalized recovery, I show that the city's post-Katrina topography still contains signs of social, economic, and geographic vulnerabilities.

The subsequent chapters presented empirical evidence on the uneven consequences of post-Katrina rebuilding. Chapter 2 offers an important context showing how federal disaster policy was designed to incentivize local actors to invest in economic development without considering its long-term consequences. I then juxtapose the dual effects of civic activism, whereby some neighborhoods enjoy the benefits of active engagement while others are left with unbalanced and undercoordinated redevelopment. For example, tracking the patterns of building permit issuance, chapter 3 shows that pre-Katrina civic engagement affected neighborhood residential reconstruction by facilitating the speed and frequency of government service delivery. This chapter also found that, as a result, the city ultimately lost its hold on controlling the pace and scope of rebuilding and thus witnessed patchworked patterns of reconstruction. Furthermore, chapter 4 describes the ways in which civically oriented recovery may exacerbate any preexisting problems of vulnerability and inequality rather than remedy them. Communities with geographic vulnerabilities—those located below sea level and exposed to the risk of hurricanes, flooding, and land subsidence—had also endured socioeconomic disadvantages such as depopulation, deinstitutionalization, and disinvestment, and this chapter found that revitalizing these communities through rebuilding may ultimately place them at greater risk. Not only have the low-lying neighborhoods become more vulnerable than their above-sea-level counterparts, they have also attracted more socially vulnerable demographics, rendering an already disadvantaged group further exposed to poverty, immobility, and flood risks. This chapter also points out that federal disaster programs, designed to compensate victims based on the pre-disaster market values of their damaged properties, inadvertently retained the residents who could only afford to return to the city's most precarious areas. In this sense, the role of civic capacity is more complex and variegated than being uniformly positive or negative. Although civic capacity helped provide people with the freedom to return and rebuild, the communal structure and civic actions fundamentally changed the social landscape of the city in a way that concentrates disadvantages in the city's vulnerable areas. As climate change continues to increase the frequency of catastrophes such as hurricanes and flooding, active civic participation in these communities may disproportionately jeopardize those who returned to high-risk areas, which will ultimately weaken the entire city's resilience.

The limited purchase of civic-oriented recovery does not only manifest itself in the city's most vulnerable communities, but it also creates tension within and between communities that have successfully rebuilt themselves. Chapter 5 demonstrates that the idea and practice of post-Katrina community development were part and parcel of the city's historically decentralized governance. When recovery outputs tend to be shared within, rather than beyond, preexisting neighborhood boundaries, the city's disadvantaged subpopulations such as the old, the poor, and renters, who are mostly African Americans, do not enjoy the fruits of redevelopment as much as their neighbors—homeowners and people with stable incomes and employment—would. As Stan Norwood's poignant comment reminds us, community organizers and city officials paid attention to blight reduction and economic revitalization but not so much to bringing back friends and family, who faced the dual difficulty of losing their homes and their old community at the same time. Even though some returned to the same geographical place, the changing look and feel of neighborhoods meant that they needed to make additional efforts to resettle themselves back into their neighborhoods. Stan's casual observation corroborates the quantitative findings that social vulnerabilities and racial sorting across the city's communities intensified in the low-lying parts of the city, creating a two-tiered city in which the socioeconomic disadvantages are stratified based on geographic vulnerabilities.

In addition to documenting the persistent effect of civic capacity on the communities' social and demographic landscape, each chapter in this book reveals various ways in which civic activism was intertwined with the direction, scope, and duration of government policies. Chapter 2 shows how local preferences for structural protection have become embedded in the design and structure of disaster policies under our federalist framework. As the smallest social units, neighborhoods are spatially embedded in larger political jurisdictions from local to federal government. Each layer of government assumes different functions to ensure the safety and prosperity of local communities, and yet the protective and compensatory responsibilities for post-disaster relief were mainly undertaken by the federal government,[5] rendering local government and neighborhoods motivated to rebuild after repeated disasters. The political effect of citizen actions was all the more direct and visible at the local level. In chapter 3, an important precondition for haphazard redevelopment was considered, namely the failure of government planning at the early stage of recovery. The city's selective rebuilding approaches, such as the building moratorium and the green dot plan to turn neighborhoods into parkland, were highly debated and eventually canceled, as citizens disagreed with the shrinking of the city proper. Instead, active civic participation facilitated permit issuance in some areas but muted a discussion on the wisdom of reconstructing flood-prone areas. Civically active communities successfully exploited the weaknesses of an underfunded city government and enjoyed greater access to its permit-granting service regardless of their location, which then led to a redevelopment of the city's vulnerable areas. Furthermore, the civic demands for building permits only reinforced the preexisting view on the limited role of the government discussed in chapter 2, because the heightened civic actions justified the view that government should pursue protection and compensation rather than prevention and regulation in making and implementing disaster policies.

In assessing the values of civic capacity, this book compels us to recalibrate the spectrum of civic activism. The meaning of civic-mindedness in a post-crisis context not only reflects the collective desire to return home, but the intent to protect and try to rebuild communities *as they were before the disaster*. This means that, like those on the lower ground who want their community back, residents on higher ground may also have a strong preference for restoring and protecting their own neighborhoods so life can resume as normal. The shared preferences for restoration left the former with limited options, who might have wished to move to a higher ground but could not due to limited financial capacity, and led to the not-in-my-backyard type of civic response from other neighborhoods. The broad-based public opposition to concentrated, compact redevelopment constrained the opportunities to build smaller but safer and more integrated communities. Without a strong government's proactive measures to assist in their relocation, the already disadvantaged population may end up being stuck in place while continuously exposed to natural hazards. Therefore, questioning the merits of civic power does not and should not mean desensitizing race and class issues. Instead, we find that racial and economic disparities continue to exist in a spatially entrenched form, even within resilient communities.

Resilience and Urban Democracy

This friction resulting from civic engagement touches upon a fundamental dilemma of democratic governance: to what extent we should follow what the public wants if it's uncertain whether popular demand actually produces what is good for the public? To this query, this book offers a sobering response. The rise of civic power as a crucial source of self-governance and recovery is certainly a welcome trend for democratic governance.[6] When people participate voluntarily in organizational activities, they develop greater trust, happiness, and understanding of each other.[7] As seen in chapter 5, promoting self-help and self-governance within communities seems an ideal way to achieve procedural justice and promote democracy at the local level, as community members can become active agents of local governance by deciding democratically such things as how to clean streets, when to hold block parties, and whether to approve the opening of a liquor store around the corner. What this book suggests, however, is that these democratic modes of local governance are necessary but not sufficient conditions for accomplishing equitable outcomes and overcoming a perpetual problem like cyclical disasters.

Evidence from this book advises caution against relegating decisions for recovery solely to citizens and their collective units. The "right to the city" approach,[8] which refers to people's collective assertions to claim urban space and resist market-oriented urbanization, emphasizes democratic inclusion and social justice in the process of post-disaster redevelopment.[9] While this approach certainly highlights the oft-neglected aspect of inequity in post-disaster recovery, it tends to gloss over the fact that in claiming the right to a city *in decline*, the normative imperative of civic empowerment may actually be detrimental to the well-being of the city's most disadvantaged population. Given that the poor are more likely to reside in geographically risky areas and the poorest citizens are more likely to claim or cling to property rights in order to protect what they do own, even if in disaster-prone communities, the greater the risk and vulnerability they tend to assume in their area. This will only increase the extent of devastation when the next cycle of natural disasters strikes. Furthermore, the uneven distribution of civic capacity is directly linked to the uneven distribution of resilience and vulnerability across the city. When recovery efforts are based in communities, these neighborhood-based activities are likely to widen the gap between the city's safe areas and risky areas, resulting in a bifurcated city structure.

Furthermore, as we saw in chapter 5, transitioning from neighborhood resilience to urban resilience is not a self-evident process, as the boundary between civic and private governance is narrow at best. Empowering communities, in this sense, does not always lead to empowering the vulnerable, disadvantaged groups within a neighborhood's boundaries. Also, community-based revitalization may not have diffusive effects across neighborhood boundaries. The comparative perspective in chapter 5 sheds a slightly skeptical light on otherwise well-meaning, constructive neighborhood efforts.

The request for equitable recovery may reinforce, rather than delegitimize, the political promise of the elites that the residents often criticize as too corrupt or self-interested. Politicians often make strong claims for the right to return to the damaged neighborhoods "without making the kinds of concrete political commitments that would enable the return of citizens to a viable, sustainable urban environment with effective services, low crime, cherished neighborhood life, and vibrant economy."[10] Without sensible planning strategies, fighting to rebuild vulnerable areas in the name of social justice may turn out to be more detrimental to the displaced population than relocating them into a safer area and shrinking the city's overall footprint. In addressing the unequal distribution of geographic opportunities, therefore, citizen empowerment—not just of the wealthy but also of average residents—and the following political actions do not always lead to better outcomes for those who are in spatially disconnected and organizationally deinstitutionalized neighborhoods.

Conceptual Guidance for Resilience

Considering the political implications of civic engagement leaves us with a question about how we can design a political framework that can effectively distribute limited resources and coordinate the varied interests of individuals and their communities. The difficulty in resolving conflicting interests among civic actors results from different conceptual approaches to community and urban resilience. To reconcile the tension, this section introduces two ideas that help bridge the gap: legitimate coercion[11] and the formation of a resilience regime. On the one hand, legitimate coercion reinstates the traditional role of government as an institution tasked with enforcing societal rules and solving collective action problems, but with the willing consent of the governed. On the other hand, the very notion of a "resilience regime" suggests a means for affecting legitimate coercion. Stemming from the urban regime analysis,[12] a "resilience regime" refers to a durable coalition of various stakeholders organized around resilience-building as a central agenda for the cites. In essence, these concepts call for understanding post-crisis rebuilding as a *political* process, in which the power of civic capacity is complemented by the governing capacity of the corresponding political institutions.

Legitimate coercion refers to the government's ability to impose restrictions on individual and collective liberty, with an informed and willing consent of the people governed under the jurisdiction.[13] It also means investing resources in strengthening the coercive capacity of the city government and inducing negotiation and cooperation from independent actors. In fact, our everyday engagement with the government could be seen as a form of coercion, as it is the traditional role of the government to give permissions and enforce sanctions, which include policing, taxation, and permit issuance, to name a few. When it comes to post-crisis resilience building, however, the degree of coercion required can be more extensive than what we conventionally conceive of as day-to-day government services. For instance, the city government may persuade residents in the high-risk areas allow it to buy out their properties and help them move to safer neighborhoods. At the same time, the government may encourage housing construction in the safe neighborhoods to accommodate this population influx at a price the refugee residents can afford while negotiating with those who want to preserve the character of the neighborhood. If the negotiation does not work, then the government may enforce sanctions, claim eminent domain, or declare a land-use change to induce contribution from all residents in the area.

Some might interpret legitimate coercion by the public authorities as equivalent to the abuse of power by big government, but the exercise of authority does not have to mean a heavy-handed encroachment of personal freedom by the state. Just as civic capacity is not always benign, coercion does not always entail curtailing individual freedom. As undemocratic as it may sound, coercing people out of harm's way can be as important as protecting land, home, and community. Furthermore, as a counterweight to coercive power, establishing legitimacy is equally important when it comes to bringing interested parties to the negotiating table. For example, persuading people on the higher ground, who are likely middle- to higher-income households, to help build low-income, assisted housing in their community, can be part of the negotiating process that involves coercion as a last resort. These types of coercion will become increasingly necessary as cities like New Orleans try to adjust their size to adapt to the changing climate and/or a shrinking economy. By rethinking civic capacity in this context, we can broaden our conception of resilience beyond communities so that it encompasses more inclusive and adaptive practices to respond to what lies ahead.

According to Jane Mansbridge, the long tradition of resistance, developed especially in the Western world, contributes to inaction by "resisting, rather than using, coercion."[14] Resistant action, however, does not always yield a democratic outcome, as it fails to solve collective action problems that are common in a democratic society. Therefore, she further argues, democratic action should incorporate resistance but should not be governed by it. Although Mansbridge presented this argument in a broader context,[15] her main idea still rings true for the discussion on urban resilience, as it requires various sorts of collective action to mitigate and adapt to natural threats while maintaining the economic prospects of the overall city.

A good example of legitimate coercion happened over twenty years ago, in a town in the American Midwest. Dennis Knobloch, the mayor of Valmeyer, Illinois, successfully mobilized residents to relocate to the higher ground after the Great Midwest Flood of 1993.[16] Located just east of the Mississippi River, this small town of about twelve hundred people experienced massive flooding that ran as high as twenty feet and lingered for several weeks. Instead of rebuilding their flooded town, residents in Valmeyer decided to move the entire village to higher ground and rebuild their community anew. In so doing, they used financial assistance from the same federal government agencies that reimbursed Katrina's damages, but in a different way. Families sold their damaged houses to FEMA and combined the proceeds with payments from the NFIP, Small Business Association loans, and their savings to create a new community.

Admittedly, Valmeyer's achievement would be more complicated for larger cities to accomplish. Compared to small-town politicians who work with relatively few people under homogeneous settings, city leaders often must address a larger and more heterogeneous demographic as well as multiple local community groups with disparate interests.[17] For a deeply divided city like New Orleans, it would be difficult, or at least challenging, for local political entrepreneurs to muster enough political power to influence the course of debate in favor of retreat or rightsizing, not to mention enforcing these policy goals.

New Orleans's government did not have sufficient resources or authority to enforce such legitimate coercion for its post-Katrina governance.[18] Instead, an incompetent government fueled reactionary community-based activities based in part on a long history of citizen distrust. Combined with declining economic conditions, entrenched political corruption and nepotism eroded public trust and raised uncertainties about the prospect of government-led post-disaster plans. Louisiana, after all, has one of the lowest levels of trust in state government[19] and is one of the most corrupt American states.[20] The degree of patronage, corruption, and nepotism has been notably extensive in the region, the most recent example being ex-mayor Ray Nagin's federal conviction and ten-year jail sentence for bribery and money laundering related to post-Katrina reconstruction projects.[21] As distrust grew among residents who witnessed the rent-seeking behaviors of public officials, citizens refused to support policies that could have strengthened the city's mitigation capacity in the long term but might place a rein upon their property rights. A core objective of individuals and their collective entities was to protect their homes and communities from external or governmental interventions—federal, state, or local.

The more people share communitarian ideals and advocate for small, self-governing communities, the more likely they are to believe that their immediate social circles, such as families and communities, are better agents of post-crisis rebuilding than governmental agencies. This belief, or norm of behavior, further reinforces the idea that it is in their best interest to protect and preserve their communities. Thus, the (relatively) small group that bears the immediate cost of building resilience, usually neighborhoods, is likely to become cohesive while the rest of the citizenry, though large in number, may remain under-organized. It is more difficult, therefore, to make residents participate in a citywide discussion than to have them organize neighborhood meetings to discuss how to rebuild a single community.

The idea of legitimate coercion is closely related to the urban regime framework in which negotiation, persuasion, and coercion may occur in urban settings. As a durable political arrangement among various stakeholders, the concept of regime is widely discussed in urban politics, and there are several advantages to considering the concept as a politically feasible alternative for building resilience in urban context. First, contrary to the traditional notion of political power as controlling other parties' behavior or interests, the regime concept emphasizes the "capacity" dimension of power, thus taking a pragmatic approach to achieving certain goals set by stakeholders.[22] This approach resonates with the primary objective of legitimate coercion: solving collective action problems to secure free-access goods.[23] Here, the coercive function of the government does not aspire to domination and control but aims at inducing compliance and consensus to resolve an underlying conflict of interests. In this context, communities with a strong civic capacity are less concerned with resistance or protesting against the government action than with turning their energies to demanding an equally powerful position as that of the privileged actors.

Another advantage of regime is its durability. Once formed, a regime is relatively stable and tends to withstand the changes in city administration, which is important in not only building but also maintaining a long-term initiative for urban resilience. Of course, reconceptualizing resilience as a coordination rather than a development issue will take a tremendous effort on the part of politicians, developers, and citizens—none of whom can expect to see immediate benefits from curtailing the pace and scope of economic development. And yet, as described in the introduction, the historical patterns of urban decline suggest that economic development alone cannot guarantee the sustainability, or even existence, of a city. As Colten suggests, "The economic depictions [in New Orleans] . . . do not factor in the costs borne by the city and its private and corporate citizens to make a site suitable for economic development."[24] Therefore, a paradigmatic shift that reformulates disaster response from protection to adaptation—from redevelopment to adjustment—is necessary.

Policy Guidance for Resilience

To apply these political concepts, I suggest four policy measures to reframe the direction of post-disaster policies and maximize the capacity of local governments to invest in long-term resilience-building. First, in order for citizens to accept and promote a realistic portrait of the city's future, more systematic efforts should be made to restore trust between the citizenry and all levels of government. Trust has long been considered as the linchpin of the long-term health of a political system.[25] As we saw in New Orleans, a lack of trust can dampen the potential for any long-term policy measures initiated by the government. In the aftermath of Hurricane Katrina, low levels of political trust among the victims led to a more pessimistic projection of the communities' potential for recovery, which suggests that the explosive civic engagement may have come from people's cynicism and distrust of the government rather than from hopeful, voluntary motivations for the good of their community.[26] As stated earlier, reactive, resistant civic activism makes it difficult for the government to exercise legitimate coercion. As conventional as it may sound, building trust is one of the most baseline tasks for federal, state, and local governments to embark on in long-term hazard mitigation.

Second, it is necessary to strengthen the bureaucratic capacity of the city government. After Katrina, it was not only the political malfeasance but also the bureaucratic failure that was frequently mentioned as the cause for eroding public trust for government. The cumulative results of poor government performance—not fixing streetlights, removing debris, or issuing repair permits, for example—add up to undermine the continuity and legitimacy of government policies, including comprehensive urban planning.[27] As such, improving the performative record of bureaucratic officials can not only enhance public trust for the city government but also provide strong support for the planning authorities' efforts to implement plans for long-term hazard mitigation. A capable bureaucracy, for example, can implement innovative citywide planning strategies, such as a land swap program that offer displaced residents with an option to sell their properties and rebuild elsewhere.[28] Led by a nonprofit organization called Project Home Again, land swaps showed success in select neighborhoods by helping residents relocate from below sea level to above. Expanding such a program to the entire city requires a competent bureaucratic organization.

Furthermore, strengthening the bureaucratic capacity is particularly important given the policy characteristics of hazard mitigation. Hazard mitigation can be classified as a coercive policy that imposes severe costs for its targets—residents in high-risk areas—whereby the affected citizens are likely to organize to take political action and pressure political elites.[29] Since climate adaptation is likely to require resettlement for part of the city's subpopulation, it is important to consider how to implement it in an effective but nonconflictual manner. To the extent that bureaucrats are not regarded as shirkers but as capable workers, scholars propose to insulate the bureaucrats from the influence and pressure of their legislative principals.[30] After Katrina, many planning experts mentioned the difficulty of persuading and communicating with the public, partly because of the way in which local politicians distanced themselves from the planning officials to curry favor with voters. Also, the short tenure and nonlocal recruitment of planning officials tends to weaken the discretionary power of the planning department in the city's governance structure. The merits of democratic accountability notwithstanding, it may be a good idea to diffuse the decision-making power from the elected officials (both the mayor or the city council) to experts and establish bureaucratic autonomy.

Third, a resilience regime should incorporate the concepts of resilience and adaptation into the development agenda and organize the political arrangements accordingly. While this may seem obvious, urban regimes have traditionally pursued economic development by encouraging the cooperation of private actors and forging public–private partnerships. Under this assumption, pro-growth policies were intended to encourage private investment. However, we have learned that such a growth-oriented arrangement is no longer feasible in many declining cities, including New Orleans. A new resilience regime should thus employ a renewed perspective on growth, and the constituents of the regime need to build consensus on compact, sustainable development. For example, the city could redefine itself as an innovative urban center for climate adaptation and form public–private partnerships for equitable and sustainable development. To this end, the resilience regime should not be a short-term policy experiment but a sustaining, durable arrangement that leads to positive externalities—employment, revenue, and infrastructural improvement—so that the economic and environmental challenges can turn into development opportunities.

Finally, in the long run, it will be beneficial to participate in and mobilize a global network of cities to disseminate ideas about strengthening the regulatory framework for tackling urban crises. Despite the unique cultural and historical characteristics of each city, there exist considerable similarities in terms of the climatic and economic vulnerabilities facing cities around the world. For example, all coastal cities are dealing with common threats from global warming and rising sea levels, and an inter-city network would help these cities to develop appropriate policies and transfer necessary technologies for climate adaptation. In fact, there are examples of this happening already, for example how climate experts in Rotterdam have shared their flood mitigation solutions with New Orleans and New York.[31] Likewise, shrinking cities can be found in America's Rust Belt as well as in postindustrial cities in Europe and Asia. These cities are also undergoing population and infrastructural decline, revenue shortages, and increasing competition with their neighbor cities. In sharing experiences and expertise with the cities undergoing crisis, a global network allows for seeking bottom-up solutions that can tackle the fundamental causes of urban crises. Furthermore, alongside technical transfers, there could also be an active discussion on minimizing societal conflicts while implementing the adaptation and smart growth strategies.

Resilience, Decline, and the Future of American Cities

Cities matter. Just as the United States is not just a sum of fifty states but an institution of its own, a city is greater than the sum of its communities and has a system that performs exclusive and independent functions from its subordinate entities. As a political unit, a city maintains legislative, executive, and judicial branches, elects officials, and provides city services. As an economic unit, a city competes with neighboring municipalities to attract more taxpayers and businesses. As a social unit, many cities cultivate unique cultural and historical identities by which their residents often distinguish themselves from other city dwellers as do New Yorkers, Chicagoans, or New Orleanians. Therefore, while the basic meaning of resilience is shared to define community or urban resilience, solutions to achieve resilience can be vastly different.

In the domestic context, stories of post-Katrina recovery offer lasting lessons for politicians and policymakers who govern cities in decline but who may be reluctant to embrace shrinkage as a reality. Thus far, urban development largely meant territorial expansion and agglomeration, and increasing economic capacity and land value constituted a core of urban policy decisions. Scholarly works on urban political economy also followed this direction. Urban sociologists John Logan and Harvey Molotch,[32] for example, called a city "a growth machine" in their book *Urban Fortunes*. Viewed as a growth machine, cities are a place where public and private actors strive to increase land values, expropriate rents through speculation, and earn profits. Cities exist to serve the material interests of private developers and investors, and this pursuit of material gains distorts the balance between exchange value and use value of place.[33] In a similar vein, political scientist Paul Peterson, in his *City Limits*, also argued that local governments, because of the possibility of individual mobility and inter-city competition, must pursue economic prosperity as their primary goal instead of redistribution.[34] While the federal government can control the flow of human migration, city governments are weak political entities that cannot regulate the mobility of people and industries. To attract more resources, Peterson shows, local governments implement policies that encourage development and investment in terms of tax abatement, infrastructure building, and so forth. Normatively, *Urban Fortunes* and *City Limits* advance different claims about the role of cities; while Logan and Molotch criticize the city's function as a growth machine, Peterson sees the pursuit of growth as an inevitable fate of local governments. However, these two views commonly define urban development as a process of physical and financial expansion, by transforming land use from rural to urban, building more roads and high-rise buildings, and attracting businesses and workers.

But to what extent can cities continue to expand? Despite, or because of, the past focus on economic development and competition, cities are now facing new challenges that ultimately redefine the very notion of development. On the one hand, Rust Belt cities have gradually eroded. Population decrease, financial deficit, and downtown ghettoization are the telltale signs of urban decline, and these cities are hard-pressed to find ways to address blight and degradation while still maintaining sustainability and attractiveness. On the other hand, Sun Belt cities have begun to experience the negative externalities of rapid expansion and sprawl, such as gentrification, traffic congestion, and unbridled land conversion. The common conceptual solution that cuts through cities at both ends is "managed growth."[35] Managed growth encourages a more centralized form of development, by which a city continues to pursue economic, social, and cultural vibrancy but directs development to locations where public services can be provided more efficiently. Managed growth is the aim of many urban policies that strive to transform a city into a more resilient system that does not just boost economic affluence but also enhances sustainability and competitiveness in the long run.

In both cases, how to manage decline or growth is an important question to urban policymakers, and resilience is a useful context in which to frame the question. To fortify the resilience of a city, this book suggests that there must be a broad consensus on the sustainable and efficient urban form as a path to redevelopment. On the one hand, residents should be aware of the possibility that they might have to concede property rights to ensure public health and the safety of all citizens. On the other hand, politicians and policymakers have a responsibility to devise a sustainable and equitable long-term plan, and more importantly, to communicate with citizens about the need to sacrifice short-term interests for the benefit of the city.[36] One big mistake made by those involved in post-Katrina planning was that they failed to frame long-term resilience as a winning strategy for all. Instead, the issue was quickly politicized and strategic shrinkage in professional parlance was translated into "shrinking the footprint," which made people question whether New Orleans was worth rebuilding at all.[37] Given the disparity between what policymakers and citizens think is a "resilient city," public resistance is not a surprise but an expected outcome. When I asked what some of the greatest challenges were in working with residents and their representatives, city official Jason Abate responded without hesitation:

> Education. Just letting them know what we were doing, what needed to be done, how long it would take, and trying to assuage their angst about, you know, getting things done. We were working on the project but the process, it does take time. . . . Sometimes the patience of the constituents is just absolutely worn thin. They just can't, they would just call and swear, they'll curse you out, and sometimes that's okay. They just curse and then they calm down, and then they just want to get that hole fixed, that sewage problem to be taken care of. Or the streetlight fixed. Or they want to stop criminals, you know. So it's a process of trying to educate the citizenry as to what happens and what the process is, and constant, constant follow-up is a big help. If we can provide constant follow-up to citizens, they are reassured greatly about that somebody is on this, that they haven't let it slip through the cracks, that it just hasn't been sent to a black hole, put somewhere and forgotten because in many cases it *is* forgotten, it is slipped through the cracks, and it's happened to them again and again. Some of these folks have tried to get things fixed for years and it just hasn't got fixed. So education is a big one, trying to let them know this is happening, trying to communicate.[38]

As much as it was enraging for citizens to lose sight of what the city government was doing for them, it was equally frustrating, on the government's part, to try and let people know the difficulties of putting things together as quickly and efficiently as possible.

While this book deals with various aspects of civic inequalities after the disaster, there are still many avenues of research that need to be explored in the future. Most importantly, a deeper analysis should be in order to identify the role of government aid in post-disaster recovery. Focusing on the civic aspect, this book did not pay sufficient attention to how government intervention, or failure thereof, contributed to shaping the uneven topography of the city. Indeed, the slow and cumbersome process of individual aid application was especially hurtful for those in lower-income communities, where the level of damage was greater but the value of the properties was lower than in the higher income, less-afflicted neighborhoods. Likewise, fraudulent contractor practices further delayed reconstruction of many homes, some of which are still left unfinished. Not surprisingly, civic actions arose amid the sluggish, unreliable assistance from the government and the business sector in every step of the recovery process. Future research can examine more carefully the extent to which the public and business sectors transformed the nature of civic engagement in times of crisis.

Acknowledging the limits of civic capacity is far from arguing that citizens, or their collective will, are ill-equipped to overcome a catastrophe. Likewise, the fact that disaster victims pursue what is best for them and organize around such interests is not a demoralizing factor for building resilience. To the contrary, civic activism plays a positive role in reviving and rebuilding devastated communities, and without resilient communities, cities can hardly sustain themselves. What this book has shown is that praising the resilience of communities should not preclude us from forming a public discussion about planning a safer, more resilient city that requires a higher level of civic cooperation between communities and government as well as between cognate communities. This book shows how difficult but important it is to extend the scope of "community" beyond the geographic confines of similar home values and homogeneous conditions. In this light, let us reconsider Roark's earlier comment: "I don't want to lose my *neighborhood*, so I have more incentive than literally any human being on the planet to make this work." A resilient city will be a less vulnerable one when the word "neighborhood" is replaced with "city," and this book, I hope, offers a good rationale for doing that.

ACKNOWLEDGMENTS

I traveled to various cities while writing this book, and many people and institutions helped me navigate what lay ahead along the way. I am indebted to my advisors at the University of Chicago. Eric Oliver, chair of my dissertation committee, provided me with much-needed academic and emotional support, without which this project would not have taken off. I really loved working with him. I extend my gratitude to another member of the committee, Mario Small, for his feedback on each and every step of the publication process. Not only did he inspire me with his own work, but he also trained me with his sharp questions and warm encouragement. Michael Dawson's dedicated work on American politics and Hurricane Katrina was crucial to shaping the framework of this book. I also acknowledge that much of the fieldwork was supported by the National Science Foundation and various grants from the University of Chicago.

I am also deeply grateful to the people I met in New Orleans for their generosity and willingness to share their experiences. Their stories fascinated me and enriched the book so much, especially in chapter 5, where I tried to recount their narratives as well as I could. I sincerely hope that my scholarship can add some value to their lives.

New York City is another special place for this project. The City University of New York (CUNY), my former employer, provided me with invaluable opportunities while I wrote this book. This work benefited from PSC-CUNY grants, the Gittell Collective Fellowship, and the Faculty Fellowship Publication Program. I was fortunate to have been part of the active scholarly community of urban researchers, and the feedback and encouragement from my colleagues at CUNY—Brooklyn College was indispensable for continuing to pursue this project as a junior scholar. Furthermore, I would like to thank my editor at NYU Press, Sonia Tsuruoka, for being so open-minded and supportive throughout the publication process. Her confidence and interest in this project contributed immensely to the completion of the book.

I put the finishing touches on the book in Seoul. My alma mater, Ewha Womans University of Korea, provided generous financial assistance, as this work was supported by the Ewha Womans University Research Grant of 2018. Now that I am back on campus as a professor, I realize how formative the college experience had been in shaping the kind of intellectual curiosity and emotional resilience that were necessary for years to come. My department at Ewha still continues to serve that role, and I am happy to be on the supply side now.

My friends and family have always been there to lend me support wherever and whenever I needed it most. I am grateful to my dear friends, inside and outside academia, for their camaraderie. Even when they were not equally interested in hurricanes and disasters, they were always ready to listen to me and cheer me on. I would like to thank my family for encouraging me to stay curious and pursue my interests. My son, Alexander, has given me so much joy and fulfillment and helped me flourish both personally and professionally. I look forward to sharing this book with all of them.

METHODOLOGICAL APPENDIX

METHODOLOGY FOR CHAPTER 3

Negative Binomial Regression

The first analysis (degree of reconstruction) concerns evaluating the hypothesis that the distribution of the number of active permits is influenced by the level of community political participation. To test this hypothesis, I conduct a negative binomial regression[1] using Zelig in R.[2] Negative binomial regression is used for modeling count variables. In our study, the number of active permits is a count variable. An alternative to this model is zero-inflation negative binomial (ZINB) regression. Upon comparison, no advantage in using ZINB regression over negative binomial was found. Vuong test statistics shows that these two models are indistinguishable, with a P-value of 0.348. Therefore, I use negative binomial regression for parsimony and ease of interpretation.

The analytic model has a log-linear function and implies that the dependent variable (λ) is an exponential function of covariates, taking the following form:

$$\log(\lambda) = a + b_1 X_1 + b_2 X_2 + \ldots + b_p X_p$$

where λ is a count variable, and $X_1 \ldots X_p$ refers to a set of exogenous covariates.

Event History Analysis

The second analysis (the speed of reconstruction) tests whether the duration until a permit is issued is associated with civic engagement, and I use the event history approach.[3] Also called "survival analysis," event history analysis is ideal for modeling a dataset that contains duration and timing.[4] Since the second question involves the speed of permit issuance, event history analysis is an adequate method to study what affects the duration of each permit. The semiparametric Cox model is most common in event history analysis, but it assumes that each case is independent from the others. However, in the case of building permits, this assumption is likely to be violated, since there can be factors unidentified in the model that may affect the distribution of survival time. For example, different zoning priorities for each neighborhood may exist, such that neighborhoods like the French Quarter have more commercial establishments than primarily residential areas such as Lakeview or the Lower Ninth Ward. Since new residential and commercial permits are examined in this study, this kind of neighborhood-specific idiosyncrasy can yield biased estimates. To address such unobserved heterogeneity and improve the model fit, I use a shared-frailty model, which incorporates random effects that are constant within groups. In our case, I use neighborhood as a group-level variable because each neighborhood (such as Tremé, the Lower Ninth Ward, and the French Quarter) has its own specific social characteristics that may affect the time to permit issuance. Furthermore, neighborhoods in New Orleans constitute a base unit of post-Katrina urban planning by the city government, so it is plausible that there is a deliberate neighborhood-level variation in permit issuance.

In our dataset, an observation is "censored" when a permit application is submitted at time To, and its status is still pending at time T1 without knowledge of its being accepted or dropped after T1. Since we know the definite entry date and the termination occurs in the right tail of the time axis, the observation is referred to as right censored.[5] The hazard rate of the proportional hazards model takes the following form:

$$h(t) = h_o(t)e^{\beta_1 X_1 + \cdots + \beta_K X_K},$$

where $h_o(t)$ refers to the nonparametric baseline hazard function and X represents time-invariant covariates.[6] The covariate coefficients (β) show whether a variable increases or decreases the risk ($h(t)$). The "risk" in our study is that an application is permitted after duration T and exits the data set. Therefore, a coefficient is positive if it will

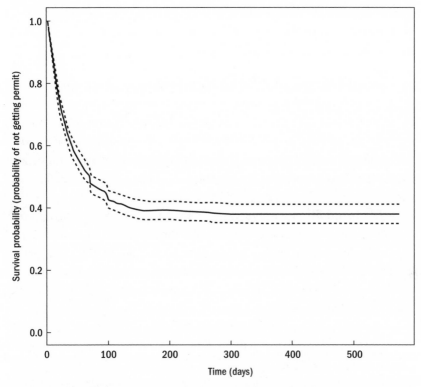

Figure A.1. Kaplan-Meier estimator of survival probability. Note: Dotted lines represent 95 percent confidence intervals.

increase the risk, meaning that the covariate shortens the duration until permit issuance.

Kaplan-Meier Curve for Permit Speed Analysis

Model specifications are categorized largely by internal technical criteria and external conditions. I include shared frailty models, whereby shared frailties represent unmeasured random factors at the neighborhood level. In general, shared frailty models (Models 2 and 4 in Table 3.2) have a better fit than nonfrailty models (Models 1 and 3), as shown with improved R-squared values. To understand how the duration of permit issuance is distributed over time, I first calculate the baseline conditional probability of the survival function, represented by a Kaplan-Meier curve (Figure A.1). A Kaplan-Meier curve is often used in estimating human mortality, whereby it estimates the probability that a person stays alive—that is, survives—beyond a specific time. Likewise, in this case, we estimate the probability that a permit application stays pending beyond a specific time. If the permit is granted, the application will be considered "dead." Based on this logic, Figure A.1 shows that not all applications are granted permits during the given period of observation, and the outcomes of many applications either remain pending or are lost to follow-up at various time points. Survival function in Figure A.1 decreases sharply for the first one hundred days and then remains at the same level until the end of the observation period. In other words, most permits are accepted within one hundred days of application, and those that are not accepted within one hundred days are likely to be pending or closed. Based on this curve, we compare whether our variable of interest (turnout) brings any change in the survival function of permit application durations.

METHODOLOGY FOR CHAPTER 4

Spatial Autoregressive Regression

To take the unit interdependence into account, I test Spatial Autoregressive Regression (SAR) models to check whether there is a spatial correlation across spatial units of analysis. SAR relaxes two OLS assumptions, that (i) errors are uncorrelated and (ii) each observation is independent from each other, and takes the following form:[7]

$$y^* = \rho W y^* + X\beta + \varepsilon,$$

where $\rho W y^*$ is a spatial lag term, W is a contiguous weights matrix that assigns weights to neighboring units with shared borders, and β is a short-run direct effect of the independent variables. Here, the value of ρ is greater than 0 and smaller than 1. An individual unit (y) is influenced by its neighbors, but the outcome y simultaneously affects other units. In turn, other units' y values are changed, and the sequence goes *ad infinitum* until a stable equilibrium is reached.[8] Here I assume that recovery process should have a positive effect on neighboring locations, hence $0 < \rho < 1$. Also, I estimate W using the rook contiguity matrix. Like a rook in chess game, the rook contiguity matrix assigns weights to those units that share line borders. In contrast, the queen contiguity matrix assigns weights to those that share not only line borders but also points.

In spatial analysis, explanatory variables can affect the outcome variable both directly and indirectly,[9] and the *coefficients* are not identical with total *effects*. β is a direct effect of x_i on y_i *before* considering spatial interdependence, and the ρ is a long-run, unit-specific equilibrium effect for the change in x_i. Since the degree of spatial connectivity (W) is different across individual units, the total equilibrium effect based on spatial connection ($\rho W y^*$) will also differ in each unit. The degree of spatial diffusion, expressed in the spatial lag coefficient (ρ), represents the indirect effect of the independent variables on the dependent variable simultaneously *through their impact on its neighbors*. To put it differently, the lag coefficient shows the degree to which community A's civic and socioeconomic conditions affect repopulation in neighboring communities, which in turn influences repopulation in community A. If the coefficient is statistically significant, it means that spatial diffusion is occurring across communities. In other words, the positive role of the civic structure is not merely limited in the host community but extends to the neighboring communities, transcending geographic boundaries. To the contrary, no spatial interaction is warranted if the coefficient does not show statistical significance.

The spatial regression results show that the value of ρ not only decreases but also becomes statistically insignificant over time, suggesting that the spatial diffusion of repopulation disappears and communities become independent of one another (Figure A.2). The recovery process was more interactive and "messy" in the early period, as civic structure not only served its target community but also contributed to the repopulation of the adjacent communities. However, as recovery unfolds, the spillover effect diminishes and the effect tends to be concentrated upon the host community. In other words, the spatial units become more autonomous as they overcome the immediate impacts of the disaster and reconstruct their communities. In the equation, we return to the following form:

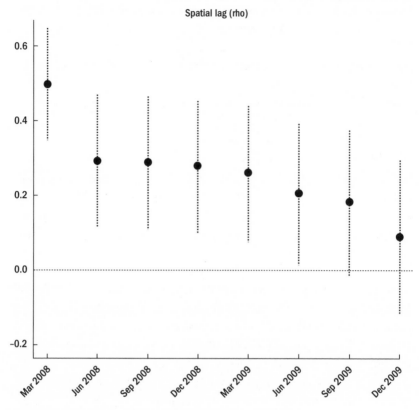

Figure A.2. Spatial lag coefficient (ρ) for repopulation, 2008–2009.

$$y^* = X\beta + \varepsilon,$$

whereby the ρWy^* term disappears because spatial lag coefficient is no longer relevant. In other words, I can run OLS regressions in the absence of spatial autocorrelation. Therefore, in this chapter, I estimate regression coefficients with the OLS method.

NOTES

1 Miet, 2005

2 Colten, 2005

3 Nance, 2009

4 Stack, 2007

5 Goldberg, 2006

6 FEMA, 2013

7 Glaeser, 2005; Blakely, 2011; Ehrenfeucht and Nelson, 2012: 133; Ryan, 2012; Dewar and Thomas, 2012a; Hummel, 2015

8 Ford, 2011

9 Goldberg, 2014

10 Interestingly, an opposite but equally paradoxical phenomenon happened in a community in Staten Island, New York. After Hurricane Sandy, residents of the affected communities supported the state government's buyout option and agreed to sell their damaged homes to relocate. In so doing, residents were mostly silent in talking about climate change because they viewed climate change as a politically controversial issue that can potentially divide communities. This "agnostic adaptation" shows how silence, rather than voicing one's opinion, may facilitate action to mitigate climate change (Koslov, 2019).

11 McQuarrie, 2013

12 Burby, 2006

13 Olshansky et al., 2012

14 Schwab, 2014

15 City of New Orleans, 2011: 7

16 Aldrich, 2012

17 Some studies warn against the negative effect of social coherence. For example, Aldrich noted that social capital produces negative externalities, primarily by not allowing necessary yet undesirable facilities into a community (Aldrich and Crook, 2008). He pointed out that social capital is in fact not always a public good, but rather can be a factor that further exacerbates existing inequalities among individuals and communities. Indeed, social capital is a "Janus-faced" property; on the one hand, members within a social ring can benefit from shared norms and feeling responsibility for each other; on the other hand, social resources can be used to exclude, ostracize, and neglect those in need of help. In disaster situations, civic inequality can reinforce preexisting inequalities by

driving out publicly shunned facilities and excluding groups with less power (women and minorities) from gaining access to aid and assistance (Aldrich, 2010). However, the negative impacts of social capital are not considered a fundamental hurdle that would hamper the recovery itself, but rather are presented as side effects or "externalities" of overzealous residents whose discriminatory behaviors cast negative impacts on the more vulnerable groups.

18 Hudson, 1991: 2000

19 Earthquakes may be located in the middle of the transitory-perpetual spectrum. Polities in earthquake-prone regions should set up necessary measures (such as strict building codes, evacuation plans, etc.) to mitigate future catastrophes, but potential epicenters are often widely dispersed and the magnitude of their impact is often difficult to predict, making human habitation less bound.

20 Dawson, 2011

21 US Department of the Interior, and US Geological Survey, 2003

22 Ibid., 67

23 Campanella, 2008

24 Airriess et al., 2008

25 Leong et al., 2007; Li et al., 2008

26 Earle Jr., 1975

27 Ibid., 330–31

28 City of New Orleans, 2006

29 Sayer, 2014

30 Plyer, 2014

31 Plyer, 2015

32 Dolfman et al., 2007

33 Hoople, 2013

34 These hurricanes include Jeanne (2004), Frances (2004), Ivan (2004), Charley (2004), Rita (2005), Wilma (2005), and Katrina (2005).

35 Insurance Information Institute, 2010

36 Barnett et al., 2013

37 Ehrenfeucht and Nelson, 2011: 137

38 Census, 2010

39 Gibson, 1998

40 Fuchs (1992) argues that New York City's fiscal crisis stems from the city's weak political system, which led to the proliferation of interest groups and the decentralization of the budgeting process. The mayor of New York City, according to Fuchs, responded to the rising demands for social services by increasing the expenditure of the city. In contrast, in Chicago, the mayor could divert the similar kinds of demand by mobilizing his Democratic Party machine and creating special districts without increasing the city expenditure. Furthermore, the taxing rates in New York City were also constrained by state mandates, while Chicago had relatively flexible taxing authority due to its Home Rule.

41 Gerring, 2004: 344

42 Aldrich and Crook, 2008; Schaeffer and Kashdan, 2010

43 Mill, 1843

44 Elliot et al., 2010; Seidman, 2013

45 King et al., 1994

46 Schaeffer and Kashdan, 2010

47 Van Evera, 1997

48 Gerring, 2004: 345

49 Schaeffer and Kashdan, 2010

50 Gotham and Greenberg, 2014

51 Horowitz, 2014

52 Platt, 1999; Chamlee-Wright and Storr, 2009

53 Small, 2011

54 Ibid.

55 Census Bureau, 2001

1. RESILIENT COMMUNITIES IN A VULNERABLE CITY

1 Van Houten, 2016; Davenport and Robertson, 2016

2 Klinenberg, 2013

3 Buettner and Chen, 2014

4 HUD "National Disaster Resilience Competition Overview," https://portal.hud. gov/hudportal/documents/huddoc?id=NDRCFactSheetFINAL.pdf

5 Colten and Giancarlo, 2011

6 Aldrich, 2011a: 7

7 Aldrich and Meyer, 2015: 2

8 Rockefeller Foundation, n.d.

9 Please see Klinenberg (2002); however, for the critique of Klinenberg's approach, see Duneier (2004).

10 Aldrich and Meyer, 2014

11 Ibid.

12 A lengthier, more comprehensive definition of urban resilience can be found in the urban planning literature, referred to as "the ability of an urban system—and all its constituent socio-ecological and socio-technical networks across temporal and spatial scales—to maintain or rapidly return to desired functions in the face of a disturbance, to adapt to change, and to quickly transform systems that limit current or future adaptive capacity" (Meerow et al., 2016: 39).

13 Adger, 2006

14 Gotham and Greenberg, 2014

15 Adams, 2013

16 Hamel et al., 2015

17 Akerlof et al., 2016

18 Garcia, 2013: 28

19 Glaeser, 2005; Russell, 2008; Ehrenfeucht and Nelson, 2011 and 2012

20 National Oceanic and Atmospheric Administration, n.d.; Koslov, 2019

21 Siders, 2013
22 Daniels et al., 2006
23 Cheong, 2011
24 *New York Times*, Urbina, 2016
25 Koslov, 2019
26 Bidgood, 2016
27 Groβman et al., 2013; Hackworth, 2015; Hummel, 2015
28 Ryan, 2012
29 Ehrenfeucht and Nelson, 2011
30 Neuman, 2005
31 Rybczynski and Linneman, 1999; Ehrenfeucht and Nelson, 2011; Martinez-
    Fernandez et al., 2012; Dewar and Thomas, 2012; Hackworth, 2015
32 Ehrenfeucht and Nelson, 2011
33 Ehrenfeucht and Nelson, 2012: 143
34 Rivlin, 2015
35 District E Public Meeting, 3/29/2010
36 Gratz, 2012
37 Meitrodt and Donze, 2005
38 Krupa, 2010
39 Nelson et al., 2007
40 New Orleans City Planning Commission, 2010: 14.2
41 Cutter et al., 2006
42 National Public Radio Cities Project, 2014
43 Ostrom, 1990: 34–35
44 Pekkanen et al., 2012
45 Means and Kuo, 2016: 20
46 PolicyLink and PERE, 2017
47 Wooten, 2012; Seidman, 2013
48 Chamlee-Wright and Storr, 2011
49 Livlin, 2006
50 Leong et al., 2007
51 Aldrich and Crook, 2008: 9
52 Sampson et al., 2005
53 de Sam Lazaro, 2005
54 Seidman, 2013
55 Larsen et al., 2004
56 Saegart et al., 2004: 4, requited from Larsen et al., 2004
57 Hawkins and Maurer, 2010
58 Klinenberg, 2002

2. FEDERALISM AND THE CONSTRUCTION OF PROTECTION FROM BETSY TO KATRINA

 1 Requoted from Colten (2009: 47).

2 LeSieur, 1965: 2

3 As the name of the organization suggests, many of the activities by *Levees.org* are based on an online platform. "Levees.org logs 900,000 visitors to its website," http://levees.org/.

4 "Mission and Goals of Levees.org," http://levees.org.

5 Colten, 2005: 188

6 Hamel et al., 2015

7 Roberts, 2013

8 Lester and Krejci, 2007

9 Wolensky and Wolensky, 1990; Henstra, 2010

10 Burby, 2006

11 Tiebout, 1956

12 Peterson, 1981; 68

13 Peterson, 1995

14 Roberts, 2013: 177–79

15 Peterson classifies FEMA emergency planning, preparedness, and mitigation as developmental programs, while defining disaster relief as a redistributive program (Peterson, 1995: 199; see appendix). Given that Peterson advances a functional-ist theory of federalism whereby the two levels of governments adapt to perform developmental and redistributive functions, such classification implies that the federal government spends more on individual disaster relief than on emergency preparedness and mitigation. However, this does not mean that state and local governments undertake the latter function, as emergency mitigation contributes to the economic well-being of a city only in the long term. Considering the short time horizon of elected local officials, it is unlikely that these representatives con-sider emergency preparedness as part of the development strategy (2013).

16 Colten, 2009: 19

17 *American Journal of History*, 2007

18 Colten, 2009: 20

19 Mittal, 2005

20 Ibid., 3

21 Kysar and McGarity, 2006

22 US Government Printing Office, 2006

23 Colten, 2009: 75

24 Go, 2012

25 US Government Printing Office, 2006

26 Kysar and McGarity, 2006

27 Biographical note, Earl K. Long Library. Archival data were collected from Inven-tory at David P. Levy Collection, University of New Orleans, http://library.uno .edu/specialcollections/inventories/265.htm.

28 Memo of Meeting, 1976; ibid., 2

29 Ibid.

30 White, 1937; Colten, 2009

31 Burby, 2006

32 Peterson, 1995

33 Healy and Malhotra, 2009

34 Reeves, 2011

35 Chen, 2013

36 Interview with city official (anonymous), 2/26/2010

37 Louisiana Recovery Office, 2013

38 FEMA, 2013

39 Not all HMGP grants are directed toward fortifying existing properties by elevating them or using stronger materials. State and local governments may set different priorities in strengthening resilience. In New York and New Jersey, the HMGP funding was used primarily to buy out damaged properties in flood-prone areas (Bova-Hiatt et al., 2014). Rather than rebuilding on a higher basis, state and local governments in New York and New Jersey directed the funding toward relocating individuals to less vulnerable areas by purchasing the properties and leaving the damaged region undeveloped.

40 Hammer, 2012b

41 Hammer, 2012a

42 Ibid.

43 Bureau of Governmental Research, 1996

44 Wardlaw and Anderson, 1988

45 Wardlaw and Anderson, 1988: C-4

46 Key, 1949

47 Wardlaw and Anderson, 1988

48 National League of Cities, n.d

49 Morial and Whelan, 2000: 213

50 Please see Russell (2004); ironically, inconsistent valuation worked in the opposite direction after Katrina. The city properties had been reassessed right after Katrina to reflect storm damages and reduced market value. When the state conducted a reappraisal of the same properties for recovery assistance, however, the taxable assessed valuation actually increased from $2.14 billion in 2005 to $2.54 billion in 2006 (Hildreth, 2009).

51 Alm and Adhikari, 2015: 2

52 Hildreth, 2009

53 Public Affairs Research Council of Louisiana and the Bureau of Governmental Research, 2006: 26

54 Ibid.

55 Joint Legislative Committee on the Budget, 2011

56 The Advocate, 2013

57 Buchanan, 2012

58 Giegengack and Foster, 2006: 29

59 Buchanan, 2012

60 McCarthy, 2014

61 Louisiana State University Public Policy Research Lab, 2014

62 Vaughan and Turner, 2013

63 Go, 2016

64 Part IV-A Louisiana Uniform Construction Code 1730.40 B

65 In contrast, insurance companies and federal agencies welcome strict building codes because they are directly affected by lax building codes. They prefer stricter building codes that can minimize property damage.

66 Burby et al., 1999

67 Four building codes exist: The Uniform Building Code developed by the International Congress of Building Officials; the Basic Building Code by the Building Officials Conference of America; the Southern Standard Building Code by Southern Building Code Congress; and the National Building Code by the American Insurance Association (Kelly 1996: 350–51).

68 FEMA, 2006

69 Edwards, 2010

70 American Planning Association/AICP Planning Assistance Team, 2006

71 FEMA, 2013

72 Go, 2012

73 Mumford, 1961: 426

74 Brooks and Young, 1993

75 Ibid., 262

76 Not all White residents lived in communities on higher ground, such as the French Quarter and Uptown. Many wealthy Whites also lived in neighborhoods close to Lake Pontchartrain, including Lakeview and Lake Vista. These areas, with a beautiful view of the lake, were significantly flooded during Katrina.

77 Census, 1998

78 Ibid.

79 FEMA, 2012

80 "The President's Remarks upon Arrival at New Orleans Municipal Airport," University of Texas Library, www.lbjlib.utexas.edu/johnson/AV.hom/Hurricane/audio_transcript.shtm.

81 Hass, 2014: 241

82 FEMA, 2002

83 Knowles and Kunreuther, 2014

84 US Government Accountability Office, 2015

85 Ibid. As of 2019, FEMA published a new rating system, in which the insurance premiums are based on multiple factors including the distance of a building from a water source, the cost of rebuilding, and various types of flooding. The new rating system is likely to increase the insurance premium for the properties in New Orleans and other coastal communities, which may reduce the financial deficit for the NFIP.

86 Germany, 2007: 75

87 Ibid., 76

88 Ibid., 75. In 1954, Louisiana repealed portions of its urban renewal act. As a result, Louisiana had been classified as not having adequate legislation related to urban renewal and did not receive much from the federal urban renewal program. In the 1960s, community activists in New Orleans's urban areas tried to overturn the repealed state legislation and eventually succeeded in enacting and enabling legislation. The significant damage by Hurricane Betsy aided the process, as it enabled the formation of a political coalition that sought to use the federal funding for fixing street, sewage, and drainage problems (Germany, 2007: 184–85 and "The Federal Urban Renewal Program," Quintin Johnstone, 312, footnote 51 http://digi talcommons.law.yale.edu/cgi/viewcontent.cgi?article=2924&context=fss_papers).

89 Alpert, 2013b

90 Alpert, 2014

91 Knowles, 2011: 256

92 Braden, 2015

93 Schleifstein, 2015a

94 "Ruling on Katrina Flooding Favors Homeowners," *New York Times*, November 18, 2009, www.nytimes.com.

95 "St. Bernard Parish Government v. United States," United States Court of Appeals for the Federal Circuit, April 20, 2018, http://blogs2.law.columbia.edu/climate-change-litigation/wp-content/uploads/sites/16/case-documents/2018/20180420_docket-16-2301-16-2373_opinion-1.pdf

96 Klein, 2015

97 Ibid.

98 Roberts, 2013: 11

99 Birkland and Waterman, 2008

100 Katz and Bradley, 2014

3. REBUILDING THE CITY

1 Hauser, 2005

2 Newman, 2012

3 Interview with Abate, 3/10/2010

4 A building permit is "a document issued by the Department of Safety and Permits that allows—or permits—the owner of a property to construct a new building, or repair, alter, or demolish an existing building" (Department of Safety and Permits. 2010: 1). This chapter focuses on new residential construction permits and excludes permits for repair, renovation, and addition to the existing structure because some repair permits were processed through an electronic system and thus did not require a direct interaction between applicants and staff.

5 Liu et al., 2006

6 McKarthy et al., 2006: 34

7 Roberts, 2006

8 Ibid.

9 Whoriskey, 2006

10 Nossiter, 2006

11 Olshansky and Johnson, 2010

12 Gillis and Barringer, 2012

13 Roig-Franzia, 2006

14 Whoriskey, 2006

15 Colten, 2009

16 Colten, 2009: 161

17 Roig-Franzia, 2006

18 Associated Press, 2006

19 Ibid.

20 Contrary to the presumption that this segregation is the direct consequence of slavery, which had historically been entrenched in New Orleans and in the South, residential isolation in New Orleans is rather a modern phenomenon (Spain, 1979). Even if social and economic segregation had been already pervasive during the nineteenth century, it did not lead to residential segregation until the Jim Crow era, when the residential topography began to resemble that of large cities in the north (Spain, 1979: 83). This was due to the "backyard pattern" of slave residence, whereby slaves used to live close to their employers and thus were racially more integrated than in later periods (ibid.). This pattern began to change at the turn of the century. Between the 1900s and 1950s, more than 25 percent of African Americans began to congregate in a few wards, and this process was accelerated by urban renewal and public housing projects. As a result of urban renewal, such as the construction of the Interstate and Superdome, in 1960, over 40 percent of all Blacks lived in only two wards—the Seventh and the Ninth—compared to the 27 percent to 36 percent in earlier years (Spain, 1979: 91).

21 Ibid.

22 Johnson, 2011: 199

23 Simons, 2007

24 Johnson, 2011: 217

25 Make It Right Foundation. "How Many Homes Have You Built in New Orleans?" retrieved at http://makeitright.org/about/faq/#q3. Accessed on January 12, 2016.

26 Johnson, 2011

27 Allen, 2015

28 Holt and Vann, 2015

29 On the City of New Orleans website, the duration for residential permit is two to five days; for commercial projects, twenty to thirty days. See "Renovation (Non-Structural) Permit," City of New Orleans, www.nola.gov/onestop/building/construction/renovation-%28non-structural%29-permit/. Accessed on December 30, 2015.

30 Department of Safety and Permits, 2010

31 Aldrich and Crook 2008; Aldrich 2011b

32 Almond and Verba, 1963

33 Almond and Verba, 1963: 191

34 Oliver and Ha, 2007

35 Aldrich and Crook, 2008

36 Kaufmann, 2004

37 Oliver and Ha, 2007; Hajnal, 2009

38 Jones, 1981: 688

39 Putnam, 2000

40 Fischel, 2001

41 Cingranelli, 1981: 676

42 Jones, 1981; Marwell, 2007

43 However, Chamlee-Wright and Storr (2011) note that in the disaster context, community-based groups can engage in rent-seeking and lobbying behaviors to compete against other communities for government assistance.

44 I measure vulnerability through *elevation*, calculated with the average of five points randomly selected within every census tract.

45 Department of Safety and Permits, 2010

46 Ibid.

47 Coefficients are presented with standard errors in parentheses. Positive coefficient means a larger number of permit applications.

48 Coefficients are presented with standard errors in parenthesis. Negative coefficient means longer durations until permit issuance.

49 Prediction is based on Cox semiparametric model.

50 Interview with a city planning official, January 28, 2011.

51 Burns and Thomas, 2015: 48

52 District E Public Meeting, 3/29/2010

53 Elliott, 2015

54 Manney, 2010

55 Roig-Franzia, 2006

56 Nelson et al., 2007

4. RETURNING TO THE CITY

 1 Pierce and Dreher, 2015

 2 Gafford, 2013

 3 Gotham and McLachlan, 2010

 4 Gafford, 2010

 5 Sampson et al., 2005; Sampson, 2012

 6 Sampson et al., 2005

 7 de Sam Razaro, 2005

 8 Tran, 2011

 9 Nolan, 2010

10 Rivlin, 2015

11 Geaghan, 2011

12 Residential addresses encompass individual housing (such as apartments and condominiums), businesses, and other living quarters such as a group of

dorm rooms, FEMA trailers, and mobile homes—PO Boxes are not included
(GNOCDC 2008; see Ortiz and Plyer, 2008, for a complete description of data
acquisition and compilation process). Typically, neighborhood recovery stabilizes
after three years (Campanella, 2011), so 2008 is a good year to examine the long-
term pattern of redevelopment after the initial phase of recovery.

13 Philip, 2015

14 In contrast, *ancillary civic structure* comprises a set of establishments whose
primary objective is not civic or public and yet provides opportunities for social
interactions. Examples include restaurants, barbershops, and beauty salons.
Although the primary function of these venues is to provide essential services to
residents for profit, they nonetheless provide people opportunities to build social
relationships and opinions on a daily basis (Harris-Lacewell, 2004). This measure
captures the spatial structure of these informal relationships. In this chapter,
however, I mainly report findings on primary civic structure because ancillary
civic structure did not show significant association with repopulation or social
vulnerabilities.

15 Lake and Huckfelt, 1998; McClurg 2003

16 Sampson et al., 2005

17 Both flood and elevation are point data that should be aggregated up to the census
tract or neighborhood levels. In order to measure average level of flooding and
elevation, I randomly drew five X and Y coordinates in each unit from areal maps
provided by the United States Geological Survey and calculated their average
values.

18 Sampson, 2012

19 Tobler, 1970: 236

20 Coefficients are presented with standard errors in parentheses. Note: Number of
organizations is predicted with negative binomial regression models. Two-tailed
test. *:p<0.1, **:p<0.05, ***:p<0.01.

21 Ancillary social organizations show somewhat different patterns from primary organizations. First, areas with high unemployment have fewer of these commercial
establishments, suggesting that barbershops, beauty salons, and restaurants are located in economically active areas or that these businesses actually drive up local
employment. Second, more ancillary social organizations are located in areas with
a greater number of renter properties than homeowners. This is also expected, as
businesses tend to be concentrated in commercial rather than residential areas.

22 Small, 2004

23 The distribution of ancillary social organizations shows that for both categories,
economic viability is an important determinant for their spatial distribution.
Areas with high unemployment tend to have a lower number of restaurants,
barbershops, and beauty salons, and the proportion of rental properties in an area
is positively associated with the number of these businesses. What differentiates
these two types of businesses is the percentage of Black population in the area.
Barbershops and beauty salons are more likely to be located in African American

communities, whereas restaurants are more frequently found in more White areas (See appendix).

24 Sampson and Wilson, 1995

25 Small 2004; Small and Stark 2005

26 Oliver, 2001

27 Gafford, 2013

28 Predicted values are based on ordinary least square regression results. All coefficients are statistically significant. Two-tailed test.

29 If the population ratio is 1 (presented with the dotted line), it means that a neighborhood has gained all of its pre-Katrina population in a given year.

30 Whitfield, 2015

31 Mean values are presented. The compiled neighborhood-level data profile is provided by the Data Center. Pre-Katrina measures are taken from the 2000 Census, and post-Katrina measures are taken from the American Community Survey (2010–2014).

32 Glock and Haussermann, 2004

33 In order to test whether these results stem from the arbitrary cutoff (below and above sea level), I divided the sample by a different standard, i.e., one meter above sea level. The results are consistent with those presented here: Neighborhoods located below one meter of elevation are worse off than their higher-ground counterparts. The disparities are actually greater with a new cutoff, suggesting that the neighborhoods slightly above and below sea level are exposed to greater risks than areas located much higher than the sea level.

34 The city opened a website, Katrina10.org, that commemorates post-Katrina reforms and achievements.

35 All coefficients are statistically significant.

36 Klinenberg, 2002

37 Hammer, 2010

38 Ehrenfeucht and Nelson, 2011

39 The entire list of civic associations is as follows (host neighborhood in parentheses): Broadmoor Development Corp. (Broadmoor), Central City Collaborative (Central City), Make It Right (Lower Ninth Ward), Lower Ninth Ward Neighborhood Empowerment Network Association (NENA) (Lower Ninth Ward), Pontchartrain Park Community Development Corp. (Pontchartrain Park), Project Home Again (Gentilly), Rebuilding Together New Orleans (Citywide), Saint Bernard Project (Gentilly), and UNITY-Common Ground Institute and Renaissance Neighborhood Development Corp. (Mid-City).

40 NORA. 2013. "Neighborhood Stabilization Program: Annual Report." www.nora works.org/documents/neighborhood-stabilization-program-nsp2-annual-report/ download.

41 Ehrenfeucht and Nelson, 2011

42 State of Louisiana Office of Community Development, 2020

43 Hammer, 2015

44 Ehrenfeucht and Nelson, 2013; Nelson and Ehrenfeucht 2016

45 Green and Olshansky, 2012; Nelson, 2014

46 State of Louisiana Office of Community Development, 2020

47 Finger, 2008; Gotham and Greenberg; 2014

48 Sharp, 2012; Michener, 2018

49 Hammer, 2015

50 Census, 2010

51 In the model, the total number of civic organizations (primary plus ancillary) is statistically significant. The predicted values are estimated based on the regression mode with all other variables held at the mean.

52 Louisiana State University Public Policy Research Lab, 2014

53 Small, 2009

5. THE MAKING OF RESILIENT COMMUNITIES

1 Blakely 2011: 103

2 Ibid., 101

3 Ibid; Blakely further mentioned that these chasms were racialized, such that most affluent communities not affected by flooding are predominantly White while heavily damaged areas are occupied mostly by Blacks. The racial differences in geography led to varied interpretation of the city's master plan, as many Black residents believed that the city's new comprehensive plan would eventually marginalize and exclude Black communities and perpetuate the White dominance in the city.

4 Ibid.

5 Ford, 2011; Seidman, 2013; Ehrenfeucht and Nelson, 2012: 133; Hummel, 2015

6 City of New Orleans, 2011

7 Ibid., 147–48

8 Interview, 2/24/10

9 District E Public Meeting, 3/29/2010

10 Elliot et al., 2010

11 Helsley and Strange, 1998; Baer and Feiock, 2005

12 Adams, 2013

13 Johnson, 2011

14 Ibid., xxiv

15 Sampson, 2012

16 Anselin, 1988; 2013

17 Campanella, 2008

18 Ibid.

19 Small, 2009

20 Wooten, 2012; Seidman, 2013

21 McQuarrie, 2013

22 Thayer, 1979

23 Ibid., 110–111

24 Ibid.
25 Thayer, 1979: 105
26 US HUD and Office of Evaluation, 1975
27 Ibid.
28 Moore, 2010
29 Eggler, 2012
30 Mayor Marc Morial, 1999
31 Carll, 1980
32 Brandt, 1982: 9
33 Sylvain, 2001:10; Lowe and Bates, 2012
34 Lowe and Bates, 2013
35 Lowe and Bates, 2012: 156–57
36 Ibid.
37 NORA, 2013: 62
38 Evans and Lewis, 2009; 44–45
39 Ibid., 47.
40 Ibid., 57.
41 Orr ed., 2007
42 *Times-Picayune*, 1929: 2
43 Ibid.
44 Ibid.
45 Political protest was not entirely absent at the initial stage of organizing because the electoral dynamic in 2006 placed a significant constraint on Mayor Nagin, who needed votes from the city's less-well-off population. Roark and others knew this and consciously showed their political power by marching in front of City Hall to signal their resistance to Nagin.
46 Interview with Roark, February 27, 2010
47 For the detailed renovation process of the library, see chapter 3 in Seidman (2013).
48 "2 Million Carnegie Corporation Grant Catalyzes Community Redevelopment Effort in Heart of New Orleans." Carnegie Corporation of New York Press Release. 6/19/2007. www.carnegie.org.
49 Broadmoor Neighborhood Meeting Transcript, March 15, 2010
50 Ibid.
51 Ibid.
52 Ibid.
53 Interview with Gray, March 10, 2010
54 Interview with Larry, March 12, 2010
55 Ibid.
56 Ibid.
57 Broadmoor Neighborhood Meeting Transcript, March 15, 2010
58 The program is called Project Home Again. Established by the chairman of Barnes & Noble, this project built environmentally friendly houses in Gentilly, and homeowners could apply for acquiring these houses in exchange for their

storm-damaged and uninhabited houses in select neighborhoods. Broadmoor just qualified for one of the neighborhoods that are eligible for a housing swap with Gentilly.

59 Seidman, 2013; McClendon, 2015

60 BIA website, www.broadmoorimprovement.com/.

61 Eggler, 2012

62 Warner, 2011

63 Census, 2000

64 Jacobs, 1961

65 Warner, 2001: 330

66 Ibid., 324

67 Freret's NU is a case where neighborhood association crossed neighborhood boundaries. At the time of my last fieldwork in 2010, the NU had its base in Freret. Historically, the association had served residents in both the Freret and Milan neighborhoods, and during the interviews, the community organizers implied that their clients encompass both neighborhoods. As of January 9, 2013, NU officially merged with Milan Focus Group to create Freret-Milan Neighbors United.

68 The Neighborhood Housing Services (NHS) is another social service organization located in Freret, whose mission is to educate first-time home buyers and increase homeownership for low-income families. However, people I interviewed did not mention the NHS as their community organization, perhaps because they cover broader areas across New Orleans and other cities. After Katrina, NHS established a sister organization called the Freret Neighborhood Center (FNC) that specifically addresses the needs of Freret residents. The FNC mostly runs educational and recreational programs for children and the elderly. It seldom deals with economic or social issues related with post-Katrina recovery. The people I interviewed in Freret rarely mentioned the FNC or NHS as organizations that represented their interests or needs.

69 Interview with Amacker, February 18, 2010

70 Ibid.

71 NU Neighborhood Meeting Transcript, 2010

72 Interview with Norwood, March 8, 2010

73 "Freret Neighborhood Planning District 3 Neighborhood Rebuilding Plan," www.nolaplans.com/plans/Lambert%20Intermediate/District_3_Plan_FINAL%20PLAN%20REPORT%20Freret%2009-29-06.pdf.

74 Ibid.

75 Harris-Lacewell, 2004

76 Conversation in Dennis' Barber Shop, March 8, 2010

77 Morris, 2013

78 Anderson and Thompson, 2012

79 Price, 2015

80 Interview with Norwood, March 8, 2010

81 Interview with Torres, March 15, 2010
82 Ironically, this transitional period provided an opportunity for better representation, and Stan Norwood became the president of the NU in 2014. His main
objective is to ensure fair access to the neighborhood new resources, which have
become expensive and less affordable to the city's old residents (Morris, 2013).
83 Orr, 2007; McQuarrie, 2013

CONCLUSION

1 Katz and Bradley, 2014; Glaeser, 2011
2 Alesina and La Ferrara, 2000
3 Glaeser, 2011
4 Hirschman, 1970
5 Dauber, 2013
6 Skocpol and Fiorina, 1999
7 Putnam, 2000
8 Lefebvre, 1979; Harvey, 2008
9 Gotham and Greenberg, 2014
10 Johnson, 2011: 1999
11 Williams, ed., 2018
12 C. Stone, 1989 and 1993; Mossberger and Stoker, 2001
13 Ellermann, 2005; Cripps, 2011; Mansbridge, 2012
14 Mansbridge, 2012: 1, 2014
15 In her presidential address to the American Political Science Association, Mansbridge presented legitimate coercion as the central idea to solve collective action
problems to acquire free-access goods in human society. She argues that political
science can find its value in providing solutions to collective action problems,
which become increasingly common as interdependence grows among jurisdictions (2014).
16 Koslov, 2016
17 Schneider and Teske, 1992
18 Burns and Thomas, 2006; 2015
19 Gallup, 2014
20 Liu and Mikesell, 2014
21 Robertson, 2014
22 Stone, D., 1989
23 Mansbridge, 2012; 2014
24 Colten, 2005: 7–8
25 Warren ed., 1999
26 Nicholls and Picou, 2013
27 Ibid.
28 Nelson, 2014
29 Ellermann, 2005
30 Brehm and Gates, 1997; Ellermann, 2005

31 MacAusland, 2017

32 Logan and Molotch, 1987

33 Ibid.

34 Peterson, 1981

35 Burchell and Mukerji, 2003

36 Ford, 2011

37 Many public discussions were held around this question at the local as well as the national level. For example, see the *Times-Picayune*, "9th Ward and All, New Orleans Deserves to Be Rebuilt: Editorial," May 6, 2015, www.nola.com; Jack Shafer, "Don't Refloat: The Case Against Rebuilding the Sunken City of New Orleans," *Slate*, September 7, 2005, www.slate.com; John M. Barry, "A City Worth Saving," *USA Today*, August 29, 2006. http://usatoday.com.

38 Interview with Abate, 3/10/2010

METHODOLOGICAL APPENDIX

1 Hilbe, 2007; Aldrich and Crook, 2008

2 Imai et al., 2009

3 Blossfeld et al., 1989; Hosmer et al., 2008; Box-Steffensmeier and Jones, 1997; Ko, 2010

4 Box-Steffensmeier and Jones, 1997

5 Hosmer et al., 2008: 6

6 Steffensmeier and Jones 1997:1433

7 Anselin, 1988

8 Lin et al., 2006; Anselin, 1988

9 Franzese and Hays, 2006

BIBLIOGRAPHY

Abramson, Larry. 2008. "Database Key in Restoring New Orleans." *Special Series: Gulf Coast's Everyday Heroes*. National Public Radio, March 11. www.npr.org.

Adams, Vincanne. 2013. *Markets of Sorrow, Labors of Faith: New Orleans in the Wake of Katrina*. Durham, NC: Duke University Press.

Adger, Neil. 2003. "Social Capital, Collective Action, and Adaptation to Climate Change." *Economic Geography* 79 (4): 387–404.

———. 2006. "Vulnerability." *Global Environmental Change* 16: 268–81.

The Advocate. 2013. "Disaster Officials Criticize Budget Funding Cut," June 30. http://theadvocate.com/home/6369217-125/disaster-officials-criticize-budget-funding.

Airriess, Christopher, A., Wei Li, Karen J. Leong, Angela Chia-Chen Chen, and Verna M. Keith. 2008. "Church-Based Social Capital, Networks and Geographical Scale: Katrina Evacuation, Relocation, and Recovery in a New Orleans Vietnamese American Community." *Geoforum* 39 (3): 1333–46. doi:10.1016/j.geoforum.2007.11.003.

Akerlof, Karen, Edward W. Maibach, Dennis Fitzgerald, Andrew Cedeno, and Amanda Neuman. 2013. "Do people 'personally experience' global warming, and if so how, and does it matter?" *Global Environmental Change*. 23: 81–91.

Aldrich, Daniel. 2010. "Separate and Unequal: Post-Tsunami Aid Distribution in Southern India." *Social Science Quarterly* 91: 1369–89.

———. 2011a. "Social Not Physical Infrastructure: The Critical Role of Civil Society after the 1923 Kobe Earthquake." *Disasters: The Journal of Disaster Studies, Policy and Management* 36: 398–419.

———. 2011b. "The Power of People: Social Capital's Role in Recovery from the 1995 Kobe Earthquake." *Natural Hazards* 56: 595–611.

———. 2012. *Building Resilience: Social Capital in Post-Disaster Recovery*. Chicago: University of Chicago Press.

Aldrich, Daniel, and Kevin Crook. 2008. "Strong Civil Society as a Double-Edged Sword: Siting Trailers in Post-Katrina New Orleans." *Political Research Quarterly* 61: 379–89.

Aldrich, Daniel, and Michelle Meyer. 2015. "Social capital and community resilience." *American Behavioral Scientist* 59 (2): 254–69.

Alesina, Alberto, and Eliana La Ferrara. 2000. "The Determinants of Trust." *NBER Working Paper* W7621. www.nber.org/system/files/working_papers/w7621/w7621.pdf.

Allard, Scott, and Mario Small. n.d. "Reconsidering the Urban Disadvantaged: The Role of Systems, Institutions, and Organizations." *Annals of the American Academy of Political and Social Science* 647 (1): 6–20.

Allen, Greg. 2015. "Ghosts of Katrina Still Haunt New Orleans' Shattered Lower Ninth Ward." *Morning Edition*. National Public Radio, August 3.

Alm, James, and Bibek Adhikari. 2015. "The Role of Tax Exemptions and Credits." Working Paper 1526. Tulane University Working Paper Series. https://ideas.repec .org/p/tul/wpaper/1526.html.

Almond, Gabriel, and Sidney Verba. 1963. *The Civic Culture: Political Attitudes and Democracy in Five Nations*. Princeton, NJ: Princeton University Press.

Alpert, Bruce. 2013a. "How Controversial Biggert-Waters Flood Insurance Bill Became Law." *Times-Picayune*, August 13. www.nola.com.

———. 2013b. "Mary Landrieu Offers Bill to Delay Increases in Flood Insurance Premiums." *Times-Picayune*, May 21. www.nola.com.

———. 2014a. "FEMA out with New Flood Insurance Rates, Reflecting March Law's Changes." *Times-Picayune*, May 30. www.nola.com.

———. 2014b. "Senate Passes Bill Averting Largest Flood Insurance Increases under Biggert-Waters." *Times-Picayune*, March 13. www.nola.com.

American Planning Association/AICP Planning Assistance Team. 2006. "Old Mandeville Redevelopment Strategy." www.planning.org.

Anderson, Alena, and Michelle Thompson. 2012. "Where Y'at? An Evaluation of Commercial Corridor Revitalization Programs in New Orleans." *Planning and Urban Studies Reports and Presentations Paper 11*. https://scholarworks.uno.edu/ plus_rpts/11.

Aneshensel, Carol, and Clea Sucoff. 1996. "The Neighborhood Context of Adolescent Mental Health." *Journal of Health and Social Behavior* 37: 293–310.

Anselin, Luc. 1988. *Spatial Econometrics: Methods and Models*. New York: Kluwer Academic.

———. 2013. *Spatial Econometrics: Methods and Models*. Vol. 4. Springer Science & Business Media.

Applebome, Peter. 1993. "In the Hurricane Belt, a New, Wary Respect." *New York Times*, August 18.

Associated Press. 2006. "Some Residents Angry over New Orleans Plan," January 11. www.nbcnews.com.

———. 2012. "Persistent Gas Shortage after Sandy Prompts Rationing Plan in New York City Area," November 8. www.foxnews.com.

Baer, Susan, and Richard Feiock. 2005. "Private Governments in Urban Areas: Political Contracting and Collective Action." *American Review of Public Administration* 35 (1): 42–56.

Baggetta, Matthew. 2010. "Civic Opportunities in Associations: Interpersonal Interaction, Governance Experience and Institutional Relationships." *Social Forces* 88 (1): 175–99.

Barnett, Jon, Colette Mortreux and W. Neil Adger. 2013. "Barriers and Limits to Adaptation: Cautionary Notes." In *Natural Disasters and Adaptation to Climate Change*, edited by Sarah Boulter, Jean Palutikof, David John Karoly, and Daniela Guitart, 223–35. London: Cambridge University Press.

Baumgartner, Frank, and Bryan Jones. 1993. *Agendas and Instability in American Politics*. Chicago: University of Chicago Press.

Bear, William C. 1985. "Just What Is Urban Service, Anyway?" *Journal of Politics* 47 (3): 881–98.

Bellin, Eva. 2000. "Contingent Democrats: Industrialists, Labor, and Democratization in Late-Developing Countries." *World Politics* 52 (2): 175–205.

Bergal, Jenni, Sara Hiles, Frank Koughan, John McQuaid, Jim Morris, Katy Reckdahl, and Curtis Wilkie. 2007. *City Adrift: New Orleans before and after Katrina*. Baton Rouge: Louisiana State University Press.

Bidgood, Jess. 2016. "A Wrenching Decision Where Black History and Floods Intertwine." *New York Times*. December 9. www.nytimes.com.

Biesbroek, G. Robbert, Catrien J. A. M. Termeer, Judith E. M. Klostermann, and Pavel Kabat. 2014. "Rethinking Barriers to Adaptation: Mechanism-Based Explanation of Impasses in the Governance of an Innovative Adaptation Measure." *Global Environmental Change* 26 (May): 108–18. doi:10.1016/j.gloenvcha.2014.04.004.

Birkland, Thomas, and Sarah Waterman. 2008. "Is Federalism the Reason for Policy Failure in Hurricane Katrina?" *Publius: The Journal of Federalism* 38 (4): 692–714.

Blake, Eric, Todd Kimberlain, Robert Berg, John Cangialosi, and John Beven II. 2013. "Tropical Cyclone Report: Hurricane Sandy." National Hurricane Center. www.nhc.noaa.gov/data/tcr/AL182012_Sandy.pdf.

Blakely, Edward. 2011. *My Storm: Managing the Recovery of New Orleans in the Wake of Katrina*. Philadelphia: University of Pennsylvania Press.

Blossfield, Hans-Peter, Alfred Hamerle, and Karl U. Meyer. 1989. *Event History Analysis*. London: Lawrence Erlbaum Associates.

Bolotin, Fredric, and David L. Cingranelli. 1983. "Equity and Urban Policy: The Underclass Hypothesis Revisited." *Journal of Politics* 45 (1): 209–19.

Bova-Hiatt, Lisa, Matt Millea, and John Redente. 2014. "Rising Waters and Storm Resiliency." Paper presented at the Thirteenth Annual Land Use and Sustainable Development Conference, Pace University Law School, New York, December 5. http://law.pace.edu/sites/default/files/LULC/Conference_2014/Rising%20Waters.pdf.

Box-Steffensmeier, Janet M., and Bradford S. Jones. 1997. "Time Is of the Essence: Event History Models in Political Science." *American Journal of Political Science* 41 (4): 1414–61.

Boyle, John, and David Jacobs. 1982. "The Intracity Distribution of Municipal Services: A Multivariate Analysis." *American Political Science Review* 76 (2): 371–79.

Braden, Susan. 2015. *St. Bernard Parish v. The United States*. 05–1119 L. The US Court of Federal Claims.

Brandt, James. 1982. "Neighborhood Based Multi-Purpose Special Tax Districts." In *Neighborhoods: A Revival*, 1–14. School of Urban and Regional Studies: University of New Orleans.

Brehm, John, and Scott Gates. 1997. *Working, Shirking and Sabotage: Bureaucratic Response to a Democratic Public*. Ann Arbor: University of Michigan Press.

Brenhouse, Hillary. 2010. "Plans Shrivel for Chinese Eco-City." *New York Times*, June 24.

Briggs, Xavier de Souza, ed. 2005. *The Geography of Opportunity: Race and Housing Choice in Metropolitan America*. Washington, DC: Brookings Institution Press.

Brooks, Jane S., and Alma H. Young. 1993. "Revitalising the Central Business District in the Face of Decline: The Case of New Orleans, 1973–1993." *Town Planning Review* 64 (3): 251–71. doi:10.2307/40113232.

Buchanan, Sarah. 2012. "Landrieu Says Region Must Rethink Its Coastal Remedies." *Louisiana Weekly*, March 19. www.louisianaweekly.com.

Buettner, Russ, and David Chen. 2014. "Hurricane Sandy Recovery Program in New York City Was Mired by Its Design." *New York Times*, September 4.

Burby, Raymond, Emil Malizia, and P. J. May. 1999. "Beating the building code burden: Code enforcement strategies and Central City success in capturing new housing." University of New Orleans College of Urban and Public Affairs [CUPA] Working Papers, 1991–2000. http://scholarworks.uno.edu/ cupa_wp/17.

Burby, Raymond J. 2006. "Hurricane Katrina and the Paradoxes of Government Disaster Policy: Bringing about Wise Governmental Decisions for Hazardous Areas." *Annals of the American Academy of Political and Social Science* 604: 171–91. doi:10.2307/25097787.

Burchell, Robert, and Sahan Mukherji. 2003. "Conventional Development Versus Managed Growth: The Costs of Sprawl." *American Journal of Public Health* 93 (9): 1534–40.

Bureau of Governmental Research. 1996. "Property Taxes in New Orleans: Who Pays? Who Doesn't? And Why?" www.bgr.org/wp-content/uploads/2017/07/PropertyTax esInNewOrleans.pdf.

Burkett, V. R., D. B. Zilkoski, and D. A. Hart. 2003. "Sea-Level Rise and Subsidence: Implications for Flooding in New Orleans, Louisiana." In *U.S. Geological Survey Subsidence Interest Group Conference: Proceedings of the Technical Meeting, Galveston, Texas, November 27–29, 2001*, edited by Keith Prince and Devin Galloway, 63–70. US Geological Survey. http://pubs.er.usgs.gov/publication/2000794.

Burns, Peter. 2006. *Electoral Politics Is Not Enough: Racial and Ethnic Minorities and Urban Politics*. Albany: State University of New York Press.

Burns, Peter, and Matthew Thomas. 2006. "The Failure of the Nonregime: How Katrina Exposed New Orleans as a Regimeless City." *Urban Affairs Review* 41 (4): 517–27.

———. 2015. *Reforming New Orleans: The Contentious Politics of Change in the Big Easy*. Ithaca: Cornell University Press.

Campanella, Richard. 2008. *Bienville's Dilemma: A Historical Geography of New Orleans*. Lafayette: University of Louisiana at Lafayette/Garrett County Press.

———. 2011. "The Build/No-Build Line: Mapping out the philosophies on the future land use of New Orleans." *Metropolitics*. June 1. www.metropolitiques.eu/The-Build -No-Build-Line.html.

Carll, Angela. 1980. "United: Residents of Eastern N.O. Development Have Conquered Their Growing Pains." *Times-Picayune/States Item*, September 20.

Carnegie Corporation of New York. 2012. "New Orleans Celebrates Opening of Carnegie Corporation-Funded Rosa F. Keller Library and Community Center." March
13. http://carnegie.org.

Census. 2003. "Poverty:1999. Census 2000 Brief." www.census.gov/prod/2003pubs
/c2kbr-19.pdf.

———. 2010. www.census.gov.

———. n.d. "Poverty Rate of Persons in 1969, 1979 and 1989 for Cities with a Population of 100,000 or More." Historical Census Data. www.census.gov/data/tables/time
-series/dec/cph-series/cph-l/cph-l-185.html.

Chamlee-Wright, Emily, and Virgil Henry Storr. 2009. "There's No Place Like New Orleans: Sense of Place and Community Recovery in the Ninth Ward After Hurricane
Katrina." *Journal of Urban Affairs* 31 (5): 615–34.

———. 2010. "The Role of Social Entrepreneurship in Post-Katrina Community Recovery." *International Journal of Innovation and Regional Development* 2 (1–2): 149–64.

———. 2011. "Social Capital, Lobbying and Community-Based Interest Groups." *Public
Choice* 149 (1/2): 167–85. doi:10.1007/s11127-011-9834-7.

Chang, I-Chun Catherine, and Eric Sheppard. 2013. "China's Eco-Cities as Variegated1
Urban Sustainability: Dongtan Eco-City and Chongming Eco-Island." *Journal of
Urban Technology* 20 (1): 57–75. doi:10.1080/10630732.2012.735104.

Chaskin, Robert. 2001. "Building Community Capacity: A Definitional Framework
and Case Studies from a Comprehensive Community Initiative." *Urban Affairs
Review* 36 (3): 291–323.

Chen, Jowei. 2013. "Voter Partisanship and the Effect of Distributive Spending
on Political Participation." *American Journal of Political Science* 57 (1): 200–17.
doi:10.1111/j.1540-5907.2012.00613.x.

Cheong, So-Min. 2011. "Policy solutions in the US." *Climatic Change* 106 (1): 57–70.

Chief of Staff (Anonymous). 2008. Interview with Chief of Staff, Councilman A, New
Orleans City Council.

Cingranelli, David. 1981. "Race, Politics and Elites: Testing Alternative Models of Municipal Service Distribution." *American Journal of Political Science* 25 (4): 664–92.

City of New Orleans. 2006. "Village De l'Est Neighborhood Planning District 10
Rebuilding Plan." www.nolaplans.com/plans/Lambert%20Final/District_10_Fi-
nal_Village%20de%20L%27est.pdf.

———. 2011. *Neighborhood Participation Program.* New Orleans: City of New Orleans.
https://nola.gov/nola/media/Neighborhood-Engagement/Files/City-NPP-Book.pdf.

Cohen, Cathy, and Michael Dawson. 1993. "Neighborhood Poverty and African American Politics." *American Political Science Review* 87 (2): 286–302.

Coleman, James. 1988. "Social Capital in the Creation of Human Capital." *American
Journal of Sociology* 94: 95–120.

Col, Jeanne-Marie. 2007. "Managing Disasters: The Role of Local Government." *Public
Administration Review* 67 (December): 114–24. doi:10.1111/j.1540-6210.2007.00820.x.

Colten, Craig. 2005. *An Unnatural Metropolis: Wresting New Orleans from Nature.*
Baton Rouge: Louisiana State University Press.

———. 2009. *Perilous Place, Powerful Storms: Hurricane Protection in Coastal Louisiana.* Jackson: University Press of Mississippi.

Colten, Craig, and Alexandra Giancarlo. 2011. "Losing Resilience on the Gulf Coast: Hurricanes and Social Memory." *Environment: Science and Policy for Sustainable Development* 53 (4): 6–19.

Cook, Brian. 2010. "Arenas of Power in Climate Change Policymaking." *Policy Studies Journal* 38 (3): 465–86.

Crean, Sarah. 2013. "Storm Surge: An Interview with Climate Change Expert Klaus Jacob On NYC's Post-Sandy Future." *Gotham Gazette*, January 13. www.gothamgazette.com.

Cripps, Elizabeth. 2011. "Climate Change, Collective Harm and Legitimate Coercion." *Critical Review of International Social and Political Philosophy*, 14 (2): 171–93.

Cutter, Susan L., Christopher T. Emrich, Jerry T. Mitchell, Bryan J. Boruff, Melanie Gall, Mathew C. Schmidtlein, Christopher G. Burton, and Ginni Melton. 2006. "The long road home: Race, class, and recovery from Hurricane Katrina." *Environment: Science and Policy for Sustainable Development* 48 (2): 8–20.

Daniels, Ronald, Donald Kettl, and Howard Kunreuther, eds. 2006. *On Risk and Disaster: Lessons from Hurricane Katrina.* Philadelphia: University of Pennsylvania Press.

Dasgupta, Partha. 2003. "Social Capital and Economic Performance: Analytics." In *Foundations of Social Capital*, 309–50. edited by Elinor Ostrom and T. K. Ahn. Cheltenham, UK: Edward Elgar.

Dauber, Michelle Landis. 2013. *The Sympathetic State: Disaster Relief and the Origins of the American Welfare State.* Chicago: University of Chicago Press.

Davenport, Coral, and Campbell Robertson. 2016. "Resettling the First American 'Climate Refugees.'" *New York Times*, May 2. www.nytimes.com.

Davey, Monica. 2013. "Financial Crisis Just a Symptom of Detroit's Woes." *New York Times*, July 9. www.nytimes.com.

Dawson, Michael. 2011. *Not in Our Lifetimes: The Future of Black Politics.* Chicago: University of Chicago Press.

Dear, Michael. 2002. "Los Angeles and the Chicago School: Invitation to a Debate." *City & Community* 1 (1): 5–32. doi:10.1111/1540–6040.00002.

DeFillipis, James. 2001. "The Myth of Social Capital in Community Development." *Housing Policy Debate* 12: 781–806.

Department of Safety and Permits. 2010. "Guideline for Building Permits." Technical Report. New Orleans: City of New Orleans. www.nola.gov/nola/media/One-Stop-Shop/Safety%20and%20Permits/SP-Brochure-Guidelines-for-Building-Permits.pdf.

Derthick, Martha. 2007. "Where Federalism Didn't Fail." *Public Administration Review* 67: 36–47.

de Sam Lazaro, Fred. 2005. "Hurricane Katrina Faith-Based Relief Efforts." *Religion and Ethics Newsweekly*. PBS.

de Tocqueville, Alexis. 2003. *Democracy in America.* New York: Penguin Books.

Dewar, Margaret, and June Manning Thomas, eds. 2012. *The City after Abandonment*. Philadelphia: University of Pennsylvania Press.

Dolfman, Michael L., Solidelle Fortier Wasser, and Bruce Bergman. 2007. "The Effects of Hurricane Katrina on the New Orleans Economy." New York: Bureau of Labor Statistics. www.bls.gov/opub/mlr/2007/06/art1full.pdf.

Duneier, Mitchell. 2004. "Scrutinizing the Heat: On Ethnic Myth and the Importance of Shoe Leather." *Critical Sociology* 33 (2): 139–50.

Dynes, Russell. 1974. *Organized Behavior in Disaster*. Columbus: Disaster Research Center, Ohio State University.

Earle, D. W. Jr. 1975. "Land Subsidence Problems and Maintenance Costs to Homeowners in East New Orleans, Louisiana." PhD diss., Department of Oceanography & Coastal Sciences: Louisiana State University.

Eaton, Leslie. 2006. "A New Landfill in New Orleans Sets Off a Battle." *New York Times*, May 8. www.nytimes.com.

Echeverria, John. 2015. "Ruling in MR-GO Takings Lawsuit." *Takings Litigation* (blog). May 2. www.takingslitigation.com/2015/05/02/ruling-in-mr-go-takings-lawsuit.

Edwards, Wanda. 2010. "Five Years after Katrina Gulf Coast Building Codes Still Inadequate." *Insurance Journal*. August 30. www.insurancejournal.com/news/south central/2010/08/30/112857.htm

Eggler, Bruce. 2012. "Three New Orleans Neighborhoods to Vote on Security Districts Nov. 6." *Times-Picayune*, October 25. www.nola.com.

Ehrenfeucht, Renia, and Marla Nelson. 2011. "Planning, Population Loss and Equity in New Orleans after Hurricane Katrina." *Planning Practice and Research* 26 (2): 129–46.

———. 2012. "Recovery in a Shrinking City: Challenges to 'Rightsizing' Post-Katrina New Orleans." In *The City after Abandonment*, edited by Margaret Dewar and June Manning Thomas, 133–50. Philadelphia: University of Pennsylvania Press.

Ellermann, Antje. 2005. "Coercive capacity and the politics of implementation: Deportation in Germany and the United States." *Comparative Political Studies*. 38 (10): 1219–244.

Elliot, James, Timothy Haney, and Petrice Sams-Abiodun. 2010. "Limits to Social Capital: Comparing Network Assistance in Two New Orleans Neighborhoods Devastated by Hurricane Katrina." *Sociological Quarterly* 51 (4): 634–48.

Elliott, Debbie. 2015. "New Orleans Neighborhoods Scrabble for Hope in Abandoned Ruins." *All Things Considered*. National Public Radio, August 22. www.npr.org.

Enserink, Bert, Dille Kamps, and Erik Mostert. 2003. "Public Participation in River Basin Management in the Netherlands: (Not) Everybody's Concern." Workpackage 4. The HarmoniCOP Project. Delft University of Technology. www.harmonicop .uni-osnabrueck.de/_files/_down/Netherlands.pdf.

Erikson, Kai. 1976. *Everything in Its Path: Destruction of Community in the Buffalo Creek Flood*. New York: Simon and Schuster.

Erikson, Robert S. 1995. "State Turnout and Presidential Voting—a Closer Look." *American Politics Quarterly* 23 (4): 387-96.

Evans, Pat, and Sarah Lewis. 2009. "A Reciprocity of Tears: Community Engagement after a Disaster." In *Civic Engagement in the Wake of Katrina*, edited by Amy Koritz and George Sanchez, 44–58. Ann Arbor: University of Michigan Press.

Feiock, Richard. 1994. "The Political Economy of Growth Management." *American Politics Research* 22 (2): 208–20.

FEMA. 2002. "National Flood Insurance Program: Program Description." www.fema .gov/media-library-data/20130726-1447-20490-2156/nfipdescrip_1_.pdf.

————. 2006. "FEMA 549, Hurricane Katrina in the Gulf Coast: Mitigation Assessment Team Report, Building Performance Observations, Recommendations, and Technical Guidance." www.fema.gov/media-library/assets/documents/4069.

————. 2012. "The History of Building Elevation in New Orleans." www.fema.gov /media-library-data/20130726-1919-25045-5921/cno_history_bldg_elev_042313 .pdf.

————. 2013. "Chapter 9. Mitigation Successes and Best Practices." Mitigation Assessment Team Report. www.fema.gov/media-library-data/20130726-1520- 20490-9868/549_ch9.pdf.

————. 2014. "Mitigation Best Practices Portfolio: Hurricane Katrina—Louisiana." www.fema.gov/mitigation-best-practices-portfolio/mitigation-best-practices -portfolio-hurricane-katrina-louisiana.

Finger, David. 2008. "Stranded and Squandered: Lost on the Road Home." *Journal for Social Justice* 7 (1): 59–100.

Fischel, William A. 2001. *The Homevoter Hypothesis: How Home Values Influence Local Government Taxation, School Finance, and Land-Use Policies.* Cambridge, MA: Harvard University Press.

Fisher, Robert, and Eric Shragge. 2007. "Contextualizing Community Organizing: Lessons from the Past, Tensions in the Present, Opportunities for the Future." In *Transforming the City: Community Organizing and the Challenge of Political Change*, edited by Marion Orr, 193–217. Lawrence: University Press of Kansas.

Ford, Kristina. 2011. *The Trouble with City Planning: What New Orleans Can Teach Us.* New Haven, CT: Yale University Press.

Forgette, Richard, Marvin King, and Bryan Dettrey. 2008. "Race, Hurricane Katrina, and Government Satisfaction: Examining the Role of Race in Assessing Blame." *Publius* 38 (4): 671–91. doi:10.2307/20184997.

Foster, Sheila. 2013. "Collective Action and the Urban Commons." *Notre Dame Law Review* 87 (1): 57–134.

Francaviglia, Richard. 1978. "Xenia Rebuilds: Effects of Predisaster Conditioning on Postdisaster Redevelopment." *Journal of the American Institute of Planners* 44 (1): 13–24.

Franzese, Robert, and Jude Hays. 2006. "Spatio-Temporal Models for Political-Science Panel and Time-Series-Cross-Section Data." www.personal.umich.edu/~franzese/ FranzeseHays.S.ST.EconometricsForPS.PolMeth06.pdf.

Fuchs, Ester. 1992. *Mayors and Money: Fiscal Policy in New York and Chicago.* Chicago: University of Chicago Press.

Fukuyama, Francis. 1995. *Trust: The Social Virtues and the Creation of Prosperity.* New York: Free Press.

Fussell, Elizabeth. 2006. *Leaving New Orleans: Social Stratification, Networks, and Hurricane Evacuation.* Social Science Research Council. https://items. ssrc.org/understanding-katrina/leaving-new-orleans-social-stratification-networks-and-hurricane-evacuation.

Gallup. 2014. "Illinois Residents Least Trusting of Their State Government." www .gallup.com/poll/168251/illinois-residents-least-trusting-state-government.aspx.

Garcia, Andrew W. 2013. "Hurricane Katrina and the City of New Orleans." In *Natural Disasters and Adaptation to Climate Change,* edited by Sarah Boulter, Jean Palutikof, David John Karoly, and Daniela Guitart, 21-30. Cambridge: Cambridge University Press.

Gafford, Farrah D. 2010. "Rebuilding the park: The impact of Hurricane Katrina on a black middle-class neighborhood." *Journal of Black Studies* 41 (2): 385-404.

———. 2013. "'It Was a Real Village' Community Identity Formation among Black Middle-Class Residents in Pontchartrain Park." *Journal of Urban History* 39 (1): 36-58.

Geaghan, Kimberly. 2011. "Forced to Move: An Analysis of Hurricane Katrina Movers." US Census Bureau. www.census.gov/programs-surveys/ahs/research/ working-papers/HK_Movers-FINAL.html.

Germany, Kent. 2007. *New Orleans after the Promises: Poverty, Citizenship, and the Search for the Great Society.* Athens: University of Georgia Press.

Gerring, John. 2004. "What Is a Case Study and What Is It Good For?" *American Political Science Review* 98 (2): 341-54.

Gibson, Campbell. 1998. "Population of the 100 Largest Cities and Other Urban Places in the United States: 1790 to 1990." US Census Bureau. www.census.gov/library /working-papers/1998/demo/POP-twps0027.html.

Giegengack, Robert, and Kenneth Foster. 2006. "Physical Constraints on Reconstructing New Orleans." In *Rebuilding Urban Places After Disaster: Lessons from Hurricane Katrina,* edited by Eugenie Birch and Susan Wachter, 13-33. Philadelphia: University of Pennsylvania Press.

Gillis, Justin, and Felicity Barringer. 2012. "As Coasts Rebuild and U.S. Pays, Repeatedly, the Critics Ask Why." *New York Times,* November 18. www.nytimes.com.

Glaeser, Edward. 2005. "Should the Government Rebuild New Orleans, Or Just Give Residents Checks?" *The Economists' Voice* 2 (4): 1-7.

———. 2011. *Triumph of the City: How Our Greatest Invention Makes Us Richer, Smarter, Greener, Healthier, and Happier.* New York: Penguin Books.

Glaeser, Edward, Matt Resseger, and Kristina Tobio. n.d. "Inequality in Cities." *Journal of Regional Science* 49 (4): 617-46.

Glock, Birgit, and Harmut Haussermann. 2004. "New Trends in Urban Development and Public Policy in Eastern Germany: Dealing with the Vacant Housing Problem at the Local Level." *International Journal of Urban and Regional Research* 28 (4): 1-7.

Go, Min Hee. 2012. "The Federal Disaster: The Failed Logic of Disaster Prevention in New Orleans." *Disasters, Hazards, and Law* 17: 155–74.

———. 2014. "The Power of Participation: Explaining the Building Permits Explosion in Post-Katrina New Orleans." *Urban Affairs Review*. 50 (1): 34–62.

_____. 2016. "Building a Safe State: Hybrid Diffusion of Building Code Adoption in American States." *American Review of Public Administration*. 46 (6): 713-33.

———. 2018. "The Tale of a Two-Tiered City: Community Civic Structure and Spatial Inequality in Post-Katrina New Orleans." *Journal of Urban Affairs*. 40 (8): 1093–114.

Goldberg, Michelle. 2006. "Saving the Neighborhood." *Salon*, February 24. www.salon.com/2006/02/24/broadmoor.

Goldberg, Suzanne. 2014. "Eight Ways Climate Change Is Making the World More Dangerous." *Guardian*, July 4. www.theguardian.com.

Gomez, Rafael, and Eric Santor. 2001. "Membership Has Its Privileges: The Effect of Social Capital and Neighbourhood Characteristics on the Earnings of Microfinance Borrowers." *Canadian Journal of Economics* 34 (4): 943–66.

Goodyear, Sarah. 2013. "We're in This Together: What the Dutch Know about Flooding That We Don't." *Bloomberg: CityLab*, January 9. www.citylab.com/politics/2013/01/were-together-what-dutch-know-about-water-we-dont/4355.

Gordon, Peter, and Sanford Ikeda. 2007. "Power to the Neighborhoods: The Devolution of Authority in Post-Katrina New Orleans." Policy Comment 12. *Mercatus Policy Series*, Policy Comment No. 12, Arlington, VA: Mercatus Center at George Mason University.

Gotham, Kevin, and Miriam Greenberg. 2014. *Crisis Cities: Disaster and Redevelopment in New York and New Orleans*. New York: Oxford University Press.

Gotham, Kevin, and John McLachlan, eds. 2010. "New Orleans—Urban Long-Term Research Area Exploratory (ULTRA-Ex) Project." Tulane University. http://tulane.edu/liberal-arts/upload/ULTRA-Annual-Report-pdf.

Grabosky, Peter. 2013. "Beyond Responsive Regulation: The Expanding Role of Non-State Actors in the Regulatory Process." *Regulation & Governance* 7 (1): 114–23.

Granovetter, Mark. 1973. "The Strength of Weak Ties." *American Journal of Sociology* 78 (6): 1360–80.

Gratz, Roberta Brandes. 2012. "What Cities Looking to Shrink Can Learn from New Orleans." City Lab. April 5. www.citylab.com/equity/2012/04/what-cities-looking-shrink-can-learn-new-orleans/1685.

Greater New Orleans Data Center. 2009.

Großman, Katrin, Marco Bontje, Annegret Haase, and Vlad Mykhnenko. 2013. "Shrinking Cities: Notes for the Future Research Agenda." *Cities* 35: 221–25.

Groves, David, Christopher Sharon, and Debra Knopman. n.d. "Planning Tool to Support Louisiana's Decisionmaking on Coastal Protection and Restoration." Santa Monica: Gulf Policy Institute, Rand Corporation. www.rand.org/pubs/technical_reports/TR1266.html.

Gutierrez, Alan. 2008. "A Spreadsheet with Every Permit Issued in Orleans Parish since January of 2005." *Think NOLA*. http://thinknola.com/post/permits-spreadsheets.

Gutierrez, Roberto. 2002. "Parametric Frailty and Shared Frailty Survival Models." *Stata Journal* 2: 22–44.

Haas, Edward. 2014. *Mayor Victor H. Schiro: New Orleans in Transition, 1961–1970.* Jackson: University Press of Mississippi.

Hackworth, Jason. 2015. "Rightsizing as Spatial Austerity in the American Rust Belt." *Environment and Planning A: Economy and Space* 47 (4): 766–82.

Hajnal, Zoltan. 2009. *America's Uneven Democracy: Race, Turnout, and Representation in City Politics.* New York: Cambridge University Press.

Hall, Jim. 2015. "How a Children's Playground Protects Rotterdam from Flooding." *Guardian*, February 11. www.theguardian.com.

Hamel, Liz, Jamie Firth, and Mollyann Brodie. 2015. "New Orleans Ten Years After the Storm: The Kaiser Family Foundation Katrina Survey Project." Kaiser Family Foundation. www.kff.org/other/report/new-orleans-ten-years-after-the-storm-the -kaiser-family-foundation-katrina-survey-project/.

Hammer, David. 2010. "New Orleans Redevelopment Authority Gets $30 Million Federal Grant to Fight Blight." *Times-Picayune*, January 14.

———. 2012a. "Homes Were Raised after Katrina with Taxpayer Money, Then Abandoned." *Times-Picayune*, June 24.

———. 2012b. "State's Post-Katrina Home Elevation Program Was Cut off by FEMA." *Times-Picayune*, June 24.

———. 2015. "Examining Post-Katrina Road Home Program." *Advocate*. August 23. www.theadvocate.com/baton_rouge/news/article_f9763ca5-42ba-5a62-9935 -c5f7ca94a7c4.html.

Haas, Edward. 2014. *Mayor Victor H. Schiro: New Orleans in Transition, 1961–1970.* Jackson: University Press of Mississippi.

Hardin, Garett. 1968. "The Tragedy of the Commons." *Science* 162: 1243–48.

Harris, Gardiner. 2014. "Borrowed Time on Disappearing Land." *New York Times*, March 28.

Harris-Lacewell, Melissa. 2004. *Barbershops, Bibles, and B.E.T: Everyday Talk and Black Political Thought.* Princeton, NJ: Princeton University Press.

Harvey, David. 2008. "The right to the city." *The City Reader.* 6 (1): 23–40.

Hastings, Sally. 1995. *Neighborhood and Nation in Tokyo, 1905–1937.* Pittsburgh: University of Pittsburgh Press.

Hauser, Christine. 2005. "Mayor of New Orleans Announces Layoffs of City Workers." *New York Times*, October 5.

Hawes, Daniel, Rene Rocha, and Kenneth Meier. 2013. "Social Capital in the 50 States: Measuring State-Level Social Capital, 1986–2004." *State Politics & Policy Quarterly* 13 (1): 121–38.

Hawkins, Robert, and Katherine Maurer. 2010. "Bonding, Bridging, and Linking: How Social Capital Operated in New Orleans Following Hurricane Katrina." *British Journal of Social Work* 40 (6): 1777–93.

Healy, Andrew, and Neil Malhotra. 2009. "Myopic Voters and Natural Disaster Policy." *American Political Science Review* 103 (3): 387–406.

Helsley, Robert and William Strange. 1998. "Private Government." *Journal of Public Economics* 69 (2): 281–304.

Henderson, Michael, and Wayne Parent. 2008. "Louisiana." In *Political Encyclopedia of U.S. States and Regions*, edited by Donald P. Haider-Markel, 233–44. Washington, DC: CQ Press.

Henstra, Daniel. 2010. "Evaluating Local Government Emergency Management Programs: What Framework Should Public Managers Adopt?" *Public Administration Review* 70 (2): 236–46.

Hero, Rodney. 1986. "The Urban Service Delivery Literature: Some Questions and Considerations." *Polity* 18 (4): 659–77.

Higgins, Andrew. 2012. "Lessons for U.S. From a Flood-Prone Land." *New York Times*, November 14.

Hilbe, Joseph M. 2007. *Negative Binomial Regression*. 2nd ed. Cambridge: Cambridge University Press.

Hildreth, W. Bartley. 2009. "The Financial Logistics of Disaster: The Case of Hurricane Katrina." *Public Performance & Management Review* 32 (3): 400–36.

Hirayama, Yosuke. 2000. "Collapse and Reconstruction: Housing Recovery Policy in Kobe after the Hanshin Great Earthquake." *Housing Studies* 15 (1): 111–28. doi:10.1080/02673030082504.

Hirsch, Arnold. 1983. *Making the Second Ghetto: Race and Housing in Chicago 1940–1960.* Chicago: University of Chicago Press.

Hirschman, Albert. 1970. *Exit, Voice and Loyalty: Responses to Decline in Firms, Organizations, and States.* Cambridge, MA: Harvard University Press.

Holbein, Andrew. 2009. "Building a Recovery Department: New Orleans Attacks Blight through Code Enforcement." *Planning (Chicago, Ill. 1969)* 75 (2): 36–339.

Holt, Lester, and Matthew Vann. 2015. "This Is the Only Grocery Store in the Lower Ninth Ward after Katrina." *NBC Nightly News.* www.nbcnews.com/nightly-news/its-last-grocery-store-standing-lower-ninth-ward-n417971.

Hoople, Daniel. 2013. "The Budgetary Impact of the Federal Government's Response to Disasters." Congressional Budget Office Official Website. September 23. www.cbo.gov/publication/44601.

Horowitz, Andy. 2014. "Hurricane Betsy and the Politics of Disaster in New Orleans' Lower Ninth Ward, 1965–1967." *Journal of Southern History* 80 (4): 893–934.

Horwich, George. 2000. "Economic Lessons of the Kobe Earthquake." *Economic Development and Cultural Change* 48 (3): 521–42. doi:10.1086/452609.

Hosmer, David W., Stanley Lemeshow, and Susanne May. 2008. *Applied Survival Analysis: Regression Modeling of Time to Event Data.* 2nd ed. New York: Wiley-Interscience.

Hudson, Blake. 1991. "Reconstituting Land-Use Federalism to Address Transitory and Perpetual Disasters: The Bimodal Federalism Framework." *Brigham Young Law Review.* http://digitalcommons.law.byu.edu/lawreview/vol2011/iss6/6.

Hummel, Daniel. 2015. "Right-Sizing Cities in the United States: Defining Its Strategies." *Journal of Urban Affairs*, 37 (4): 397–409. doi:10.1111/juaf.12150.

Imai, Kosuke, Gary King, and Olivia Lau. 2009. *Zelig: Everyone's Statistical Software.* http://gking.harvard.edu/zelig.

Insurance Information Institute. 2010. "Hurricane Katrina Fact File." New York: Insurance Information Institute. www.iii.org/sites/default/files/docs/pdf/HurricaneKa trinaFactFile-032010.pdf.

Jackman, Robert, and Ross Miller. 1998. "Social Capital and Politics." *Annual Review of Political Science* 1: 75–93.

Jacobs, Jane. 1961. *The Death and Life of Great American Cities.* New York: Random House.

Johnson, Cedric, ed. 2011. *The Neoliberal Deluge: Hurricane Katrina, Late Capitalism, and the Remaking of New Orleans.* Minneapolis: University of Minnesota Press.

Louisiana Division of Administration. 2011. "Executive Budget, 2011–2012." March 11. www.doa.la.gov/opb/pub/FY12/FY12ExecutiveBudget.pdf.

Jones, Bryan. 1981. "Party and Bureaucracy: The Influence of Intermediary Groups on Urban Public Service Delivery." *American Political Science Review* 75 (3): 688–700.

Jones, Bryan, Saadia Greenberg, and Joseph Drew. 1980. *Service Delivery in the City: Citizen Demand and Bureaucratic Rules.* New York: Longman.

Journal of American History. 2007. "New Orleans's Levee System: Timeline." http:// archive.oah.org/special-issues/katrina/resources/levee.html.

Kamel, Nabil. 2012. "Social Marginalisation, Federal Assistance and Repopulation Patterns in the New Orleans Metropolitan Area Following Hurricane Katrina." *Urban Studies* 49 (14): 3211–31.

Kaniasty, Krzysztof, and Fran Norris. n.d. "A Test of the Social Support Deterioration Model in the Context of Natural Disaster." *Journal of Personality and Social Psychology* 64 (3): 395–408.

Katz, Bruce, and Jennifer Bradley. 2014. *The Metropolitan Revolution: How Cities and Metros Are Fixing Our Broken Politics and Fragile Economy.* Washington, DC: Brookings Institution Press.

Kaufmann, Karen. 2004. *The Urban Voter: Group Conflict and Mayoral Voting Behavior in American Cities.* Ann Arbor: University of Michigan Press.

Kelly, Eric Damian. 1996. "Fair Housing, Good Housing, or Expensive Housing? Are Building Bodes Part of the Problem or Part of the Solution?" *John Marshall Law Review.* 29 (2): 349–68.

Kennedy School of Government. 2009. "Case Study of Broadmoor's Community Based Recovery." "Broadmoor Lives": A New Orleans Neighborhood's Battle to Recover from Hurricane Katrina. Harvard University. www.belfercenter.org/publication /case-study-broadmoors-community-based-recovery.

Kershner, Jessi. 2010. "Restoration and Managed Retreat of Pacifica State Beach [Case Study on a Project of ESA PWA]." Product of EcoAdapt's State of Adaptation Program. www.cakex.org/case-studies/restoration-and-managed-retreat-pacifica -state-beach.

Key, V. O. 1949. *Southern Politics in State and Nation.* Knoxville: University of Tennessee Press.

Kimmelman, Michael. 2013. "Going with the Flow; Dutch Engineers Turn to 'Controlled Flooding' to Protect Land from Storms." *International Herald Tribune*, February 16. www.lexisnexis.com/lnacui2api/api/version1/getDocCui?lni=57RW-DCV1-JC85-N4YW&csi=270944,270077,11059,8411&hl=t&hv=t&hnsd=f&hns=t&hgn=t&oc=00240&perma=true.

King, Gary, Robert Keohane, and Sidney Verba. 1994. *Designing Social Inquiry: Scientific Inference in Qualitative Research*. Princeton, NJ: Princeton University Press.

Kingdon, John. 2011. *Agendas, Alternatives, and Public Policies*. New York: Longman.

Kirk, David S. 2009. "A Natural Experiment on Residential Change and Recidivism: Lessons from Hurricane Katrina." *American Sociological Review* 74 (3): 484–505.

Klein, Jennifer. 2015. "Potential Liability of Governments for Failure to Prepare for Climate Change." Sabin Center for Climate Change Law: Columbia Law School. http://web.law.columbia.edu/sites/default/files/microsites/climate-change/klein_-_liability_of_governments_for_failure_to_prepare_for_climate_change.pdf.

Klinenberg, Eric. 2002. *Heat Wave: A Social Autopsy of Disaster in Chicago*. Chicago: University of Chicago Press.

———. 2013. "Adaptation." *New Yorker*, January 7. www.newyorker.com.

Knack, Stephen. 2000. *Social Capital and the Quality of Government: Evidence from the States*. Policy Research Working Paper. Washington, DC: The World Bank. https://elibrary.worldbank.org/doi/abs/10.1596/1813-9450-2504.

Knowles, Scott Gabriel. 2011. *The Disaster Experts: Mastering Risk in Modern America*. Philadelphia: University of Pennsylvania Press.

Knowles, Scott Gabriel, and Howard Kunreuther. 2014. "Troubled Waters: The National Flood Insurance Program in Historical Perspective." *Journal of Policy History* 26 (3): 327–53.

Ko, Maeda. 2010. "Two Modes of Democratic Breakdown: A Competing Risks Analysis of Democratic Durability." *Journal of Politics* 72 (4): 1129–43.

Koritz, Amy, and George Sanchez. n.d. *Civic Engagement in the Wake of Katrina*. Ann Arbor: University of Michigan Press.

Koslov, Liz. 2016. "The Case for Retreat." *Public Culture*. 28.2 (79): 359–87.

———. 2019. "Avoiding Climate Change: 'Agnostic Adaptation' and the Politics of Public Silence." *Annals of the Association of American Geographers* 109 (2): 568–80.

Kotkin, Joel. 2013. "America's Fastest-Growing Cities Since the Recession." *Forbes*, June 18. www.forbes.com.

Kreps, Gary, and Susan Bosworth. 1993. "Disaster, Organizing, and Role Enactment: A Structural Approach." *American Journal of Sociology* 99 (2): 428–63.

Krupa, Michelle. 2010. "Five Years after Katrina, New Orleans Faces Bill for Keeping Its Footprint." *Times-Picayune*, August 4.

Kysar, Douglas A., and Thomas O. McGarity. 2006. "Did Nepa Drown New Orleans? The Levees, the Blame Game, and the Hazards of Hindsight." *Duke Law Journal* 56 (1): 179–235. doi:10.2307/40040543.

Lai, Elisa Chih-Yin. 2009. "Climate Change Impacts on China's Environment: Biophysical Impacts." A China Environmental Health Project Research Brief.

Wilson Center. www.wilsoncenter.org/publication/climate-change-impacts
-chinas-environment-biophysical-impacts.

Lake, Ronald La Due, and Robert Huckfelt. 1998. "Social Capital, Social Networks and
Political Participation." *Political Psychology* 19 (3): 567–84.

Larsen, Larissa, Sharon Harlan, Robert Bolin, Edward J. Hackett, Diane Hope, Andrew
Kirby, Amy Nelson, Tom R. Rex, and Shaphard Wolf. 2004. "Bonding and bridging:
Understanding the relationship between social capital and civic action." *Journal of
Planning Education and Research.* 24 (1): 64–77.

Leanning, Jennifer, and Debarati Guha-Sapir. 2013. "Natural Disasters, Armed Conflict,
and Public Health." *New England Journal of Medicine* 369 (19): 1836–42.

Lefebvre, Henri. 1979. "Space: Social Product and Use Value." In *Critical Sociology:
European Perspective,* edited by J.W. Freiberg, 285–95. London: Halsted Press.

Leong, Karen J., Christopher A. Airriess, Wei Li, Angela Chen, and Verna M. Keith.
2007. "Resilient History and the Rebuilding of a Community: The Vietnamese
American Community in New Orleans East." *Journal of American History* 94 (3):
770–79.

LeSieur, Kenneth. 1965. "Re: Master Plan for Hurricane Flood Control." Institute for
Water Resources. https://biotech.law.lsu.edu/katrina/hpdc/docs/19651124_Citizen
_group_suggestions.pdf.

Lester, William, and Daniel Krejci. 2007. "Business 'Not' as Usual: The National
Incident Management System, Federalism, and Leadership." *Public Administration
Review* 67 (December): 84–93. doi:10.1111/j.1540-6210.2007.00817.x.

Levi, Margaret. 1996. "Social and Unsocial Capital: A Review Essay of Robert Putnam's
Making Democracy Work." *Politics and Society* 24 (1): 45–55.

Lewis, Oscar. 1966. *La Vida: A Puerto Rican Family in the Culture of Poverty–San Juan
and New York.* New York: Random House.

Li, Wei, Christopher Airriess, Angela Chia-Chen Chen, Karen J. Leong, Verna M.
Keith, and Karen L. Adams. 2008. "Surviving Katrina and Its Aftermath: Evacuation and Community Mobilization by Vietnamese Americans and African Americans." *Journal of Cultural Geography* 25 (3): 263–86. doi:10.1080/08873630802476235.

Lin, Tse-Min, Chine-En Wu, and Feng-Yu Lee. 2006. "Neighborhood Influence on the
Formation of National Identity in Taiwan: Spatial Regression with Disjoint Neighborhoods." *Political Research Quarterly* 59 (1): 35–46.

Lipsky, Michael. 1980. *Street-Level Bureaucracy: Dilemmas of the Individual in Public
Services.* New York: Russell Sage Foundation.

Liu, Amy, Matt Fellowes, and Mia Mabanta. 2006. "Special Edition of the Katrina
Index: A One-Year Review of Key Indicators of Recovery in Post-Storm New
Orleans." Washington, DC: Brookings Institution. www.brookings.edu/research
/special-edition-of-the-katrina-index-a-one-year-review-of-key-indicators-of
-recovery-in-post-storm-new-orleans.

Liu, Cheol, and John L. Mikesell. 2014. "The Impact of Public Officials' Corruption on
the Size and Allocation of U.S. State Spending." *Public Administration Review* 74 (3):
346–59. doi:10.1111/puar.12212.

Liu, Coco. 2011. "Shanghai Struggles to Save Itself from the Sea." *New York Times*, September 27.

Livlin, Gary. 2006. "In Rebuilding in the Disaster, Wealth and Class Help Define New Orleans." *New York Times*, April 25.

Logan, John. 2006. *The Impact of Katrina: Race and Class in Storm-Damaged Neighborhoods.* Brown University: Spatial Structures in the Social Sciences (Initiative). https://s4.ad.brown.edu/Projects/Hurricane/report.pdf.

Logan, John, and Harvey Molotch. 1987. *Urban Fortunes: The Political Economy of Place.* Berkeley: University of California Press.

Louisiana Recovery Office. 2013. "Louisiana Recovery." Federal Emergency Management Agency. www.fema.gov/louisiana-recovery.

Louisiana State University Public Policy Lab. 2014. "2014 Louisiana Survey." LSU Manship School of Mass Communication. http://pprllsu.com/wp-content/uploads/2015/12/LA-Survey-2014.pdf.

Lowe, Jeffrey S., and Lisa K. Bates. 2012. "Missing New Orleans: Lessons from the CDC Sector on Vacancy, Abandonment, and Reconstructing the Crescent City." In *The City after Abandonment*, edited by Margaret Dewar and June Manning Thomas, 151-73. Philadelphia: University of Pennsylvania Press.

Lowi, Theodore. 1962. *Legislative Politics U.S.A.* Boston: Little Brown.

MacAusland, Dorothy Brayton. 2017. "Exporting Expertise? Rotterdam's Planners and the Flood Adaptation Industry." PhD diss. Department of Architecture and Planning. Columbia University.

Maestas, Cherie D., Lonna Rae Atkeson, Thomas Croom, and Lisa A. Bryant. 2008. "Shifting the Blame: Federalism, Media, and Public Assignment of Blame Following Hurricane Katrina." *Publius: The Journal of Federalism* 38 (4): 609-32.

Malhotra, Neil, and Alexander G. Kuo. 2008. "Attributing Blame: The Public's Response to Hurricane Katrina." *Journal of Politics* 70 (1): 120-35.

Manney, Dave. 2010. "Getting Back on Track." *HOUR Detroit*, January 22. www.hour detroit.com/Hour-Detroit/February-2010/Getting-Back-on-Track.

Mansbridge, Jane. 2012. "On the Importance of Getting Things Done." *PS: Political Science & Politics.* 45 (1): 1-8.

———. 2014. "Presidential Address: What Is Political Science For?" *Perspectives on Politics.* 12 (1): 8-17.

Martinez-Fernandez, Cristina, Ivonne Audirac, Sylvie Fol, and Emmanuele Cunningham-Sabot. "Shrinking Cities: Urban Challenges of Globalization." *International Journal of Urban and Regional Research* 36 (2): 213-25.

Marwell, Nicole. 2000. "Social Networks and Social Capital as Resources for Neighborhood Revitalization." PhD dissertation. Social Service Administration. University of Chicago.

———. 2007. *Bargaining for Brooklyn: Community Organizations in the Entrepreneurial City.* Chicago: University of Chicago Press.

Mayor's Press Office. 2011. "Mayor Emanuel Announces New Efficiencies in Building Permitting Process." City of Chicago, August 10. www.chicago.gov/city/en/depts

/mayor/press_room/press_releases/2011/august_2011/mayor_emanuel_announces
newefficienciesinbuildingpermittingproces.html.

McCarthy, Justin. 2014. "Louisiana Tilting Democratic in 2014." Gallup. www.gallup.
com/poll/177560/louisiana-tilting-democratic-2014.aspx.

McClurg, Scott. 2003. "Social Networks and Political Participation: The Role of Social
Interaction in Explaining Political Participation." *Political Research Quarterly* 56 (4):
448–64.

McKarthy, Kevin, D. J. Peterson, Narayan Sastry, and Michael Pollard. 2006. "The
Repopulation of New Orleans after Hurricane Katrina." Technical Report. Santa
Monica: RAND Corporation. www.rand.org/content/dam/rand/pubs/technical
_reports/2006/RAND_TR369.pdf.

McPherson, J. Miller, and Lynn Smith-Lovin. 1982. "Women and Weak Ties: Differences by Sex in the Size of Voluntary Organizations." *American Journal of Sociology*
87 (4): 883–904.

McQuarrie, Michael. 2013. "Community Organizations in the Foreclosure Crisis: The
Failure of Neoliberal Civil Society." *Politics & Society* 41 (1): 73–101.

McRoberts, Omar. 2003. *Streets of Glory: Church and Community in a Black Urban
Neighborhood.* Chicago: University of Chicago Press.

Means, Benjamin, and Susan S. Kuo. 2016. "Collective Coercion." *Boston College Law
Review.* 57 (5): 1599.

Meerow, Sara, Joshua Newell, and Melissa Stults. 2016. "Defining urban resilience: A
review." *Landscape and Urban Planning.* 147: 38–49.

Meitrodt, Jeffrey, and Frank Donze. 2005. "Plan Shrinks City Footprint." *Times-
Picayune,* December 14.

"Memo of Meeting: Louisiana Pontchartrain, La. & Vicinity Hurricane Protection
Project." 1976. Baton Rouge, LA. LSU Law, Science, and Public Health Program
Site. http://biotech.law.lsu.edu/katrina/hpdc/docs/19760406_Meeting_with_oppo-
nents_of_barrier_plan.pdf.

Menzel, Donald. 2006. "The Katrina Aftermath: A Failure of Federalism or Leadership?" *Public Administration Review* 66 (6): 808–12.

Michigan Legislature. 2012. *Local Financial Stability and Choice Act 436.* www.legisla
ture.mi.gov/%28S%28whgij4o3utts5lfihqjyjwrd%29%29/mileg.aspx?page=getObject
&objectName=mcl-141-1549.

Michener, Jamila. 2018. *Fragmented Democracy: Medicaid, Federalism, and Unequal
Politics.* New York: Cambridge University Press.

Miet, Hannah. 2005. "Broadmoor Neighborhood's Recovery Has Reached a Plateau."
Times-Picayune, November 28.

Mill, John Stuart. 1843. *System of Logic: Ratiocinative and Inductive.* New York: Long-
mans, Green and Co.

Miranda, Rowan A., and Ittipone Tunyavong. 1981. "Patterned Inequality? Reexam-
ining the Role of Distributive Politics in Urban Service Delivery." *Urban Affairs
Review* 29 (4): 509–34.

Mittal, Anu. 2005. "Army Corps of Engineers: Lake Pontchartrain and Vicinity Hurricane Protection Project." United States Government Accountability Office. www.gao.gov/products/GAO-05-1050T.

Mlandeka, Kenneth. 1981. "The Urban Bureaucracy and the Chicago Political Machine: Who Gets What and the Limits to Political Control." *American Political Science Review* 74 (4): 991–98.

Moore, Katie. 2010. "More N.O. Neighborhoods Seek Security Taxes." WWLTV.

Morenoff, Jeffrey, and Robert Sampson. 1997. "Violent Crime and the Spatial Dynamics of Neighborhood Transition: Chicago, 1970–1990." *Social Forces* 76 (1): 31–64.

Morenoff, Jeffrey, Robert Sampson, and Stephen Raudenbush. 2001. "Neighborhood Inequality, Collective Efficacy and the Spatial Dynamics of Homicide." *Criminology* 39 (3): 517–60.

Morial, Marc. 1999. "Community Development Block Grant Success Stories—Treme Neighborhood." The United States Conference of Mayors. www.usmayors.org /bestpractices/cdbg/pub67.htm.

Morial, Marc, and Robert Whelan. 2000. "Privatizing Government Services in New Orleans." In *Making Government Work: Lessons from America's Governors and Mayors*, edited by Paul J. Andrisani, Simon Hakim, Eva Leeds, 211–22. New York: Rowman & Littlefield.

Morlan, Robert L. 1982. "Sub-Municipal Governance in Practice: The Rotterdam Experience." *The Western Political Quarterly* 35 (3): 425–41. doi:10.2307/447555.

Morris, Robert. 2013. "Good neighbors: Freret's revival has largely avoided the issues that often accompany gentrification." *Uptown Messenger*, August 12. http://uptown messenger.com/2013/08/good-neighbors-frerets-revival-has-largely-avoided-the -issues-that-often-accompany-gentrification.

Mossberger, Karen, and Gerry Stoker. 2001. "The Evolution of Urban Regime Theory: The Challenge of Conceptualization." *Urban Affairs Review* 36 (6): 810–35.

Mumford, Lewis. 1961. *The city in history: Its origins, its transformations, and its prospects*. San Diego: Harcourt, Brace and World.

Myers, Ben. 2015. "Sea to Swallow New Orleans Eventually Regardless of Carbon Limits, Scientists Say." *Times-Picayune*, October 12.

Nance, Earthea. 2009. "Responding to Risk: The Making of Hazard Mitigation Strategy in Post-Katrina New Orleans." *Journal of Contemporary Water Research & Education*. 141(1): 21–30.

National League of Cities. 2016. "Revenue from Taxes." Official Website. www.nlc.org /resource/cities-101-revenue-structures.

National Oceanic and Atmospheric Administration. n.d. "Managed Retreat Strategies Case Studies: Pacifica State Beach Adopts Managed Retreat Strategy." US Department of Commerce. http://coastalmanagement.noaa.gov/initiatives/shoreline_ppr _retreat.html#1.

National Public Radio Cities Project. 2014. "MAP: FEMA Is Buying Out Flood-Prone Homes, But Not Where You Might Expect." October 20. www.npr.org/sections

/thetwo-way/2014/10/20/357611987/map-femas-buying-out-flood-prone-homes
-but-not-where-you-might-expect.

National Research Council. 2015. "Tying Flood Insurance to Flood Risk for Low-Lying
Structures in the Floodplain." Washington, DC: The National Academies Press. doi:
10.17226/21720.

Nelson, Marla. 2014. "Using land swaps to concentrate redevelopment and expand
resettlement options in post-Hurricane Katrina New Orleans." *Journal of the American Planning Association.* 80 (4): 426–37.

Nelson, Marla, Renia Ehrenfeucht, and Shirly Laska. 2007. "Planning, Plans and
People: Professional Expertise, Local Knowledge, and Government Action in Post-
Hurricane Katrina New Orleans." *Cityscape: A Journal of Policy Development and Research* 9 (3): 23–52.

Neuman, Michael. 2005. "Compact City Fallacy." *Journal of Planning Education and Research* 25 (1): 11–26.

Newman, Andy. 2012. "Hurricane Sandy vs. Hurricane Katrina." *New York Times,*
November 27.

New Orleans City Planning Commission. "Adopted Master Plan." www.nola.gov/nola
/media/City-Planning/Ch-13-Combined-w-Opportunity-Sites.pdf.

———. "Land Use Plan." www.nola.gov/getattachment/431b50b4-9559-473c-b927-
fcdf0fb4265e/Vol-2-Ch-14-Land-Use-Plan.

New Orleans Redevelopment Authority. 2013. "Neighborhood Stabilization Program
Phase Two Report." www.noraworks.org/programs/residential/nsp2.

Nicholls, Keith, and J. Steven Picou. 2013. "The impact of Hurricane Katrina on trust in
government." *Social Science Quarterly.* 94(2): 344-361.

Nolan, Bruce. 2010. "N.O. Priest Leaves Parish to Work for Church Tribunal." *Times-Picayune,* June 30.

Nossiter, Adam. 2006. "Rebuilding New Orleans, One Appeal at a Time." *New York Times,* February 5.

OECD. 2014. "Cities and Climate Change." www.oecd.org/env/cc/Cities-and-climate
-change-2014-Policy-Perspectives-Final-web.pdf.

Oliver, J. Eric. 2001. *Democracy in Suburbia.* Princeton: Princeton University Press.

Oliver, J. Eric, and Shang E. Ha. 2007. "Vote Choice in Suburban Elections." *American Political Science Review* 101 (3): 393–408.

Oliver, Melvin. 1988. "The Urban Black Community as Network: Toward a Social Network Perspective." *Sociological Quarterly* 29 (4): 623–45.

Olshansky, Robert, Lewis Hopkins, and Laurie Johnson. 2012. "Disaster and Recovery:
Processes Compressed in Time." *Natural Hazards Review* 13 (3): 173–78.

Olshansky, Robert, and Laurie Johnson. 2010. *Clear as Mud: Planning for the Rebuilding of New Orleans.* Chicago: American Planning Association Press.

Orr, Marion ed. 2007. *Transforming the City: Community Organizing and the Challenge of Political Change.* Lawrence: University Press of Kansas.

Ortiz, Elaine, and Allison Plyer. 2008. "Valassis Lists Data as an Indicator of Population Recovery in the New Orleans Area." Greater New Orleans Data Center.

Oshitani, Shizuka. 2006. *Global Warming Policy in Japan and Britain*. Manchester: Manchester University Press.

Ostrom, Elinor. 1990. *Governing the Commons: The Evolution of Institutions for Collective Action*. Cambridge: Cambridge University Press.

———. 2000. "Social Capital: A Fad or a Fundamental Concept?" In *Social Capital: A Multifaceted Perspective*, edited by Ismail Serageldin and Partha Dasgupta, 172–214. Washington, DC: World Bank Publications.

Peacock, Walter Gillis, and Hugh Gladwin, eds. 1997. *Hurricane Andrew: Ethnicity, Gender, and Sociology of Disasters*. New York: Routledge.

Pekkanen, Robert. 2006. *Japan's Dual Civil Society: Members without Advocates*. Palo Alto, CA: Stanford University Press.

Pekkanen, Robert, Yuko Kawato, and Yutaka Tsujinaka. 2012. "Civil Society and the Triple Disasters." In *Natural Disaster and Nuclear Crisis in Japan*, edited by Jeff Kingston,78–93. London: Routledge.

Peterson, Paul E. 1981. *City Limits*. Chicago: University of Chicago Press.

———. 1995. *The Price of Federalism*. Washington, DC: Brookings Institution.

Phillip, Abby. 2015. "White People in New Orleans Say They're Better Off after Katrina. Black People Don't." *Washington Post*, August 24.

Pierce, Wendell, and Rod Dreher. 2015. *The Wind in the Reeds: A Storm, a Play, and the City that Would Not Be Broken*. New York: Penguin.

Platt, Rutherford H. ed. 1999. *Disasters and Democracy: The Politics of Extreme Natural Events*. Washington, DC: Island Press.

Plyer, Allison. 2014. "Facts for Features: Katrina Impact." The Data Center. www.data centerresearch.org/data-resources/katrina/facts-for-impact.

Plyer, Allison, and Elaine Ortiz. 2011. *Fewer Jobs Means Fewer People and More Vacant Housing*. The Data Center. www.datacenterresearch.org/reports_analysis /jobs-population-and-housing.

Portes, Alejandro. 1998. "Social Capital: Its Origins and Applications in Modern Sociology." *Annual Review of Sociology* 24: 1–24.

PolicyLink and PERE, 2017. "An Equity Profile of New Orleans." https://nationalequity atlas.org/sites/default/files/EP-New-Orleans-june21017-updated.pdf.

Price, Todd A. 2015. "Dunbar's returns, out-of-town chefs and 9 more Eat-Drink-Cook stories you might've missed." *Times-Picayune,* December 7. www.nola.com/ entertainment_life/eat-drink/article_21ecde44-7534-58b6-970f-87d8ca3e207a. html.

Public Affairs Research Council of Louisiana, and Bureau of Governmental Research. 2006. "Municipal Bankruptcy in Perspective." Joint Report. http://parlouisiana.org /wp-content/uploads/2016/03/Municipal-Bankruptcy-in-Perspective-April-2006-1 .pdf.

Putnam, Robert. 1993. *Making Democracy Work: Civic Traditions in Modern Italy*. Princeton, NJ: Princeton University Press.

———. 2000. *Bowling Alone: The Collapse and Revival of American Community*. New York: Simon and Schuster.

———. 2007. "*E Pluribus Unum*: Diversity and Community in the Twenty-First Century: The 2006 Johan Skytte Prize Lecture." *Scandinavian Political Studies* 30: 137–74.

Quarantelli, E. L. 1994. "Looting and Antisocial Behavior in Disasters." Preliminary Paper 205. University of Delaware Disaster Research Center.

Quarantelli, E. L., and Russell Dynes. 1977. "Response to Social Crisis and Disaster." *Annual Review of Sociology* 3: 23–49.

Rahm, Dianne, and Christopher G. Reddick. 2011. "US City Managers' Perceptions of Disaster Risks: Consequences for Urban Emergency Management." *Journal of Contingencies and Crisis Management* 19 (3): 136–46. doi:10.1111/j.1468-5973.2011.00647.x.

Rahman, Atiq, and DL Mallick. n.d. "Climate Change Impacts on Cities of Developing Countries: A Case Study on Dhaka." C40 Tokyo Conference on Climate Change— Adaptation Measures for Sustainable Low Carbon Cities. www.yumpu.com/en /document/read/53868517/climate-change-impacts-on-cities-of-developing-coun tries-a-case-study-on-dhaka.

Raymond J. Bubry, Emil Malizia, and Peter May. 1999. "Beating the Building Code Burden: Code Enforcement Strategies and Central City Success in Capturing New Housing." College of Urban and Public Affairs Working Papers, 1991–2000. University of New Orleans.

"Repetitive Loss Area Analysis #3." 2006. University of New Orleans Center for Hazard Assessment, Response, and Technology. http://floodhelp.uno.edu/images/docs /BroadmoorFinalReport.pdf.

Reeves, Andrew. 2011. "Political disaster: Unilateral powers, electoral incentives, and presidential disaster declarations." *Journal of Politics*. 73 (4): 1142–151.

Rivlin, Gary. 2015. *Katrina: After the Flood*. New York: Simon and Schuster.

Roark, Hal. 2010. Interview with Hal Roark.

Robert, Stephanie. 1999. "Socioeconomic Position and Health: The Independent Contribution of Community Socioeconomic Context." *Annual Review of Sociology* 25: 489–516.

Roberts, Deon. 2006. "No One Truly Knows How Many People Are Back in New Orleans." *New Orleans CityBusiness (New Orleans, LA)*, November, NEWS.

Roberts, Patrick S. 2013. *Disasters and the American State: How Politicians, Bureaucrats, and the Public Prepare for the Unexpected*. New York: Cambridge University Press.

Robertson, Campbell. 2009. "Ruling on Katrina Flooding Favors Homeowners." *New York Times*, November 18.

———. 2014. "Nagin Guilty of 20 Counts of Bribery and Fraud." *New York Times*, February 12.

———. 2015. "A Decade after Katrina, New Orleans Is Partying Again, and Still Rebuilding." *New York Times*, August 29.

Rockefeller Foundation. n.d. "Resilience." www.rockefellerfoundation.org/report /city-resilience-framework/.

Roig-Franzia, Manuel. 2006. "Hostility Greets Katrina Recovery Plan." *Washington Post*, January 12.

Roman, Caterina Gouvis, and Gretchen Moore. 2004. "Measuring Local Institutions and Organizations: The Role of Community Institutional Capacity in Social Capital." Urban Institute. http://webarchive.urban.org/publications/410998.html.

Russell, Gordon. 2004. "Dubious Value." *Times-Picayune*, April 4.

———. 2008. "It's Time for New Orleans to Admit It's a Shrinking City, Some Say." *Times-Picayune*, November 23.

Ryan, Brent D. 2012. "Rightsizing Shrinking Cities: The Urban Design Dimension." In *The City after Abandonment*, edited by Margaret Dewar and June Manning Thomas, 268–88. Philadelphia: University of Pennsylvania Press.

Rybcznski, Witold, and Peter Linneman. 1999. "How to Save Our Shrinking Cities." *Public Interest*. Spring: 30–44.

Saegert, Susan, Mark Warren, and J. Phillip Thompson. 2001. *Social Capital and Poor Communities*. New York: Russell Sage Foundation.

Sampson, Robert. 2008. "Moving to Inequality: Neighborhood Effects and Experiments Meet Social Structure." *American Journal of Sociology* 114: 189–231.

———. 2012. *Great American City*. Chicago: University of Chicago Press.

Sampson, Robert J. 1999. "What Community Supplies." In *Urban Problems and Community Development*, edited by Ronald F. Ferguson and William T. Dickens, 126–66. Washington, DC: Brookings Institution Press.

Sampson, Robert, and Stephen Raudenbush. 2004. "Seeing Disorder: Neighborhood Stigma and the Social Construction of 'Broken Widows.'" *Social Psychology Quarterly* 67 (4): 319–42.

Sampson, Robert, and Thomas Gannon-Rowley. 2002. "Assessing 'Neighborhood Effects': Social Processes and New Directions in Research." *Annual Review of Sociology* 28: 443–78.

Sampson, Robert, and William Julius Wilson. 1995. "Toward a Theory of Race, Crime, and Urban Inequality." In *Crime and Urban Inequality*, edited by John Hagan and Ruth Peterson, 37–54. Palo Alto: Stanford University Press.

Sampson, Robert J., Doug McAdam, Heather MacIndoe, and Simon Weffer-Elizondo. 2005. "Civil Society Reconsidered: The Durable Nature and Community Structure of Collective Civic Action." *American Journal of Sociology* 111(3): 673–714.

Sayer, Katherine. 2014. "Two proposals to bring back Jazzland at Six Flags site; Which one do you like?" Nola.com. March 29. www.nola.com/news/business/article _12975f63-caf2-501e-92ce-7493c7f9a8d1.html.

Schaeffer, E, and A Kashdan. 2010. "Earth, Wind and Fire! Federalism and Incentives in Natural Disaster Response." In *After Katrina: The Political Economy of Disaster and Community Rebound*, edited by Emily Chamlee-Wright and Virgil Henry Storr, 159–84. Northampton: Edward Elgar.

Schleifstein, Mark. 2015a. "Judge: Corps' MR-GO 'Took' Value of Properties in St. Bernard, Lower 9th Ward." *Times-Picayune*, May 1.

———. 2015b. "National Flood Insurance Program Rate-Setting Should Be Overhauled, National Research Council Says." *Times-Picayune*, June 19.

Schneider, Mark, and Paul Teske. 1992. "Toward a Theory of the Political Entrepreneur: Evidence from Local Government." *American Political Science Review* 86 (3): 737–47.

Schwab, James ed. 2014. *Planning for Post-Disaster Recovery: Next Generation*. American Planning Association. www.fema.gov/media-library-data/1425503479190-22edb246b 925ba41104b7d38eddc207f/APA_PAS_576.pdf.

Scott, Richard. 1992. *Organizations: Rational, Natural and Open Systems*. Upper Saddle River, NJ: Prentice Hall.

Segal, David. 2013. "A Missionary's Quest to Remake Motor City." *New York Times*, April 14.

Seidman, Karl F. 2013. *Coming Home to New Orleans: Neighborhood Rebuilding after Katrina*. New York: Oxford University Press.

Senate Proceeding. n.d. "Sen Landrieu Explaining Biggert Waters Act." Washington, DC: C-Span. www.c-span.org/video/?c4450805/ sen-lendrieu-explaining-biggert-waters-act&start=0.

Sharp, Elaine. 2012. *Does Local Government Matter? How Urban Policies Shape Civic Engagement*. Minneapolis: University of Minnesota Press.

Shaw, Clifford, and Henry McKay. 1942. *Juvenile Delinquency and Urban Areas*. Chicago: University of Chicago Press.

Shelby, Janine, and Michael Tredinnick. 1995. "Crisis Intervention with Survivors of Natural Disaster: Lessons from Hurricane Andrew." *Journal of Counseling and Development* 73 (5): 491–97.

Siders, Ann. 2013. "Managed Costal Retreat: A Legal Handbook on Shifting Development Away from Vulnerable Areas." SSRN Working Paper.

Simons, Latoya T. 2007. "Building moratorium, proposed flood zoning and expropriation after Katrina." *Loyola Journal of Public Interest Law*. 9: 39–62

Skocpol, Theda, and Morris Fiorina, eds. 1999a. *Civic Engagement in American Democracy*. Washington, DC: Brookings Institution.

Small, Mario. 2004. *Villa Victoria: The Transformation of Social Capital in a Boston Barrio*. Chicago: University of Chicago Press.

———. 2006. "Neighborhood Institutions as Resource Brokers: Childcare Centers, Interorganizational Ties, and Resource Access among the Poor." *Social Problems* 53 (2): 274–92.

———. 2007. "Racial Differences in Networks: Do Neighborhood Conditions Matter?" *Social Science Quarterly* 88 (2): 320–43.

———. 2008. "Four Reasons to Abandon the Idea of 'The Ghetto.'" *City & Community* 7: 389–98.

———. 2009. *Unanticipated Gains: Origins of Network Inequality in Everyday Life*. New York: Oxford University Press.

———. 2011. "How to conduct a mixed methods study: Recent trends in a rapidly growing literature." *Annual Review of Sociology*. 37: 57–86.

Small, Mario, and Laura Stark. 2005. "Are Poor Neighborhoods Resource Deprived? A Case Study of Childcare Centers in New York." *Social Science Quarterly* 86 (s1): 1013–36.

Small, Mario, and Michele Lamont. 2010. "Reconsidering Culture and Poverty." *Annals of the American Academy of Political Science* 629 (1): 6–27.

Spain, Daphne. 1979. "Race Relations and Residential Segregation in New Orleans: Two Centuries of Paradox." *Annals of the American Academy of Political and Social Science* 441 (1): 82–96.

Stack, Sarah, Monica Teets Farris, Shirley Laska, Norma Jean Mattei, Maggie Olivier, Iman Adeinat, Michael Wesley, and French Wetmore. 2007. "A Review of Repetitive Floodloss Data for Hoey's Basin, Jefferson Parish, Louisiana." New Orleans: University of New Orleans, CHART Repetitive Floodloss Project. http://floodhelp.uno.edu /uploads/Hoey's%20Basin%20Report_Aug%2010%202007.pdf.

Stanley, Jason. 2014. "Detroit's Draught of Democracy." *New York Times*, July 19.

State of Louisiana Office of Community Development. 2020. *The Homeowner Assistance Program Situation & Pipeline Report.* www.road2la.org/HAP/HAP_Situation AndPipelineReports.aspx.

Stone, Clarence. 1989. *Regime Politics: Governing Atlanta, 1946–1988.* Lawrence: University Press of Kansas.

———. 1993. "Urban Regimes and the Capacity to Govern: A Political Economy Approach." *Journal of Urban Affairs* 15 (1): 1–28.

Stone, Deborah. 1989. "Causal Stories and the Formation of Policy Agendas." *Political Research Quarterly* 104 (2): 281–300.

Sun, Lisa Grow. 2011. "Smart Growth in Dumb Places: Sustainability, Disaster, and the Future of the American City." *Brigham Young Law Review* 2157: 101–45.

Surowiecki, James. 2012. "Disaster Economics." *New Yorker*, December 3.

Suttles, Gerald. 1968. *The Social Order of the Slum.* Chicago: University of Chicago Press.

Sylvain, Vincent. 2001. "Housing and Neighborhood Development in the City of New Orleans: A Historical Review from May 1994–March 2001." Master's thesis, University of New Orleans.

Sze, Julie. 2014. *Fantasy Islands: Chinese Dreams and Ecological Fears in an Age of Climate Crisis.* Berkeley: University of California Press.

Tam, Laura. 2009. "Strategies for Managing Sea Level Rise." *Urbanist* Issue 487. www.spur.org/publications/urbanist-article/2009-11-01/ strategies-managing-sea-level-rise.

Thayer, Ralph E. 1979. "The Evolution of Housing Policy in New Orleans (1920–1978)." Institute for Government Studies: Loyola University of New Orleans.

Times-Picayune. 1929. "Governor Asked to Name Experts in Drainage Issue." September 12.

Tiebout, Charles M. 1956. "A Pure Theory of Local Expenditures." *Journal of Political Economy* 64 (5): 416–24.

Tierney, Kathleen. 2007. "From the Margins to the Mainstream? Disaster Research at the Crossroads." *Annual Review of Sociology* 33: 271–86.

Tobler, Waldo. 1970. "A Computer Movie Simulating Urban Growth in the Detroit Region." *Economic Geography* 46: 234–40.

Tran, Jonathan. 2011. "The Disasporic Politics of Asian-American Christianity." In *Korean Diaspora and Christian Mission*, edited by Kim S. Hun and Ma Wonsuk, 72–83. Oxford, UK: Regnum Oxford Centre for Mission Studies.

Tse-Min Lin, Chine-En Wu, and Feng-Yu Lee. 2006. "Neighborhood Influence on the Formation of National Identity in Taiwan: Spatial Regression with Disjoint Neighborhoods." *Political Research Quarterly* 59 (1): 35–46.

Turk, Austin. 2004. "Sociology of Terrorism." *Annual Review of Sociology* 30: 271–86.

Uphoff, Norman. 2001. "Understanding Social Capital: Learning from the Analysis and Experience of Participation." In *Social Capital: A Multifaceted Perspective*, edited by Partha Dasgupta and Ismail Serageldin, 215–49. Washington, DC: World Bank Publications.

Urbina, Ian. 2016. "Perils of Climate Change Could Swamp Coastal Real Estate." *New York Times*. November 24. www.nytimes.com.

US Department of Housing and Urban Development, and Community Planning and Development Office of Evaluation. 1975. "Housing and Community Development Act of 1974: Community Development Block Grant Program, a Provisional Report."

US Department of the Interior, and US Geological Survey. 2003 "U.S. Geological Survey Subsidence Interest Group Conference, Proceedings of the Technical Meeting, Galveston, Texas, November 27–29, 2001." http://pubs.usgs.gov/of/2003/ofr03-308/pdf/OFR03-308.pdf.

US Government Accountability Office. 2015. "High-Risk Series: An Update." Report to Congressional Committees. www.gao.gov/assets/670/668415.pdf.

US Government Printing Office. 2006. "Hurricane Katrina: Who's in Charge of the New Orleans Levees?" *Senate Hearing 109–616*. www.gpo.gov/fdsys/pkg/CHRG-109shrg26746/html/CHRG-109shrg26746.htm.

Van Evera, Stephen. 1997. *Guide to Methods for Students of Political Science*. Ithaca, NY: Cornell University Press.

Van Houten, Carolyn. 2016. "The First Official Climate Refugees in the U.S. Race Against Time." *National Geographic*, May 25. www.nationalgeographic.com.

Vaughan, Ellen, and Jim Turner. 2013. "The Value and Impact of Building Codes." Environmental and Energy Study Institute. www.eesi.org/papers/view/the-value-and-impact-of-building-codes.

Venkatesh, Sudhir. 2000. *American Project: The Rise and Fall of a Modern Ghetto*. Cambridge, MA: Harvard University Press.

———. 2006. *Off the Books: The Underground Economy of the Urban Poor*. Cambridge, MA: Harvard University Press.

Verchick, Robert, and Lynsey Johnston. 2013. "When Retreat Is the Best Option: Flood Insurance after Biggert-Waters and Other Climate Change Puzzles." *John Marshall Law Review*, Annual Kratovil Symposium on Real Estate Law & Practice, 47 (2): 695–718.

Wardlaw, Jack, and Ed Anderson. 1988. "GOP, Blacks May Be Keys to La. Tax Reforms." *Times-Picayune*, August 14, sec. C.

Ward, Michael, and Kristian Gleditsch. 2008. *Spatial Regression Models*. Los Angeles: Sage.

Warner, Coleman. 2001. "Freret's Century: Growth, Identity, and Loss in a New Orleans Neighborhood." *Louisiana History: The Journal of the Louisiana Historical Association*. 42 (3): 323-58.

Warner, Mildred. 2011. "Club Goods and Local Government: Questions for Planners." *Journal of the American Planning Association*. 77 (2): 155-66.

Warren, Mark ed. 1999. *Democracy and Trust*. London: Cambridge University Press.

Webb, Gary. 2002. "Sociology, Disasters, and Terrorism: Understanding Threats of the New Millennium." *Sociological Focus* 35 (1): 87-95.

Webre, Gil. 1984. "Drainage Proposals Explained by Planners." *Times-Picayune/States-Item*, April 12, sec. 1.

Wellman, Berry, and Scot Wortley. 1990. "Different Strokes from Different Folks: Community Ties and Social Support." *American Journal of Sociology* 96 (3): 558-88.

West, Mark D., and Emily M. Morris. 2003. "The Tragedy of the Condominiums: Legal Responses to Collective Action Problems after the Kobe Earthquake." *American Journal of Comparative Law* 51 (4): 903-40. doi:10.2307/3649133.

White, Gilbert. 1937. "Notes on Flood Protection and Land-Use Planning." *Journal of the American Planning Association* 3 (3): 57-61. doi:10.1080/01944363708978728.

Whitfield. Chandra. 2015. "Progress in The Park: Pontchartrain Park 10 Years After Katrina." *NBC News*, August 27. www.nbcnews.com/storyline/hurricane-katrina-anniversary/progress-park-pontchartrain-park-10-years-after-katrina-n417021.

Whoriskey, Peter. 2006. "Post-Katrina Rebuilders Hug Ground, Trust Levees; Some Say They Don't Have the Time or Money to Elevate Houses." *Washington Post*, February 26.

Williams, Melissa ed. 2018. *Jane Mansbridge: Participation, Deliberation and Legitimate Coercion*. London: Routledge.

Wilson, James Q. 1980. *The Politics of Regulation*. New York: Basic Books.

———. 1989. *Bureaucracy: What Government Agencies Do and Why They Do It*. New York: Basic Books.

Wilson, William Julius. 1987. *The Truly Disadvantaged: The Inner City, Underclass, and Public Policy*. Chicago: University of Chicago Press.

———. 1996. *When Work Disappears: The World of the Urban Poor*. New York: Knopf.

Wolensky, Robert P., and Kenneth C. Wolensky. 1990. "Local Government's Problem with Disaster Management: A Literature Review and Structural Analysis." *Review of Policy Research* 9 (4): 703-25. doi:10.1111/j.1541-1338.1990.tb01074.x.

Wolfinger, Raymond E., and Steven Rosenstone. 1980. *Who Votes?* New Haven, CT: Yale University Press.

Woolcock, Michael, and Deepa Narayan. 2000. "Social Capital: Implications for Development Theory, Research, and Policy." *World Bank Research Observer* 15 (2): 225-49.

Wooten, Tom. 2012. *We Shall Not Be Moved: Rebuilding Home in the Wake of Katrina.* Boston: Beacon Press.

Zaninetti, Jean-Marc, and Craig E. Colten. 2012. "Shrinking New Orleans: Post-Katrina Population Adjustments." *Urban Geography* 33 (5): 675–99. doi:10.2747/0272-3638.33.5.675.

Zhou, Min, and Carl L. Bankston III. 1994. "Social Capital and the Adaptation of the Second Generation: The Case of Vietnamese Youth in New Orleans East." *International Migration Review* 28 (4): 775–99.

Zhukov, Yuri. 2010. *Workshop: Applied Spatial Statistics in R.* www.people.fas.harvard.edu/~zhukov/spatial.html

INDEX

Page numbers in *italics* indicate Figures and Tables

abandonment: population loss, blight and, 117; of properties, 109–10, 114

Abate, Jason, 83–84, 197

ABFEs. *See* Advisory Base Flood Elevations

accountability, 62–63; democratic, 193; of government, 50, 166

ACORN. *See* Association of Community Organizations for Reform Now

adaptation: to climate change, 193–94; to climate risk, 16; to existing risks, 32; reconstruction and, 8; resilience as, 33–36

Advisory Base Flood Elevations (ABFEs), 69

African Americans, 11, 13, 28–29, 43; deaths of, 46; homeowners, 112; proportion of, among population, 95. *See also* Black population

Aldrich, Daniel, 30

Amacker, Andrew, 172–74

American dream, 112–13

American Planning Association (APA), 69–70

ancillary civic structure, 217n14

ancillary social organizations, 217nn21–23

Andrew H. Wilson Charter School, 163–64

antisocial capital, 41

APA. *See* American Planning Association

Army Corps of Engineers, US, 47–48, 53–58

Association of Community Organizations for Reform Now (ACORN), 157

austerity programs, 20

autonomy: federalism encouraging, 82; self-governance and, 151

barrier plan, 54–57

Base Flood Elevation (BFE), 69

BDC. *See* Broadmoor Development Corporation

Berggren, Wayne, 70

BFE. *See* Base Flood Elevation

BIA. *See* Broadmoor Improvement Association

Biggert-Waters Flood Insurance Reform Act, 76–78

Biloxi-Chitimacha-Choctaw tribe, 27

Black population: civic organization density and change in, *137*, *138*; comparing White and, 117, 120–21; susceptibility of, 139

Blakely, Edward, 143–44, 219n3

blight, 109, 114; mitigated, in post-disaster recovery, 58–61; population loss, abandonment and, 117; reducing, 133, 174–76, 179

BNOBC. *See* Bring New Orleans Back Commission

Boggs, T. Hale, 74

bonding social capital, 44–45

BP. *See* British Petroleum

BP Deepwater Horizon oil spill, 114

Braden, Susan, 78–79

bridging social capital, 44–45

Bring New Orleans Back Commission (BNOBC), 36–37, 87, 110
British Petroleum (BP), 66
Broadmoor Development Corporation (BDC), 1, 160–63, 168–70
Broadmoor Improvement Association (BIA), 134, 160–73
Broadmoor neighborhood, 1–2, 13–15, 24, 37, 134, 141–42; as civic victory, 114; community development in, 26; invisible boundaries of, 167–71; map of, *169*; meeting spaces provided in, 43; recovery of, 140; repopulation rates in, *168*; resiliency strategies of, 149, 159–67
Building, Electrical, and Mechanical Codes, 91
building codes, 6, 213n67; adoption of ex post, 67–70; enforcement of, 174–79; International Building Code, 69; strict, 213n65; Uniform Construction Code, 67–68
building moratorium, 87–89, 100–102, 185; nullifying, 111; passage of, 110
building permits, 25, 214n4; civic capacity and issuance speed of, 105–7; civic demand for, 185; commercial, 91, *98*, 103–4; explosion of, post-Hurricane Katrina, 87–89; factors influencing, for new construction, *103*; factors influencing duration of, *106*; fees for, 95; issuance of applications for, 84–86, 89–95, *96–97*, *98*–111, 202; residential, *98*, *103*, 215n29
Bureau of Governmental Research, 64
Bush, George W., 59, 93
business improvement district, 170–71
buyout programs, 34
buyouts, 39–40, 141, 207n10

Canizaro, Joseph, 36, 87–88
Cantrell, LaToya, 162–65
Carroll, Maggie, 163
Cassidy, Bill, 78

CBD. *See* Central Business District
CDA. *See* Housing and Community Development Act
CDBG. *See* Community Development Block Grant
CDCs. *See* Community Development Corporations
Centineo, Mike, 85
Central Business District (CBD), 71–72
Chehardy, Lawrence, 62
Cingranelli, David L., 93
Citizens Committee for Hurricane Flood Control, 47
City Limits (Peterson), 51–52, 195–96
city services, privatizing, 34
civic activism, 23, 33, 56, 161–62, 198; civic competence and, 110–11; dimensions of, 179, 184–85; power of, 116; successful, 168
civic activists, 54
civic activities, 5, 76, 112–13
civic actors: government interaction with, 23, 71; role of, 49–50
civic associations, 218n39
civic capacity, 8–9, 15; building permit issuance speed and, 105–7; city services and, 86; collective participation and, 151; disaster mitigation influenced by, 70–71; geography, reconstruction and, 94; limits of, 29; natural disasters and, 20; beyond neighborhoods, 45; new construction patterns guided by, 101–4; potential, 118; rebuilding impacted by high levels of, 42–43; reconstruction and, 23; reevaluation of, 20; resilience and, 33; role of, 183–84; as spatially bounded, 46; uneven distribution of, 44, 187; urban resilience and, 24, 29; varying impact of, 46; voter turnout and, 91
civic competence, 91–94, 110–11
civic discontent, 56–58

civic engagement, 21, 186; in context of natural disasters, 22; political implications of, 188; rebuilding influenced by, 25; resilience of, 91
civic interventions, 32
civic jealousy, 145, 179
civic organizations, 71, 118–21, 219n51; change in Black and White population by density of, *137*, 138; community civic structure and, 141; density of, 132; factors influencing, *122*; predicted repopulation rates by density of, *124–25*, 126; predicted vulnerability by density of, *130–31*
civic participation, 9–10, 184; active, 92–93; impact of, 33; opportunities for, in Pontchartrain Park, 123
civic performance, 116
civic strength, 6, 24
civic vision, 143
Clarkson, Jackie, 37–38
class: desensitizing, 6, 186
climate change, 3, 10; adaptation to, 193–94; economic decline and, 12; land subsidence induced by, 12; long-term challenges of, 182–84; risks from natural disasters and, 129; shrinkage in age of, 33–36; urban resilience and, 31
Clinton Foundation, 1
CLURO. *See* Comprehensive Land-Use Regulation Ordinance
clustering redevelopment, 36
coastal erosion, 66
Coastal Protection and Restoration Authority, 66
coastal restoration, without emergency preparedness, 65–67
collective contestation, 55–56
Colten, Craig, 39, 192
communities: civic capacity of, 191; civic strength of, 24; empowering, 4; in flood-prone areas, 34–35; homeowners attachment to, 22; networks, partnership and, 28; preserv-

ing culture of, 38; repopulation and interactions of, 23; resilience projects oriented to, 49; rise of self-reliant, 152–59; risk perception in coastal, 33; social meaning of, 42; social resources across, 118–19; socioeconomic backgrounds of, 45; spatial scale of, 29; viability of, 43; vulnerabilities in, 8–9; vulnerable resilience generated in, 39–45
community-based organizations, 44, 216n43; mobilization through, 113; as source of civic competence, 94; urban resilience, vulnerability and, 114
community boundaries, 44
community civic structure: boundaries of, 141; civic organizations and, 141; land elevation and, 129; leadership and, 113–14; measuring, 118–19; in neighborhoods, 120–23; racialized geography and, 136; repopulation contributed to by, 123–24; resilience, repopulation and, 126–27
community development: in Broadmoor neighborhood, 26; disaster recovery and, 179; in Freret neighborhood, 26; history of, 150; property values and, 93
Community Development Block Grant (CDBG), 135, 148
Community Development Corporations (CDCs), 112, 157–59
community resilience, 9, 109, 146, 151; defining, 30–33; as localized, 46; measuring vulnerability and, 116–17
comparative case studies, 20–21
Comprehensive Land-Use Regulation Ordinance (CLURO), 70
Crescent City Rebuilding Authority, 87

DDD. *See* Downtown Development District
deaths: from Hurricane Betsy, 53; from hurricanes, 15

Delta Works, 66
Department of Agriculture, US, 74–75
Department of Housing and Urban Development, US (HUD), 27, 77, 81, 158
depopulation, 35–36, 128
disaster management programs, 51–52
disaster mitigation: civic capacity influence on, 70–71; methods of, 80–81; structure for, 49
disaster policy, 6, 49, 80
disaster prevention, 51, 57
disaster relief grants, 64–65
disaster response agency, 21
disasters: declarations of, securing electoral support, 59; federalizing, 74–77; human-made, 9–10; individual relief and mitigated blight in recovery from, 58–61; mitigating, at federal level, 53–61; negative impact of, 30; overcoming adversities of, 30; probability of, 111; transitory, 10; unpredictability of, 182; vulnerability to, 15
Downtown Development District (DDD), 71–72
drainage systems, 7, 12–13, 24, 39, 74, 159–60
drift, 32
dry infrastructure, 31
Dunbar, Celestine, 177
Duval, Stanwood, Jr., 79

Earl, George G., 159
earthquakes, 10, 21, 32, 208n19
Echeverria, John, 80
ecological conditions, 10, 21–22
economic decline, 71; climate change and, 12; impact of, 20
economic development, 25, 46; without government, 67; opportunities for, 61; pace of, 192; stifling of local, 68; strategies for, 66; tax burdens and policies for, 71
economic expansion, 34

economic geography, 12
economic insecurities, 73–74
Edwards, Edwin, 61
EIS. *See* Environmental Impact Statement
elevation, land, 148; requirements, 85–86; social vulnerabilities, Hurricane Katrina and, *128*; standards, 68
emergency preparedness, 81; coastal restoration without, 65–67; at state level, 61–65
empowerment, 5
environmental change, 31
Environmental Impact Statement (EIS), 55
environmental litigation, 56
Evans, Pat, 158
event history analysis, 201–2

FDPA. *See* Flood Disaster Protection Act
Federal Circuit Court of Appeals, US, 79
Federal Claims Court, 79
federal disaster programs, 7, 183
Federal Emergency Management Agency (FEMA), 21, 211n15; buyouts from, 39–40; funding through, 58; rating system for, 213n85; reports from, 70
federal engineering projects, 48–49
federal grants, 49, 59–60, 64
Federal Housing Administration, US (FHA), 75
federalism: constraints within, 52; innovation and autonomy encouraged by, 82; promoting urban resilience under, 51–53
federalist structure, 46, 51, 184–85
federal policies, 50
FEMA. *See* Federal Emergency Management Agency
FIRMs. *See* Flood Insurance Rate Maps
Flood Control Act, 53–54
flood depth, 99
Flood Disaster Protection Act (FDPA), 76

flooding, 2–3; depth of, 148; magnitude and duration of, 80; reducing risk of, 65–66; serial, 48
flood insurance: federally subsidized, 75–76; individualized programs for, 81; premium increases, 77; reduction in, 70
Flood Insurance Rate Maps (FIRMs), 78
flood level, 102
floodplains, 53
flood protection, 36
floods: civic strength of victims of, 40; cyclical impact of, 53; loss due to, 12; recurring, 39
floodwalls, 7; constructing, 54; improved, 74; safer and taller, 48
FNC. *See* Freret Neighborhood Center
Foley, Gene, 75
Ford, Kristina, 144–45, 179
forgiveness bill, 75
French Quarter, 63, 73, 154
Freret neighborhood, 24, 141–42, 221n67; community development in, 26; economic resilience of, 171–78; resilience strategies for, 149
Freret Neighborhood Center (FNC), 221n68
Freret renaissance, 177
Future Land Use Map, 38–39

GAO. *See* Government Accountability Offices
Garden District, 63, 73, 88
Gentilly neighborhood, 37, 134, 169
gentrification, 177
Geographic Information System (GIS), 93–94, 119
ghettoization, 196
GIS. *See* Geographic Information System
GMP. *See* Growth Management Program
GOHSEP. *See* Governors Office of Homeland Security and Emergency Preparedness

governance: decentralized, 184; democratic, 111; privatized, 9, 146
government: accountability of, 50, 166; anger toward, 136; civic actors interaction with, 23, 71; distrust of, 144, 192–93; economic development without, 67; failures of, 111; incentives for, 51, 183; layers of, 185; power of, 189; private, 146; protection recommendations from, 69; role of, in recovery, 198; subnational, 51–52; territorial expansion pursued by, 73
Government Accountability Offices, US (GAO), 76
Governors Office of Homeland Security and Emergency Preparedness (GOHSEP), 65
grassroots privatization, 146–47
Gray, Aida, 165–66
Great Chicago Fire, 10–11, 21
Great Midwest Flood of 1993, 190
Great Storm of 1915, 3
Growth Management Program (GMP), 71–72

hazard mitigation, long-term, 25, 192–93
Hazard Mitigation Grant Program (HMGP), 34, 60, 212n39
hazardous development, 65–67
Head, Stacy, 83
Heat Wave (Klinenberg), 30
Hébert, F. Edward, 74–75
HFIAA. *See* Homeowner Flood Insurance Affordability Act
Hirschman, Albert, 182
HMGP. *See* Hazard Mitigation Grant Program
Holy Cross neighborhood, 146
HOME. *See* Home Ownership Made Easy
Home Improvement Association, Pontchartrain Park, 112–13
Homeowner Flood Insurance Affordability Act (HFIAA), 76, 78

homeowners: African American, 112; community attachment of, 22; community leaders as, 114; concerns for, 41; costs of subsidence for, 14; home elevation requirements bypassed by, 85; insurance for, 70; interests of, 50; in Pontchartrain Park, 134–35; of repetitive-loss properties, 2; socioeconomic conditions for, 26
Home Ownership Made Easy (HOME), 157
Home Rule Charter, 67–68
homestead exemption, 61–65
Housing and Community Development Act (CDA), 153
housing deterioration, 15
housing elevation projects, 60
housing patterns, lower density, 74
HUD. *See* Department of Housing and Urban Development
Hurricane Betsy, 3, 7, 15, 53, 74–77, 214n88
Hurricane Camille, 15
Hurricane Charley, 208n34
Hurricane Frances, 208n34
Hurricane Georges, 15
Hurricane Gustav, 79
Hurricane Ike, 79
Hurricane Ivan, 15, 208n34
Hurricane Jeanne, 208n34
Hurricane Katrina, 1–2, 7, 21, 76, 208n34; arrival of, 69; building permits explosion after, 87–89; financial losses from, 15; as human-made disaster, 9–10; inequalities after, 197–98; lawsuits following, 50; magnitude of, 80; memory of, 11–12; physical infrastructure destroyed by, 83–84; political trust after, 192; social vulnerabilities, land elevation and, 128; spatial gap widened by, 127; as unprepared-for disruption, 181
Hurricane Rita, 69, 79, 208n34
hurricanes, 11; cyclical impact of, 53; deaths from, 15

Hurricane Sandy, 27–28, 35, 76, 207n10
Hurricane Wilma, 208n34

Impact Neighborhood Strategy, 154–55
Industrial Canal, 13, 54
inequalities, 22, 46, 182; in neighborhoods, 44; post-Hurricane Katrina, 197–98; racial, 139; spatial, 115–16, 139; urban, 5
innovation: federalism encouraging, 82; urban, 181
International Building Code, 69
inundation, 48
Isle de Jean Charles, 27–28
isolation, residential, 45–46, 215n20

jack-o-lantern effect, 109
Jazzland, 14–15
Jindal, Bobby, 65
Johnson, Cedric, 146–47
Johnson, Lyndon B., 74–75, 148

Kaplan-Meier curve, for permit speed analysis, *203*, 204
Kerry, John, 93
Klinenberg, Eric, 30
Knobloch, Dennis, 189–90
Kresge Foundation, 113
Kuo, Susan, 41

Lake Borgne, 56
Lake Pontchartrain, 13, 56
Lake Pontchartrain and Vicinity Hurricane Protection Project (LPVHPP), 53–56
Lakeview neighborhood, 13, 87–88, 100, 154
Landrieu, Mary, 65–66, 77–78
Landrieu, Mitch, 38, 65
land subsidence, 22, 39, 153; climate change inducing, 12; costs of, for homeowners, 14
land use, 6, 50

Land Use Plan, 144–45
land-use regulations, 49, 68, 70, 78
Larsen, Larissa, 44
leadership, community civic structure and, 113–14
League of Women Voters, 55
legitimate coercion, 46, 188–93
LeSieur, Kenneth, 47–48
levees, 7, 24; delays in construction of, 55–56; failure of, 47–48; importance of, 48; preference for, 49; reconstruction of, 50
Levees.org, 47–48
Levy, David P., 56–57
Lewis, Sarah, 158
light-rail systems, 110
Livingston, Robert, 55
Local Initiatives Support Corporation, 157
Logan, John, 195–96
logincome, 95, 119
Long, Russell, 74–75
Lower Ninth Ward, 13, 28–29, 87, 100; basic infrastructure of, 145–46; MIR in, 88–89; recovery in, 133–34; regeneration of, 37–38; successful lobbying for, 77
Lower Ninth Ward Neighborhood Council, 77
LPVHPP. *See* Lake Pontchartrain and Vicinity Hurricane Protection Project

macroeconomic downturn, 16
Make It Right Foundation (MIR), 88–89, 133–34
managed coastal retreat, 34
managed growth, 196
Mansbridge, Jane, 189, 222n15
market-based activities, 34–35
market value, tax valuation and, 63
Master Plan, 38–39
Means, Benjamin, 41
Menendez, Robert, 78
method of agreement, 20
method of difference, 20

Meyer, Michelle, 30
MIR. *See* Make It Right Foundation
Mississippi River Commission, 53
Mississippi River–Gulf Outlet (MRGO), 79–80
Mitigation Best Practice cases, 70
mixed-methods approach, 22–23
mobility: limited, 92–93; regulation of, 51–52
Molotch, Harvey, 195–96
Morial, Marc, 157
MRGO. *See* Mississippi River–Gulf Outlet
Mumford, Lewis, 71

NAACP. *See* National Association for the Advancement of Colored People
Nagin, Ray, 38, 68, 83, 87, 93–94, 190, 220n45
Napoleon Canals Project, 2
National Association for the Advancement of Colored People (NAACP), 88
National Disaster Resilience Competition (NDRC), 27
National Environment Policy Act (NEPA), 55
National Flood Insurance Act, 75–76
National Flood Insurance Program (NFIP), 16, 70–71, 74–77, 213n85
natural disasters, 9–10; civic capacity and, 20; civic engagement in context of, 22; as federal responsibility, 81; risks from climate change and, 129
natural hazards, 31
nature, bringing back, 9–11
NDRC. *See* National Disaster Resilience Competition
negative binomial regression, 201
neighborhood action, 43–44
neighborhood associations, 141
Neighborhood Empowerment Network Association (NENA), 158
neighborhood groups, 152–56
Neighborhood Housing Services (NHS), 221n68

Neighborhood Participation Plan, 8
neighborhoods, 23; application response
time by, *101*; boundaries around, 152;
civic capacity beyond, 45; community
civic structure in, 120–23; competition
among, 144; inequalities in, 44; marginalized, 39; percentage of undervaluation
in, *64*; preserving character of, 38–39;
privatization, competition and marketability of, 147; restricting recovery of,
36; self-governance of, 154; vulnerability
of, 6. *See also specific topics*
Neighborhood Stabilization Program
(NSP), 134, 158
Neighbors United (NU), 171–74
NENA. *See* Neighborhood Empowerment
Network Association
NEPA. *See* National Environment Policy
Act
nepotism, 190
new construction: civic capacity guiding
patterns of, 101–4; factors influencing
permits for, *103*
New Orleans. *See specific topics*
New Orleans East, 13–14, 37
New Orleans Redevelopment Authority
(NORA), 110, 134, 158
NFIP. *See* National Flood Insurance
Program
Nguyen, Vien, 114
NHS. *See* Neighborhood Housing Services
Nixon, Richard, 153
NORA. *See* New Orleans Redevelopment
Authority
Norwood, Stan, 174–76, 178, 184, 222n82
NSP. *See* Neighborhood Stabilization
Program
NU. *See* Neighbors United

Obama, Barack, 27
O'Brien, Miles, 110
OECD. *See* Organisation for Economic
Co-operation and Development

OLS. *See* Ordinary Least Squares
regression
100 Resilient Cities initiative, 27
Ordinary Least Squares regression (OLS),
119–20
Organisation for Economic Co-operation
and Development (OECD), 12
organizational diversification, 161
Ostrom, Elinor, 40, 50
Outer Continental Shelf, 66
owner tenure, 95

patronage, 190
Pennington, Richard, 93
Peterson, Paul E., 51–52, 195–96, 211n15
Pierce, Wendell, 112–16
Pitt, Brad, 88–89
place attachment, 42
Planning Assistance Team program, 70
planning strategies, politicization and
rejection of, 88
political corruption, 62–63, 182, 190
political engagement, 92
political participation, 105; high levels of,
25; at local and national level, 91–93
Pontchartrain Park: homeowners in,
134–35; participation and mobilization
opportunities in, 123; Pierce dedication
to, 112–16; poverty in, 114; recovery
of, 126
population change, *99*; in Rust Belt cities,
17; in Sun Belt cities, *18*
population decline, 71, 117, 196
population density: decrease in, 35–36; in
Rust Belt cities, *19*
poverty, 103–4, 117, 142; accelerated development and growing, 71–74; definition
of, 95; exacerbated by White flight, 73;
gap, 133; in Pontchartrain Park, 114;
urban, 182
private entity, 158
private governments, 146
Project Home Again, 220n58

properties: abandonment of, 109–10, 114; acquisition of, 36; buyouts for, 35; compensating vulnerable, 78–80; income-producing, 63–64; raising value of, 42; reappraisal of, 212; vacant or abandoned, 20

property rights, 50; conceding, 196; protection of, 111; violation of, 87

property taxes, 61–63

property values, community development and, 93

protection: costs of, 31; federal responsibility to provide, 50; flood, 36; government recommendations for, 69; of property rights, 111; rebuilding and, as primary reaction, 40; of shoreline, 34; storm, 7, 36

protests, 43, 220n45

Public Affairs Research Council of Louisiana, 64

public housing, 152–53

public service provisions, 20

public transportation, 20, 36, 73

public works projects, 7

race, 121; desensitizing, 6, 186; geography of, 136–38; neighborhood recovery and, 162

racial disparities, 25, 88, 116, 184–86

racial inequality, 139

racial transformation, 117

Rault, Joseph, 159

Rebuild by Design, 28

rebuilding, 8–9; assistance for, 58; civic engagement influencing, 25; consequences of, 86, 183; high levels of civic capacity impacting, 42–43; protection and, as primary reaction, 40; reconstruction, repopulation and, 32, 107–11; regulations on, 69; sustainability impacted by, 85

reconstruction: adaptation and, 8; civic capacity and, 23; of civic facilities, 108–9; continual, 15; costs of, 21;

geography, civic capacity and, 94; of levees, 50; mapping, 2005-2008, 95, 96–99; pace of, 108; post-disaster, 22; rebuilding, repopulation and, 32, 107–11; urban service provision and, 89–95

recovery, 216n12; of Broadmoor neighborhood, 140; civic-oriented, 184; collective action of community members for, 113; community-based, 45–46; community-based organizations and, 44; community development and, 179; equitable, 89; funding, 15–16; government role in, 198; from hardship, 4; individual relief in post-disaster, 58–61; inequity in, 186; in Lower Ninth Ward, 133–34; pace of, 82; patterns of, 7, 98–99, 148–49; of Pontchartrain Park, 126; post-Katrina, 1, 3; race and neighborhood, 162; repopulation as core condition for, 117; restricting neighborhood, 36; social capital facilitating, 8; standard recovery plans, 10

Red Cross, 8, 75

redevelopment, 174; clustering, 36; expansion and, 31; privatized mode of, 178; resilience, revitalization and, 31; uneven pattern of, 134

redistributive good, federal assistance as, 58

relief grants, 50

relocation, from threatened area, 34

repetitive development, 8

repetitive-loss properties, 2

repopulation, 8, 115; community civic structure, resilience and, 126–27; community civic structure contributing to, 123–24; community interaction and, 23; as core condition for disaster recovery, 117; predicted rates of, by civic organizational density, 124–25, 126; rates of, in Broadmoor neighborhood, 168; reconstruction, rebuilding and, 32, 107–11; as slow, 108–9

reproduction, patterns of, 32

rescue and relief missions, 59

resettlement patterns, 109

residents: collective interests of, 22; economic bases of, unsettled, 72; socioeconomic backgrounds of, 45; vulnerabilities of, 60–61

resilience: as adaptation, 33–36; Broadmoor strategies for, 149, 159–67; civic capacity and, 33; of civic engagement, 91; community civic structure, repopulation and, 126–27; community-oriented projects for, 49; competing notions of, 29–33; conceptual guidance for, 188–92; contemporary definition of, 48; decision-makers utilizing, 27; decline, future of cities and, 195–98; economic, 149; economic, of Freret, 171–78; fostering, 4; Freret strategies for, 149; gentrified, 173–78; geography of, 123–27; levels of, 116; long-term, 28, 46, 197; neighborhood action as obstacle for long-term, 43–44; policy guidance for, 192–94; revitalization, redevelopment and, 31; self-governance and, 171, 178–79; social, 149, 164–66; urban democracy and, 186–87. See also community resilience; urban resilience; vulnerable resilience

resilience building, 7, 188–89; citywide, 68–69; fundamental dilemma of, 9–10; long-term, 26

resilience regime, 188–94

resistant civic action, 39, 42–43, 189–90, 192

resources, 23, 30; ability to distribute, 31; availability of, 115–16; across communities, 118–19; community-based, 4–5; competing for, 44; extraction of natural, 62; harnessing, 110; limited, 20; mobilization of collective, 40–41; possession of, 107; reliance on civic, 123; social, 13

Resources and Ecosystems Sustainability, Tourist Opportunities, and Revived Economies of the Gulf Coast States Act (RESTORE Act), 77

retreat: managed coastal, 34; refusal to, 40; rightsizing and, 37

revitalization, 5, 42, 104, 187; Blakely plan for, 143–44; corporate-centered, 72; deferring redevelopment and, 9–10; economic, 184; of real estate market, 160; resilience, redevelopment and, 31; urban, 151

Richmond, Cedric, 78

rightsizing, 3, 35, 37

risks: from climate change and natural disasters, 129; in coastal communities, 33; internalizing, at local level, 70–71; limited scope of, 46; reducing, of flooding, 65–66

Road Home grant, 60, 135, 166

Roark, Hal, 1, 160–62, 198, 220n45

Roberts, Patrick, 52

Rockefeller Foundation, 27, 30

Roemer, Charles, 61–62

Rosa F. Keller Library, 161–63

Rosenthal, Sandy, 47–48

Rust Belt cities, 16, 110, 196; population change in, 17; population density in, 19

Saint Bernard Parish, 56, 78–80

Saint Bernard Parish v. United States, 78–80

Salvation Army, 113–15

Sampson, Robert, 118–20, 147

San Francisco Earthquake, 10

Save Our Wetlands v. Early Rush, 55–56

SBA. See Small Business Administration

Scalise, Steven, 78

Schiro, Victor, 74–75

Schumer, Chuck, 78

security, false sense of, 57–58

seismic resiliency design, 32

seismic threat, 11

self-governance: autonomy and, 151; facilitating, 154; resilience and, 171, 178–79
self-reliance, 25–26, 142, 146, 151, 152–59, 164
service delivery, 35–36
settlement patterns, 36
shrinkage, 50; in age of climate change, 33–36; resisting, 38; unplanned, 115
shrinking-city debate, 4
shrinking strategy, 35–37
Six Flags, New Orleans, 14–15
sketch, 95
slaves, 215n20
Small Business Administration (SBA), 75, 190
Small Rental Property Program, 135
social assets, 44
social boundaries, 73
social capital, 207n17; deficit in, 44; high levels of, 41; manifestations of, 20; recovery facilitated by, 8
social disorganization, 123
social disparities, 25
social insecurities, 73–74
social justice, 186–87
social networks, egocentric, 45
socioeconomic backgrounds, 45
Southeast Hurricane Disaster Relief Act, 75
Southeast Louisiana Urban Flood Control Project, 2
spatial autoregressive regression, 204–5
spatial diffusion, 120, 147–48
spatial inequality, 115–16, 139
spatial lag regression, 23, 206
spatial methods, 23
spatial recovery, 5
spatial scale, 45
spatial variation, 149
Special Flood Hazard Areas, 69
SPH. See Standard Project Hurricane
Stafford Disaster Relief and Emergency Assistance Act of 1988, 58

Standard Project Hurricane (SPH), 57
standard recovery plans, 10
state budget funds, 65
structural protection, 53–54, 184–85
structural solutions, 48
submergence, 15
Sun Belt cities, 18
survival probability, 107
sustainability, rebuilding impacting, 85
swampland, 53
Swamp Land Acts of 1849, 53

Tax Assessment District, 64
tax base: disparities in, 156; shrinking, 61–65
tax burden, 50, 71
tax credits, 63–64
tax exemption laws, 65
tax reforms, 62–63
tax valuation, market value and, 63
territorial contraction, 38
territorial expansion, 10, 48, 73, 195
time horizons, 40
Tobler, Waldo, 120
Torres, Rick, 177–78
tourism, 34, 72, 177–78
transitory-perpetual spectrum, 10, 208n19
transit projects, 67
tsunamis, 20

undervaluation, 63, 64
unemployment, 119–23
unemployment compensation, 64
Uniform Construction Code, 67–68
unions, 72–73
United Houma Nation tribe, 27
United States (US), 195; Army Corps of Engineers, 47–48, 53–58; Department of Agriculture, 74–75; Federal Circuit Court of Appeals, 79; FHA, 75; GAO, 76; HUD, 27, 77, 81, 158; SBA, 75, 190
Uptown, 63, 88
Uptown Audubon, 100

urban democracy, resilience and, 186–87
urban development, vulnerabilities and, 22
Urban Fortunes (Logan and Molotch), 195–96
urban inequality, 5
urbanization patterns, 39
Urban Land Institute, 36, 38, 87
urban planning, 193
urban renewal, 77, 215n20
urban renewal act, 214n88
urban resilience, 9, 20, 191, 209n12; civic capacity and, 24, 29; climate change and, 31; community-based organizations, vulnerability and, 114; defining, 29–33; federalist structure and, 51; promoting, under federalism, 51–53;resistant civic action and, 39; successful, 27
urban service provision, reconstruction and, 89–95
US. *See* United States

vacancy rates, housing, 117, 121, 128, 132
variable of interest, 21
vehicles: access to, 128; ownership of, 117
Vietnamese community, 11, 13–14, 43
Village de l'Est neighborhood, 8, 13–15, 155; newspaper coverage for, *156*; protests in, 43; recovery in, 140
Vitter, David, 78
voter myopia, 58, 79
voters, civic capacity and turnout of, 91

vulnerabilities: as binary variable, 94; of cities, 4–5; civic organization density and prediction of, *130–31*; in communities, 8–9; compensation for properties with, 78–80; continuation of, 32; to disasters, 15; ecological, 31; geographic, 16, 104, 119, 127–36, 183; as geographic variable, 102; geological, 39; Hurricane Katrina, land elevation and social, *128*; isolation creating, 45–46; measuring community resilience and, 116–17; of neighborhoods, 6; of residents, 60–61; social, 115–17; sustained, 70–71; urban development and, 22; urban resilience, community-based organizations and, 114
vulnerable resilience, 5, 39–45

Warehouse District, 71
War on Poverty, 76
welfare, 67
wetland erosion, 27
White flight, poverty exacerbated by, 73
White population, 213n76; civic organization density and change in, *137, 138*; comparing Black and, 117, 120–21
The Wind in the Reeds (Pierce), 112
Worlds Fair, 1984, 71–72
World War II, 13, 16, 74

zero-inflation negative binomial regression (ZINB), 201
zoning, 50, 174

ABOUT THE AUTHOR

Min Hee Go is Associate Professor in the Department of Political Science and International Relations at Ewha Womans University, South Korea. Prior to joining Ewha, Go received her PhD at the University of Chicago and was previously an assistant professor at Brooklyn College, the City University of New York, and William Paterson University of New Jersey.